Shaping Sound Musicians

Shaping Sound Musicians

An innovative approach
to teaching comprehensive musicianship through
performance

Patricia O'Toole

Contributions from CMP Master Teachers:

Mike George, Susan McAllister, Kathy Punwar,
Leyla Sanyer, Mary Schmidt, Laura Sindberg,
Patty Schlafer, Randy Swiggum, Rich Tengowski,
Jan Tweed, Rebecca Winnie, Gary Wolfman

GIA Publications, Inc.
Chicago • www.giamusic.com

G-5739
Copyright © 2003
GIA Publications, Inc.
7404 S. Mason Ave.
Chicago, IL 60638
www.giamusic.com

ISBN: 1-57999-211-0

Printed in the U.S.A

Table of Contents

Part II: Practical Realities of Teaching CMP

Orchestra

This book is dedicated to Mike George,
who has been able to transform an inspired vision
into a stunning reality while nurturing
the best teacher in all of us.

Introduction

A Tribute

It is my greatest hope that, as a result of reading this book, you will be motivated to find your "inner-inspired teacher." That was my experience when I met teachers from the Wisconsin Comprehensive Musicianship Project (CMP) ten years ago. As I attended the annual workshop, experienced the comprehensive approach to teaching music in ensembles, and listened to extraordinary stories of profound student learning, I was inspired to raise my ensemble teaching to a higher level. After that initial workshop I became a CMP master teacher but have since moved to another state. However, distance from the CMP project has only created a greater appreciation for the depth of thought, the remarkable teaching abilities, and the commitment to continual growth that these Wisconsin teachers demonstrate.

This book is the collective wisdom of band, choir, and orchestra master teachers (both middle and high school level) from the last 25 years in Wisconsin. Every idea is classroom-tested, which is important to remember when you read an example and think, "That would never work." All of these ideas have worked within the context of an ensemble learning to perform with a meaningful understanding of musical concepts and aesthetic awareness, which is the goal of CMP.

It may be reassuring to know that all of these master teachers developed their skills and insights over time. I find this idea encouraging because it means that really good teachers are the result of hard work, self-reflection, and self-motivation—ingredients available to all who are eager to grow professionally. Hopefully this book will ignite your imagination and inspire you to continue to grow as a teacher, as this process has done for many who have studied CMP and worked with the Wisconsin master teachers.

Comprehensive Musicianship
through Performance (CMP)

The concept of comprehensive musicianship has been discussed since 1965 and refers to the interdisciplinary study of music. Although performing ensembles might seem like the logical place to teach across disciplines, many directors focus solely on performing skills. In this manner, all an instrumentalist might learn from playing 15 pieces of music in a band is 15 second-clarinet parts. Many teachers have been troubled by Charles Benner's (1972) summary of the problem:

> It can be inferred that performing group participation has little effect on musical behavior other than the acquisition of performance skills, unless there is a planned effort by the teacher to enrich the performing experience with additional kinds of musical understanding (p. 10).

There have been a number of projects that have addressed these issues and that have created models for teaching music comprehensively: The Hawaii Curriculum Project (1967-1972), *Teaching Musicianship in the High School Band* by Joseph Labuta (1972), *Teaching Comprehensive Musicianship through Classroom Music* by William Thomson (1974), and *Blueprint for Band* by Robert Garofalo (1976). All of these projects served as resources for the Wisconsin CMP Project (est. 1977).

Description of Chapter Contents

This book offers ensemble directors a model for how to teach students to perform with a historical and theoretical understanding of the music and the creative process. The model is called Comprehensive Musicianship through Performance (CMP) and is represented by a five-point star:

Each point of the model is fully

explained in chapters one through five. Chapter one, "Score Analysis," begins with a user-friendly process to help discover the inner-workings of a composition as well as the historical and social context, all of which leads to planning thoughtful instruction. Once the score is analyzed, you are ready to choose your teaching goals. Chapter two, "Outcomes," describes several different types of learning outcomes (skill, musical knowledge, and affective outcomes) and provides examples for how to design each type of outcome. Chapter three, "Strategies," shows you how to design a variety of teaching strategies that are sensitive to learning styles and promote a student-centered classroom. Chapter four, "Assessment," offers a variety of models for assessing student learning within ensembles, including paper-and-pencil tests, observational and performance assessments, journals, and portfolios. The last part of the model is chapter five, "Music Selection." The key to good teaching is working with quality literature and this chapter discusses elements of quality music and provides evaluative checklists to determine the breadth of your repertoire selection over a three to six year period.

To help demonstrate the CMP model, three compositions are used as examples in each chapter: Holst, *First Suite for Military Band*—I. Chaconne; Handel, *Hallelujah Chorus*; Mozart, *Eine Kleine Nachtmusik*—I. Allegro. You can choose to follow the example from your specific area, or examine how the model works with repertoire across all three ensemble types.

The second part of the book, *Practical Realities of Teaching CMP*, provides additional information regarding some of the specifics mentioned in the first part of the book. The sixth chapter, "Becoming a Different Kind of Ensemble Director," offers insights from a variety of experienced teachers into the process of implementing CMP. The seventh chapter, "Effectively Using Journals," describes how to design and implement successful journal assignments and includes several examples of student journal responses. Chapter eight, "Homework and Listening Assignments," includes tips and insights for assigning homework, using listening in the classroom, and managing your time and CMP program efficiently. The ninth chapter, "Concerts That Teach," is a collection of CMP concerts that teach both students and audiences musical, historical, social, and creative concepts about music. Chapter Ten, "CMP at a Glance," is designed as a quick-aid for designing teaching plans. It includes chapter summaries and templates for writing teaching plans.

The last part of the book is a collection of CMP unit plans for a variety of standard band, choral, and orchestral repertoire. These plans serve as pedagogical models to help you learn how to write unit plans and prepare daily CMP lessons.

How to Use This Book

The best way to learn the CMP model as presented in this book is to get a copy of one of the scores that is used as an example throughout the first five chapters (choose the one appropriate for you). Holst, *First Suite for Military Band*—I. Chaconne; Handel, *Hallelujah Chorus;* Mozart, *Eine Kleine Nachtmusik*—I. Allegro were chosen because they can be found in most school libraries and at music stores. By reading the chapter and following along in the scores, you will quickly learn the teaching model and develop lots of ideas for your own teaching. Then read *Part Two: Practical Realities of Teaching CMP* to help prepare and organize you for the shift in your teaching and in student responses that are a result of CMP teaching. This section is rich with teacher-tested advice and insights. Lastly, review the unit plans in the back of the book and notice the variety of ways CMP can be applied to lead students to meaningful music making.

After you have read through the book once, take a piece of music you plan to perform and walk it through the first five chapters. Do a thorough analysis, determine outcomes, write creative strategies, and plan a few assessments for your ensemble. If at any point you get stuck, review the sample unit plans in the back of the book for more ideas. After completing the first five chapters with your score, you will have written your first unit plan. All that remains is to write your first teaching plan and begin comprehensive instruction with your ensemble.

In addition to teaching a pedagogical model, this book can serve as a quick resource for inspiring creative teaching and concert programming. While all authors hope that their books will be read cover-to-cover (several times, even!), I realize that this book has hundreds of teacher-tested ideas, which makes it a good, quick resource and source of inspiration. So, you have permission to pick up the book, let the pages fall open, and begin reading knowing that you are being offered a lesson or inspiration you somehow need for the day or teaching moment.

Part I
Points of the Model

CHAPTER 1

Analysis

Within every good piece of music there is a rich curriculum waiting to be discovered by your "inner musical detective." Analyzing music provides you with a wealth of ideas for creatively teaching music because the more you know about a piece of music, the more in-depth your teaching will be. Investing time in score study is a critical component of CMP or any teaching process. The more often you do it, the easier and the more addictive it will become, and before long, you will notice your students using music vocabulary to describe what they are playing and hearing. This will translate into more significant learning and greater performances, all because you did your homework and presented thoughtful lessons.

Another good reason for analyzing your music is that it enables you to internalize and even memorize the music more quickly. If you understand how the music is constructed, you will make more effective choices when you introduce and rehearse it. Think about how easy it is to teach a piece of music the second time around. Because you know the composition well, you can anticipate most problems and teach more effectively. Investing in a thorough analysis affords you a similar level of comfort and expertise.

The more ways you interact with your scores the better you will come to understand them. This chapter suggests varied methods for analyzing music. However, if these suggestions seem overwhelming, then choose only one approach with which to begin. Starting small will bring quicker success and encourage you to do more. Soon you will be enjoying the process of pulling apart your music as you search for interesting and valuable lessons for your students.

ANALYSIS

Where to Begin

Some of you have been well trained by music theory professors and will feel the impulse to immediately do a roman numeral analysis. Althoug this can be a useful exercise because it highlights major key centers and moments of harmonic interest; this usually is not the best place to begin. Start with a broad description of the music and work your way to the specific details so that your analysis is rooted in a strong intellectual, cultural, and historical context. Begin by describing the composition you have selected for study using broad, general responses such as "this is a piece for voices," "this is a piece for full orchestra," "this is an opener," "this is an old "warhorse," "this has been highly recommended by colleagues," etc. By describing the composition in broad terms you gently open the door to a thorough analysis.

Examples of Broad Descriptions

BAND TEACHING PLAN

Holst, *First Suite for Military Band*
(I. Chaconne)

- British military band music
- Part of a suite
- Major work for wind band

CHORAL TEACHING PLAN

Handel, *Hallelujah Chorus*

- Sacred
- Four-part accompanied chorus
- Performed by many choirs at Christmas

ORCHESTRAL
TEACHING PLAN

Mozart, *Eine Kleine Nachtmusik*
(I. Allegro)

- A popular piece for strings
- A classic masterwork by Mozart

The next step involves a more specific labeling of the composition's type or genre. You may have chosen an overture, a march, a madrigal, or motet. This label reveals the next step in the analysis—exploring the history and background of the music.

Examples of Type/Genre Labels

BAND
TEACHING PLAN

Holst, *First Suite for Military Band*
(I. Chaconne)

Chaconne

CHORAL
TEACHING PLAN

Handel, *Hallelujah Chorus*

Oratorio chorus

Mozart, *Eine Kleine Nachtmusik* (I. Allegro)

- Classical period
- Serenade

Understanding the style period of your composition and how it fits into the life and style characteristics of your composer is imperative for making interpretive choices. To assemble this background information, explore the following suggestions:

Background Information
- Research the style period to determine what elements make it a characteristic or uncharacteristic example of the period.
- Research the composer's life and style characteristics. Pay particular attention to those aspects that pertain to your composition and that would interest your students.
- Explore why the composer wrote this piece (e.g. commissioned for a special event or written as part of a job) and determine whether it is a good example of his or her work.
- Determine who originally performed this piece and in what setting.
- Discuss any traditions that accompany this piece (such as the audience standing for the *Hallelujah Chorus* or the trombones standing for *The Stars and Stripes Forever*).

Additional Choral Information
- If the text is in a foreign language, translate it yourself and compare it with the given translation.
- If the text is written by a famous poet or writer, research the author and poem to determine its historical and cultural significance.
- Describe the story or mood that the text tells or creates.
- Establish whether the edition is historically accurate and check it against a more authentic version in a collected edition, if possible.

Additional Instrumental Information

- Describe solo requirements.
- Determine whether the technical challenges are appropriate for the selected age group or level.
- Describe the quality of the transcription or arrangement.
- Establish whether this is original instrumentation. If not, determine how the original was modified for this composition and why the arranger made modifications.

The above line of inquiry works well for Western Classical music, but needs to be adjusted for studying non-Western, folk, or popular music. Consider the following guidelines:

Background Information for Non-Western, Folk, or Popular Music

- Research the country and musical tradition from which this composition comes. List style characteristics of the music tradition.
- Explore the instrumentation that would be used in this music's original country, culture, or tradition.
- Determine who would have performed this music and for what reasons.
- Research the arranger's compositional style and determine how well this piece represents the musical tradition of the country.
- If your arrangement is based on a folk song, try to find the original tune.
- Translate the text if it is not in English.
- Determine what story or mood the text tells or creates.
- If the text is written by a famous poet or writer, look up the author and poem to determine its historical and cultural significance.
- Discuss any traditions or rituals that accompany this piece. Would it have just been sung, or might there be dancing and instrumental accompaniment? Think about how these answers might affect your interpretation.

Examples of Background Information

**BAND
TEACHING PLAN**

Holst, *First Suite for Military Band*
(I. Chaconne)

- Gustav Holst (1874-1934)
- Prominent 20th-century British composer who wrote this piece in a Romantic style
- Most famous orchestral work—The Planets
- Diatonic harmony
- Straightforward rhythmic devices
- Uses harmonic and melodic suspension to create tension
- Holst's *First Suite* written in 1909 for amateurs
- First major symphonic style piece for military band

**CHORAL
TEACHING PLAN**

Handel, *Hallelujah Chorus*

- George Frideric Handel (1685-1756)
- English composer of German birth
- *Messiah,* written in 1741, is Handel's most famous oratorio
- Premiered in Dublin in 1742
- Typical Baroque choral style—a mixture of homophony and polyphony, fugue, driving rhythmic energy, text repetition, extreme dynamics, and dramatic effects
- Text from Revelation 19:6, 16 and 11:15
- Climax in Part II of oratorio

ORCHESTRAL
TEACHING PLAN

Mozart, *Eine Kleine Nachtmusik*
(I. Allegro)

- Wolfgang Amadeus Mozart (1756-1791)
- Title translation: "A Little Night Music"
- Completed in Vienna on August 10, 1787
- First movement from a serenade
- Serenade was "pop" music in Vienna during Classical period
- Used as entertainment at parties, dinners, and outdoor events
- Light music but shows Mozart's craftsmanship
- Originally five movements but second one is lost
- Typical Classical period style: diatonic harmonies, triadic melodies, emphasis on I and V chords, balanced and shapely phrases, clear form, grace and elegance

Once you have discovered the historical and cultural significance of your composition, it will be time to delve into the musical aspects to figure out how it works. At this point, you will already be anticipating certain musical gestures based upon the style period and the composer's style characteristics. Your challenge is to explore how your anticipated ideas are borne out and what specific gestures the composer uses in this particular composition. To identify the compositional devices, consider your composition in light of the following elements of music:

Elements of Music

Form

What is the structure of this piece? How is the piece organized (binary, ternary, through- composed) What recognizable devices does it include (fugue, chorale, trio)

Rhythm

What are the primary motives? What note values are the most common? Is there syncopation or a peculiar time signature? Are there challenging rhythmic devices such as hemiolas and mixed meters?

Melody

What is the shape of the theme? What is the tonality—major, minor, modal, or a combination? Does it progress by step or skip? Is there a melodic motive? Is there even a melody? Are there counter-melodies that are important for the audience to hear?

Harmony

What is the harmonic rhythm? How and when does it modulate and what are the key relationships? Where are there dissonances? Are there any suspensions?

Brainstorming Compositional Devices

Articulation

Augmentation/ Diminution

Cadence

Changing Modality

Contrast

Counterpoint

Dynamics

Instrumentation

Meter Change

Modulation

Motives

Ornamentation

Repetition

Sequence

Solo/Ripieno Group

Suspensions

Text Painting

Variation

Varying Texture

Timbre

What are the colors in the piece? Is it primarily bright or dark, and what instrumentation or voicing creates the colors? How does the timbre reflect the text, title, or mood?

Texture

Is this piece primarily homophonic, monophonic, or polyphonic? Is it melody and accompaniment or monody? Does the density of the overall texture change? How does the composer contrast textures, and what effect does that create?

Expression

What are the dynamics, phrases, articulations, and tempi for this piece? How and when is each element used and applied?

Additional Considerations

How does the composer create moments of tension and release? How does the composer use and create contrast? How does the composer unify the composition? How does the composer sustain interest throughout the composition? How does the instrumentation contribute to the overall effect of the composition? How does the orchestration represent the style period?

Forms

ABA

Da capo aria

Rondo

Sonata and Allegro

Strophic

Theme and Variation

Through Composed

Imitation

Call and Response

Canon

Countermelody

Fugue

Points of Imitation

Stretto

Texture

Homophony

Melody and
    Accompaniment

Monophony

Polyphony

Having discovered the compositional devices, you are now ready to engage your best detective skills as you ask, "Why might the composer have chosen these particular musical gestures?" Acknowledging that a composition uses ABA form is not enough. You must think like the composer and figure out why he used that particular form. Most of the time the answers will be based on performance practice; nevertheless, sometimes you will have to infer or give your interpretation of what you thought the composer was intending. Perhaps the text is in ABA form, so setting the music the same way is obvious. Perhaps the composer is trying to create a particular mood of comfort by ending the composition with familiar musical material.

It is not always clear why a composer chooses a particular gesture, so consequently, you must often make an informed guess. These "guesses" will reveal your emerging interpretation. It is not enough to notice musical characteristics—the point of analyzing elements of music is to construct an interpretation. It is the act of interpreting music that makes us artists, and interpreting music based on a well-informed analysis makes us great artists. Invest time in the "why" question, because it will result in the most productive and profound interpretive insights.

Examples of Analyzing Compositional Devices and Elements of Music

BAND
TEACHING PLAN

Holst, *First Suite for Military Band* (I. Chaconne)

Form

Chaconne—variation form built over a recurring melodic theme. An unusually strict, archaic form similar to Passacaglia, popular in the Baroque period. Fifteen variations total

Melody

Eight bars long, climaxes at the end on the dominant (an important

BAND TEACHING PLAN CONT'D.

feature that helps propel each variation to the next one and keep the forward momentum

mm.

1-8   Original theme: baritone and tuba

9-16   Theme played in trombone; three countermelodies added in cornet 1 and 2 and trombone 1

17-24   Theme played in lower woodwinds, string bass; two new countermelodies presented in oboe, clarinet, alto saxophone

25-32   Theme played in low voices, arpeggiated chords in wood winds, fanfare-type figure in brass

33-40   Theme plus arpeggiated chords that are played on afterbeats

41-48   Theme played in eighth-note chords plus sixteenth-note runs in upper woodwinds

49-56   Theme played in upper woodwinds plus eighth-note accompaniment in low voices—style is *pesante*

57-65   Theme in solo horn, flowing countermelody in clarinets

66-73   Theme in solo alto saxophone; triplet-based countermelodies in flute and oboe

74-81   Theme inverted and placed in relative minor key of C-minor in horns; countermelodies in upper woodwinds

82-89   Theme inverted in cornets; basses play duple accompaniment pattern that shifts pulse and stresses "C" pedal, creating hemiola; suspended cymbal and bass drum enter

90-97   Theme presented transposed up a major third in trombones; basses continue with duple accompaniment

98-105   Theme returns to original key of E-flat, stated in trumpets and baritone; thicker texture; timpani enter

106-114 Theme presented by additional voices (flute, oboe, solo clarinet); additional accompaniment provided in low brass (chords) and lower woodwinds (eighth-note countermelody)

115-122 Theme presented by low brass; accompaniment is full and vertical (chordal); countermelodies from m. 9 return

123-132 Theme presented with altered harmonies, creating tension until the concluding E-flat major chord

The Chaconne theme is the unifying element

Harmony

- Key of E-flat
- Three variations are in C minor
- Use of pedal tones at D and E creates tension
- Dominant prolongation from E to F intensifies tension, finally released at F

Texture

Variety of cantabile countermelodies, fanfare-like motives, rushing woodwind cascades, brass chorales, and pedal tones create a kaleidoscope of shifting textures—important in variation form to help define structural points

Timber

Created by constantly changing orchestration and emphasizes form

Dynamics

Both extremes used in combination with timbral, textural, and rhythmic effects underscores form

**CHORAL
TEACHING PLAN**

Handel, *Hallelujah Chorus*

Form

- Through-composed based on text
- Each new section of text gets its own musical treatment
- Use of fugue at mm. 41-51

Melody

- Each phrase of text assigned its own melodic motive
- Five main melodic ideas:
    1. "Hallelujah!" (also used for "forever")

    2. "For the Lord God omnipotent reigneth"

    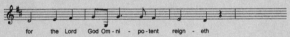

    3. "The kingdom of this world"

    4. "And He shall reign forever and ever"

    5. "King of Kings"

- Imitative
- All voices share melodic material

Harmony

- Emphasis on I, IV, and V chords gives the feeling of strength and solidarity
- Piece rarely leaves D major (only for four-measure episode), which contributes to the feeling of stability
- Successive pedal tones in soprano part (mm. 51-68) create rising tension to set up final climactic section

Rhythm

   Typical Baroque driving rhythms (i.e. almost continuous use of eighth-note pulse, many dotted rhythms, very little rhythmic repose)

- Voices used in an instrumental (rhythmic) way
- Fanfare-like rhythm in "Hallelujah!" motive
- Use of dotted rhythms suggest royalty

Timbre

- Full range of voices used effectively from bright high voicings (e.g. opening section) to lower, warmer voicings (e.g. m. 36)
- Contrast between choral *tutti* and orchestral colors, especially trumpet

Texture

- Mixture of homophony and polyphony
- Uses both strict fugue and counterpoint
- Choral unison (e.g. m. 17) versus homophonic block chords (e.g. opening)

Dynamics

- As consistent with the Baroque period, not a prominent feature
- Created by variations in texture

ORCHESTRAL
TEACHING PLAN

Mozart, *Eine Kleine Nachtmusik* (I. Allegro)

Form

- Compact *sonata-allegro* form
  Intro (fanfare) / First Theme (m. 5) / Second Theme (m. 28) / Development (m. 57) / Recapitulation (m. 77) / Coda (m.128)

Melody

- Typical galant style—tuneful, based on triadic harmony, lightly ornamented
- Popular style of the late 18th century
- Consistent with the galant style, the two main themes have contrasting character
- First theme area: fanfare bravura style
- Second theme area: elegant, lyrical, understated
- Use of sequences—e.g. violin 1 (mm. 9-10), viola/cello/bass (mm. 39-40), violin 1 (mm. 65-71)

Harmony

- In the key of G major

ORCHESTRAL
TEACHING PLAN
CONT'D.

- Second theme group in D but later returns in G m. 102 (typical for style)
- Main key areas define form—Exposition cadences in dominant (m. 56); sets up development, etc.
- Heavy use of I, IV, and V chords

Rhythm
- Continuous motor rhythm of eighth-notes
- Creates cheerful mood

Timbre
- A homogenous, blended effect of five string instruments
- Variations in color come from texture, articulation, or register change

Texture
- Melody and accompaniment
- Mozart spices up the texture with bits of imitation and counterpoint in all voices

Dynamics
- The two themes use contrasting dynamics—first theme uses *f*, second theme uses *p*
- Extreme contrast between consecutive phrases "surprises" the listener

It is possible and productive to have students analyze the music as well as the teachers. A word of encouragement and caution: having students analyze music will increase their understanding of history and compositional devices, which will lead to better overall musicianship and better performances; however, make sure that you have done your homework first so that you can easily determine the accuracy of student analyses. Also, it is more effective to have students research only one part of a composition as opposed to doing an entire analysis. Small assignments will yield higher quality work and offer students opportunities to share their emerging analysis with classmates, which will engage everyone in interesting musical conversations.

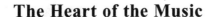
The Heart of the Music

One of the most important steps of the CMP analysis is to identify the heart of the music you are examining. This step provides the opportunity to analyze the affective (as opposed to technical) aspects of the music and explore your relationship to and desires for this composition.

We are attracted to specific musical selections for different reasons—different reasons from other musicians, and different reasons for each piece. Once you decide to perform a selection you enter into a relationship with it where you are constantly learning both about the music and about yourself through the music. Just as in the case of a long-term relationship with another person, there are qualities that attract you and sustain the relationship. CMP calls these relationship-sustaining qualities of music its "heart." There can be a number of reasons that attract you to a piece of music, so the heart is not only the sustaining attractive elements, but also that quality that makes a piece of music distinct.

Just as your reasons for remaining in a relationship with another person change or mature over time, so will your reasons for pursuing a rela-tionship with a piece of music. Remember that people fulfill a variety of roles in our lives: some are good playmates, some provide good conversation, some challenge you, and once in a while there are those who impact and touch your life forever. Music can play all of these roles. What is more, your relationship with the music and your perception of the heart will change as you present it to your students. Together, you will establish individual and collective relationships and definitions of the heart.

The following are some questions to help you determine the heart of a piece of music:

- What attracted you to this piece of music?
- What maintains your interest in it?
- What gives this piece its distinctive qualities?
- What do you learn about yourself through the eyes of this music?
- What are text-based or musical images that you find compelling?
- How has the composer created your response through compositional devices?

Often the music's heart appears to be an element of music such as the rhythm or the melody, but in actuality, this element of music is only the doorway to the heart. The heart is the reason that element attracts you. For example, if you find the rhythm to be the heart of the *Hallelujah Chorus*, then ask yourself to keep going and complete the "because" part of the sentence. In other words, the rhythm in the *Hallelujah Chorus* is the heart because it creates a drive and spirit so infectious that it literally pulls listeners to their feet. This statement has now led you to the heart (a spirit and drive so infectious it literally pulls listeners to their feet) and suggests some of the musical elements that create the heart (the rhythm).

An affective or poetic heart is ultimately more useful than a technical one. Imagine introducing the *Hallelujah Chorus* as a piece with spirited rhythm, as opposed to a piece with an infectious drive and spirit that has been known to pull listeners to their feet. Instead of asking the ensemble to *crescendo* the first dotted quarter-note on "Hallelujah" and then sing the ensuing eighth-notes crisply to accentuate the rhythm, imagine the effect of asking them to use the space provided by the length of the note on "Hal" to surround listeners with inspiration and enthusiasm and then use the remaining eighth-notes, "le-lu-jah," to arouse them to their feet. Both of these approaches are good; however, the second one is more compelling because it gets the singers immediately to the heart of the music.

Determining the heart of the composition provides you with an inspirational entry point into teaching the piece to your ensemble. It will also color your interpretations and expressive choices. Mostly, it will solidify and make tangible your relationship with your selected music.

A word of caution to choral directors: Avoid choosing the text as the heart of the music—it is far too broad of a concept. It will be more productive to determine why the text is so attractive. Perhaps the rhythm of the words, an image conjured by the text, the manner in which the story is told, or how the composer set the text to music makes the text attractive and effective. Once again, spinning out your analysis of the text provides rich ideas for understanding your affective responses to the composition.

ANALYSIS

Examples of Possible Musical Hearts

**BAND
TEACHING PLAN**

Holst, *First Suite for Military Band*
(I. Chaconne)

The unity created by repetition of a simple melody
contrasted with imaginative variations

**CHORAL
TEACHING PLAN**

Handel, *Hallelujah Chorus*

The excitement and energy of its unrelenting drive
and excellent pacing of tension/release toward the
final goal

**ORCHESTRAL
TEACHING PLAN**

Mozart, *Eine Kleine Nachtmusik*
(I. Allegro)

The charm and grace created by the melodies

Moving from Analyzing to Teaching

It is often effective combinations of musical ideas that yield quality compositions. By analyzing what elements are paramount in a chosen composition, you and your students can begin to see what is involved in creating a quality piece of music. You can discover what about a particular selection makes it worth rehearsing and performing. At this point, we can list several things that make our example compositions worth performing:

Examples of What Makes These Compositions Worth Performing

BAND TEACHING PLAN

Holst, *First Suite for Military Band*
(I. Chaconne)

- Good example of variation form
- Classic in the wind band repertoire
- Holst is a major English composer in early 20th-century music

CHORAL TEACHING PLAN

Handel, *Hallelujah Chorus*

- An icon of Western music
- A movement from an oratorio
- Masterful example of Handel's style and the high Baroque style

ORCHESTRAL TEACHING PLAN

Mozart, *Eine Kleine Nachtmusik*
(I. Allegro)

- Good example of Classical style and Mozart's craftsmanship
- Good for teaching 18th-century bowing and articulation
- All five parts have musical interest

This chapter began with the recognition that every good score houses a rich curriculum, and now, after a careful analysis, that curriculum is apparent. Incidentally, poor repertoire selections reveal themselves after a thorough analysis because there is little to analyze. Upon review of your analysis, you have found numerous teachable musical ideas. The challenge now is deciding which ideas to actually teach, because you do not have time to teach everything. Begin by surveying your concert's music for common or contrasting musical ideas. For example, you may have three pieces in three-part form, but one is ABA, one is *da capo aria,* and one is A A'A" or three strophes. Teaching about form with these three pieces would be an obvious choice.

To demonstrate how the hard work of analyzing music pays off, this chapter ends with a list of things that you could teach with the three examples:

Example: Things You Could Teach with These Compositions

BAND TEACHING PLAN

Holst, *First Suite for Military Band* (I. Chaconne)

- The chaconne variation form
- How composers create variety
- Pedal point
- Motif
- Tension and release
- Articulation
- Arched phrases
- History of British wind band music

**CHORAL
TEACHING PLAN**

Handel, *Hallelujah Chorus*

- The oratorio
- The Messiah's place in music history
- Strong rhythmic vitality (articulation, inner pulse)
- Homophonic versus polyphonic textures
- Imitation
- Characteristics of the Baroque period
- Motif
- Relationship of tonic and dominant chords
- Handel

**ORCHESTRAL
TEACHING PLAN**

Mozart, *Eine Kleine Nachtmusik* (I. Allegro)

- Sonata *allegro* form
- 18th-century ornamentation
- Mozart's style, life, and influences
- Bowing styles
- Rhythmic cohesion
- Ensemble playing
- Sequence
- Values of the Classical period
- I and V chords
- Tapered phrasing
- Cadence

Summary

By investing time in a thorough analysis, you will discover the inner workings of the composition, you will briefly stand in the mind and the historical/social setting of the composer, and you will explore your personal relationship to the music. Further, you will be better prepared to teach the composition because of the depth of your familiarity with its inner workings. Lastly, you will have discovered musical concepts and vocabulary to teach your students. Make sure that as you teach, you share your analysis with students. This does not mean that you photocopy and hand out your ten-page analysis. Rather, find moments in rehearsals to interject interesting and motivating ideas or lead students to discover important elements of the music, such as the heart (specific suggestions for how to do this are the topics of ensuing chapters). By weaving analytical information into your rehearsals, you are making the ensemble experience more educational and comprehensive.

Outcomes

It is in the defining of outcomes that the teacher's role grows in importance. Whether consciously or not, it is the teacher who prioritizes what students should know, be able to do, understand, appreciate, even value. These outcomes may be immediate and spontaneous (I want my students to be able to sing the cadence on page two in tune before the bell rings) or long-term and carefully planned (I want my students to understand many characteristics of Baroque style). They may be easily observable (I want my students to play the E-flat scale) or difficult to observe (I want my students to appreciate Bach). They may be easy to evaluate (I want my students to notate a dictated melody) or almost impossible (I want my students to be inspired). All these types of outcomes can be divided generally into three broad categories:

1. Skill outcomes
2. Knowledge outcomes
3. Affective/aesthetic outcomes

Skill (or perceptual-motor) outcomes are a natural part of every music teacher's goals for students. They include such things as technical facility on an instrument and vocal techniques for singers, spiccato bowing, double tonguing, playing chromatic scales quickly, and singing a long line in tune are all examples of skill outcomes. Other skills that enable a student to function as part of a musical ensemble such as reading notation, following a conductor, creating a *legato* line, or improvising in thirds with a melody also fall into this category. Skill outcomes are easy to understand and they are the part of music teaching that is the easiest to assess because skills are foundational to music making. Teachers are comfortable with skill development and error detection because these skills are what have been emphasized in ensemblerehearsals throughout their music teacher training programs.

CMP teachers take skill outcomes somewhat for granted in their planning and are often heard to say, "The skill is the part we already do well—lets go deeper." Deeper, for a comprehensive musician, means an understanding of how music works in terms of its theory and its historical contexts. This kind of understanding defines knowledge (or cognitive) outcomes. The ability to define text painting, to recognize polyphonic or homophonic textures, to label the themes in a symphonic movement, to identify triads, or to critique a performance using precise musical vocabulary—these are examples of knowledge outcomes.

The line between skill and knowledge is often blurry. To improvise over a 12-bar blues progression is a skill that demands a particular kind of knowledge. It is merely a skill to play a minor scale with the correct fingerings. Understanding its structure of half and whole steps or its relationship to a relative major

Examples of Knowledge Outcomes

- Students will compose changing meter.
- Students will improvise the melody and harmony in stylistically appropriate ways.
- Students will be able to analyze the musical elements of Bach Cantatas.
- Students will identify examples of melisma, be able to use the term, and be able to sing the melismas in this piece correctly.
- Students will identify and recognize parallel thirds as a harmonic device.
- Students will identify the melodic themes of the piece and describe how and where they recur.
- Students will describe and identify motives.
- Students will contrast homophony and polyphony and discuss how they are used for expressive purposes in this piece.
- Students will define the compositional principle of unity versus variety.
- Students will analyze the concept of dissonance as an expressive device.

26

key is a knowledge outcome. Even something as seemingly basic as reading musical notation seems like a skill, but has a knowledge component, especially if a students' knowledge of notation can be demonstrated by their actually writing notation themselves.

Although skill and knowledge outcomes are the easiest to define, to observe, and to assess, they are not the real essence of the musical experience. They are not the reason most students sing in choir or play an instrument, and they are not the reason most music teachers choose music as their profession. It is the humanity expressed through music that draws us to and sustains our relationship with this art form.

This intrinsic quality of humanness is addressed in affective outcomes. Sometimes they also may be referred to as aesthetic outcomes or as personal knowledge but they deal with the internal and subjective aspects of students' musical experiences—their affective responses, attitudes, values, desires, commitments, and tastes.

Affective outcomes are as diverse as the many varieties of

Examples of Affective Outcomes

- Students will evaluate compositional techniques and their descriptive effect.
- Students will express their feelings about the poem and how it pertains to their own life experiences.
- Students will examine the orchestra as a metaphor for community.
- Students will analyze Bach's expression of faith in the musical elements of this composition.
- Students will discover the importance of connection with African roots in African American culture and compare and contrast this idea with their feelings about their own heritage.
- Students will examine their understanding of and reactions to the subject of death and dying.
- Students will experiment with a variety of ways to express the loss of a loved one through music.
- Students will investigate the feelings of performing Christian music when one is not Christian.
- Students will consider the pros and cons of attending adjudicated musical events and construct a philosophical position for doing (or not doing) so, based on their feelings about the potential outcomes.

OUTCOMES

musical expression and mood. A student develops a new appreciation for Copland. A student describes the relationship between a piece's compositional devices and its ability to evoke emotion. A student relates the mood of melancholy in a Brahms partsong to her own experience of loneliness.

Just as skill and knowledge outcomes are often closely related, affective outcomes are not always so easily separated from skills and knowledge. Many kinds of learning include all three: a skill, a knowledge, and an affective dimension. For example, the feeling of creating tension and release in a long phrase demands both a technical skill and an ability to analyze the peaks of the phrase, a kind of theoretical knowledge. The essence of a musically expressive and arched phrase, however, is something that is ultimately better felt than analyzed, and its analogous relationship to an ocean wave or the movement of a ballet dancer or the life cycle of birth, growth, and death makes it an even more profound experience when addressed as such.

Writing Outcomes

Outcomes may originate from different places. They may come from your music department curriculum, your state curriculum, or even from the National Standards for Music Education, which are all written in the form of student outcomes.

The process of writing student learning outcomes can also begin at several places within the CMP model. The teacher may first assess (see chapter four, "Assessment") a particular need in her students, such as better spiccato bowing; or more knowledge of the Romantic period; or more practice at fast, Baroque melismatic singing; or more experience with mixed meters. From here, the teacher writes an outcome based on what her students need to know, and proceeds to look for a piece of music to address that outcome.

Often music selection is the starting point. Once a piece of music has been selected and identified as a quality composition, possibilities for outcomes will be revealed through analysis. It is helpful to look at each piece as a textbook of possible learning outcomes and jot them down as you analyze it (see chapter one, "Analysis").

Possible things to teach (from last part of Analysis):

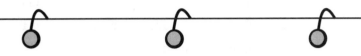

Holst: *First Suite for Military Band*

1. How to play an arched phrase
2. Variation form—what's a chaconne?
3. The balance between repetition and contrast (it's the same basic tune over and over, but it never gets dull—why not?)
4. The composer's use of color and timbre to maintain interest
5. The importance of the Suite in E-flat in wind band history
6. Different articulation styles
7. Tension and release—how a composer creates suspense, climaxes, etc.
8. Terms: pedal point, motif, hemiola, countermelody

Handel: *Hallelujah Chorus*

1. Textures: homophonic, polyphonic, monophonic
2. Fugue/imitation/counterpoint
3. Motif/theme
4. Form: the relationship of text to structure
5. The IV-I chord progression
6. Tension and release
7. Rhythmic energy and articulation of Baroque style
8. The oratorio form

Mozart: *Eine Kleine Nachtmusik*

1. Sonata-*allegro* form (terms: Theme, Exposition, Development, Recapitulation)
2. Characteristics of Classical period
3. Classical style bowing/articulation
4. Classical style phrasing
5. Compositional devices: sequence, motor rhythm, appogiaturas
6. Tension/release
7. Key relationships
8. Cadence

Analysis of the music helps sort out all the possibilities for designing outcomes, and the teacher selects those that are best suited to the piece and to her students' needs as young musicians. Rarely is it practical to teach all the possible outcomes related to a composition, although sometimes a longer, in-depth study of a piece with students will accomplish exactly that (especially if the teacher is planning long-range goals and/or more comprehensive units of study). More often, a thoughtful teacher will isolate (through analysis) the best possible outcomes from the piece to teach thoroughly, and only touch upon or perhaps briefly mention the others.

This is where discovering the heart of the piece is helpful. If you can determine the aspect of the music that is its strongest element (i.e. that unifies it, or gives it its distinction), you will have discovered at least one strong learning outcome, if not several.

When writing outcomes, it is tempting to focus on basic skills such as intonation, articulation, balance, blend, good vowels, etc.—in other words, technique. Of course these skills are important and absolutely necessary to a good performance and even a good understanding of the piece. Conscientious music teachers will teach these things already, so the challenge is to write more specific and less obvious skill outcomes, as well as compelling knowledge and affective outcomes. It is also important to identify what may be a long-term outcome, one that you will teach to over a long period of time, and what may be a short-term outcome, which can be achieved within a class period and lead to accomplishing a long-term goal. For example, long-term outcome means students will be able to judge the quality of an arrangement by considering how effectively the arranger used the elements of music. This long-term outcome would then break into short-term outcomes, such as students will define and describe form, identify and explain texture, locate and analyze compositional devices, and discover how composers/arrangers use form, texture, and compositional devices to create a mood, tell a story, or construct a quality composition. Each of these short-term outcomes will provide students with the knowledge and skills to be able to accomplish the long-term outcome.

To write an outcome, think about what you want your students to learn as opposed to how you want them to learn. Then choose an action verb stated as something students will do, know, or experience. For example:

The student will analyze sonata-allegro form by describing and labeling its parts.

When choosing verbs for skill and knowledge outcomes, it is helpful to look at different musicianly roles which the students could enact. The following is a list of those roles stated as verbs.

Assess	Compose	Move	Reflect
Analyze	Conduct	Name	Research
Arrange	Discuss	Notate	Respond
Bow	Evaluate	Orchestrate	Sightread
Breathe	Identify	Play	Sing
Classify	Improvise	Read	Write

Writing Good Outcomes

To clarify the goal for both you and your students, be as specific as possible about the desired learning opportunity. For example, an outcome such as "students will understand sequences" uses a verb that is too general and that fails to indicate important information such as what constitutes "understanding." Stating that "using a four note pattern, students will notate a sequence" indicates that through the written notation, you will have evidence that students have an "understanding" of musical sequences.

General—Students will understand sequences.

Specific—Using a four-note pattern, students will notate a sequence.

OUTCOMES ★

Another obstacle when writing outcomes is ensuring that the outcomes challenge students to think and interact on a variety of intellectual levels. It is common to ask students to memorize and repeat basic information, because lower-level cognitive interactions are quickly taught and easily assessed. For example, asking students to define an oratorio requires less time to answer than asking why a composer might write an oratorio instead of a mass.

Bloom's Taxonomy of the Cognitive Domain provides a useful tool for leading students to more sophisticated ways of thinking. Bloom argues that the lowest forms of cognitive interactions are *knowledge* and *comprehension*

Looking for substantial outcomes? Try the National Standards—they are written in action form already!

Standard 1: Playing

Standard 2: Singing

Standard 3: Improvising

Standard 4: Composing
             Arranging

Standard 5: Reading
             Notating

Standard 6: Listening
             Analyzing
             Describing

Standard 7: Evaluating

Standard 8: Relating to
             Arts and Other
             Disciplines

Standard 9: Understanding
             Music in
             Relationship
             to History and
             Culture

outcomes, which ask students to define, list, show, or explain ideas. He then places *application* and *analysis* (demonstrate, compare/contrast) as the next levels of thinking and concludes the taxonomy with *synthesis* and *evaluation* (design, critique) as the most sophisticated forms of cognition. The following chart illustrates Bloom's taxonomy, which places simple forms of knowing at the bottom and more complex forms of thinking at the top:

Bloom's Taxonomy of the Cognitive Domain

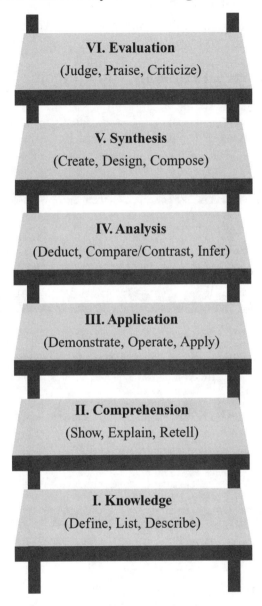

VI. Evaluation
(Judge, Praise, Criticize)

V. Synthesis
(Create, Design, Compose)

IV. Analysis
(Deduct, Compare/Contrast, Infer)

III. Application
(Demonstrate, Operate, Apply)

II. Comprehension
(Show, Explain, Retell)

I. Knowledge
(Define, List, Describe)

OUTCOMES

The taxonomy is helpful as a means to scrutinize your outcomes for balance and fortitude. For example, it does little good to have students always operating at the knowledge or comprehension level where they are basically repeating the knowledge that you have given them (defining, listing, retelling). Likewise, it is difficult for students to critique or design if they do not have foundational knowledge upon which to draw. Outcomes need to be sequenced to ensure successful learning, and they also need to be balanced so that students are intellectually challenged, and therefore gaining independence. The following chart will aid you in choosing and sequencing outcome verbs:

Bloom's Taxonomy and Outcome Verbs

MORE COMPLEX

Evaluation
Appraise, compare, critique, criticize, evaluate, support, summarize, judge, consider, recommend, weigh, relate

Synthesis
Combine, plan, role-play, invent, compose, revise, design, hypothesize, construct, create, develop, produce, organize

Analysis
Analyze, classify, survey, distinguish, categorize, subdivide, differentiate, infer, separate, select, point out

Application
Apply, chance, choose, solve, show, sketch, modify, dramatize, classify, discover, produce, prepare, use, paint

Comprehension
Convert, change, transform, rewrite, give examples, illustrate, restate, infer, relate, extend, explain, defend, predict, distinguish, generalize, summarize, interpret, compare

Knowledge
Define, describe, memorize, label, recognize, locate, name, recite, state, identify, select

LESS COMPLEX

The following example demonstrates how to alter an outcome so that it is more intellectually challenging:

1. Students will define chaconne. (Knowledge)
2. Students will analyze an unfamiliar score and discover a chaconne. (Analysis, Application)
3. Students will take a theme from one of their scores and construct a chaconne that uses this pre-existing theme. (Synthesis)

You will notice that each outcome requires interacting with basic information in more sophisticated ways. You may not have time to constantly teach at the *synthesis* and *evaluation* level of the taxonomy, but it is important to monitor outcomes to ensure the inclusion of higher-level thinking objectives so that your students are growing as thinkers and not becoming just good "mimics."

The Biggest Challenge—Writing Affective Outcomes

Music teachers know that music offers participants opportunities to grow emotionally, but having this sort of growth as an intended outcome is less familiar. While it is true that music creates a magical, affective experience, which is unique to each person, these experiences are more frequent and deeper when there is a planned effort on the teacher's part to more actively address them. An affective response includes a meaningful (e.g. spiritual, physical, or emotional) connection between the student and the music. It often results from the connection of the elements of music, personal knowledge, and accumulated experiences. The goal of the teacher is to use these responses to help students grow in personal knowledge (e.g. opinions, values, wishes, desires), awareness of the transcendent, and heightened sensitivity in their connection to humanity. The teacher can create an environment where affective experiences are more likely to occur by taking time to analyze the text, the social context for the music, the intended affect on the audience, or the reasons for performing music communally.

Because teachers are not used to writing them, affective outcomes can be challenging to conceive and construct. It helps to remember that affective outcomes are often long-range goals for our music students because it takes time to develop appreciation, inspiration, or sensitivity. To help you get started, the following chart lists actions that are focused on affective experiences:

Appreciate	Express feelings about	Respond to
Articulate opinions about	Inspired by	Show awareness of
	Make a commitment to	Value
Be open to	Motivated	Willing to explore
Be sensitive to	Perceive	
Be thoughtful about	Prioritize	
Develop a personal opinion about	Question beliefs about	

Just as there are many types of skills in music making and many kinds of musical knowledge, there are many ways to approach affective ways of knowing. Here are four ways to categorize affective outcomes:

1. **The Composer's Craft:** Students analyze the composition in terms of its affect and draw conclusions about its expressive content based on the composer's compositional choices. For example, students may describe a particularly exciting part of the piece as an "emotional rush" but never think deeply about what makes that part of the music so exciting. By teaching them to analyze and identify the aspects of the composition that contribute to its mood or emotional character, their affective/aesthetic experience is enhanced.

Examples of Affective Outcomes Based on the Composer's Craft

- Students will analyze and categorize compositional devices that create tension, and evaluate their expressive impact in the piece.

- Students will evaluate the composer's text setting for effectiveness and feeling.

- Students will compare the first and last sections of a piece in ABA form, and especially the emotional effect of the "B" on the final "A."

- Students will describe their favorite part of the piece and the compositional devices used to create that musical moment.

2. The Meaningful Performance: Just as the composer makes choices that create emotional content inherent in the piece itself, performers enhance (or detract from) that emotional content. Helping students to understand the relationship between their rhythmic precision and a mood of exhilarating joy, or the feeling of a slow musical phrase when performed with intensity of line and direction not only makes them better performers, but provides them a more thoughtful approach to music-making and a deeper understanding of how music works.

Examples of Affective Outcomes Based on the Meaningful Performance

- Students will analyze rubato as a tool of musical expression, and apply it appropriately and effectively to the composition based on the mood or tone they want to express.

- Students will compare the expressive effects of different styles of English diction (e.g. jazz or gospel style versus art song style).

- Students will create physical gestures to express the energy, articulation, and mood of each of the three themes of the piece.

> - Students will write their own prose narrative of the piece, taking into account its structure, compositional devices, and overall musical line.
>
> - Students will compare the expressive effects of different transpositions of the piece.

3. **Building the Community:** Sometimes the piece will lend itself to an outcome that enhances the group identity, builds a stronger sense of teamwork, promotes pride, creates an atmosphere of trust, openness, or sensitivity to others. These kinds of outcomes can even be addressed without a particular piece of music, through group discussions, retreats, and student-centered activities that promote sharing. However, when and if they can be tied to an excellent piece of music, both the outcome and the musical performance are enhanced.

Examples of Affective Outcomes
Based on Building Community

- Students will analyze the development section of the symphony as an analogy of a group discussion.

- Students will explore issues of group identity, nationalism, and patriotism, both healthy and destructive.

- Students will create new group goals based on the previous concert performance.

- Through musical improvisation, students will explore the tension between process and product in a performing group.

- Students will write text and melody for a band "alma mater" based on their feelings about and desires for the band.

4. Personal Knowledge: By giving students a chance to explore their own personal connections with the music they are performing, they are able to explore aspects of themselves that are practically never dealt with in school but can influence their values and feelings in a meaningful way.

Examples of Affective Outcomes
Based on Personal Knowledge

- Students will explore themes of consonance and dissonance, both in music and in their personal relationships.

- Students will define themselves as primarily a Romanticist or Classicist and explain why.

- Students will develop a rich and specific vocabulary to describe their musical tastes.

- Students will explore the idea of ambiguity and multiple meaning in the arts, and discover their own comfort or discomfort with it.

- Students will relate their own experiences of loss or grief to the piece.

OUTCOMES

BAND TEACHING PLAN

Holst, *First Suite for Military Band* (I. Chaconne)

Skill Outcomes
Students will perform arched phrases, showing understanding of tension and release

Knowledge Outcomes
Students will recognize and describe the chaconne form

Affective Outcomes
Students will explore emotions created by the idea of unity versus variety and how composers create our experience and sustain our imagination in a piece over time

CHORAL TEACHING PLAN

Handel, *Hallelujah Chorus*

Skill Outcomes
Students will perform with rhythmic vitality

Knowledge Outcomes
Students will describe polyphony, homophony, and monophony

Affective Outcomes
Students will explore their emotional responses to the music as well as their responses to concepts of popularity, durability, and the "masterpiece"

ORCHESTRAL TEACHING PLAN

Mozart, *Eine Kleine Nachtmusik* (I. Allegro)

Skill Outcomes
Students will perform Classical period bowing styles (*spiccato, legato,* etc.)

Knowledge Outcomes
Students will describe *sonata-allegro* form

Affective Outcomes
Students will describe the effect of this piece on listeners and determine how Mozart used compositional devices to create that effect

In a truly student-centered performance group, students are involved in developing outcomes. It is often instructive to listen to students describe personal goals for their musical life—they may differ from your own goals. When the outcomes are generated by students themselves, commitment to achieving them is considerably higher. Even sharing with students your outcomes for them will ensure a quicker route to their success. Once students are let in on the secret of what they should be learning, they learn it faster.

> ### Qualities of a Good Outcome
> - Interesting
> - Appropriately complex
> - Students learn something meaningful (as opposed to something obvious)
> - Integral to performing the music well
> - Specific and focused

Taking the time to carefully plan and write skill, knowledge, and affective outcomes will provide you with a set of goals, and therefore a structure for every lesson you teach. Because you have specific goals for teaching about various aspects of the music, you will be teaching your students how to perform with understanding.

References

Bloom, Benjamin S., and David R. Krathwohl. 1956. *Taxonomy of Educational Objectives.* NY: Longmans

Strategies

Teaching strategies are the teacher's playground because they are an opportunity to be creative, motivational, and fun. You have already established your outcomes, or what your students need to learn, so the strategies are how you are going to teach your students so that they achieve the outcomes. In other words, you are designing the creative journey students will take on the path to performing with greater understanding. In this chapter, you will learn to design teaching strategies specifically related to your outcomes that lead to a coherent teaching process. You will be generating strategies that teach musical concepts, that engage students in diverse musical behaviors, and that encourage them to think like composers as well as performers.

Designing Teaching Strategies

To begin designing strategies, as stated above, first consider the desired outcome.

Students will describe the characteristics of European folk music.

Take a moment to list what students need to know in order to accomplish this outcome. For example, to describe the characteristics of Western folk music students need to have experience playing, singing, or listening to it; they need to discuss the musical characteristics such as form, harmonization, and voicings; they also need to know who performs this music, where, and how. Next, select from the following actions to write the teaching strategies, because good strategies should involve student action, interaction, and discovery. These terms are useful because they position students as active participants in the learning process, which guarantees more in-depth and meaningful learning.

STRATEGIES

Acting	Classifying	Evaluating	Notating
Analyzing	Composing	Identifying	Orchestrating
Arranging	Conducting	Improvising	Playing
Articulating	Describing	Interpreting	Recording
Bowing	Designing	Journaling	Reflecting
Choreographing	Discussing	Listening	Researching
Clapping	Drawing	Moving	Sight-reading
			Singing

Some strategies for the above outcome might include:

Strategies

- *Sing and play* several folk songs with the students. Teach the songs by rote so that students experience the oral tradition. Over the course of several rehearsals, allow one of the folk song melodies to change according to what the students remember from day to day (as opposed to constantly correcting it so that they "get it right") so that students experience how folk songs develop and change over time.

- Ask the students to *describe* differences between oral and written musical traditions.

- Teach the students a traditional *dance* related to one of the folk songs and then ask them to *analyze* the interaction between the dance, the music, and the words. For example, how does music change when a dance is added?

Writing strategies is fairly straightforward once you understand that they must correspond to outcomes. Unfortunately, to open a score and begin teaching is all too common practice. Although this method can produce good performances, the lack of planning and thoughtfulness does little to teach students how to perform with understanding.

Writing Effective Teaching Strategies

It is not enough to write interesting teaching strategies. Because students' learning preferences vary greatly, one strategy does not fit all. Consequently, it is important to vary your teaching strategies to meet the needs of all learners and to develop independence and good musicianship in each student.

Learning Styles

Because of the prevalence of research on learning styles over the last two decades, most teachers are aware that they harbor personal preferences for learning, and that these preferences translate into specific teaching styles. For example, visual learners are likely to be the kind of teachers who frequently write on the blackboard or use detailed handouts in order to visualize what they are teaching.

There are three reasons for identifying your learning preference. If you know how you learn best, you can create that environment as often as possible and have more successful learning experiences. Further, you can work to strengthen the modalities in which you are weaker or less attentive to have success with teachers who teach to different strengths. Finally, as already implied, you will preference your learning mode as you design teaching strategies, which will benefit students with similar learning preferences while handicapping those with different ones. Consequently, you should vary teaching strategies in order for all students to be successful. (If you are unsure of which modality you teach in, videotape and analyze a rehearsal).

Researchers have identified numerous variables that affect learning: temperature, light, time of day, color of room, need for structure, etc. Because the field of learning styles is so diverse, we have limited ourselves to giving examples for auditory, visual, and kinesthetic learning modalities.

STRATEGIES

Teaching Strategies for Different Learning Modalities

Visual Learners

Visual learners learn best when they can see or visualize information. Writing goals on the blackboard, passing out handouts with bowings written out, and having students write in their music provide visual cues for those who learn best when they see the information.

**BAND
TEACHING PLAN**

Holst, *First Suite for Military Band* (I. Chaconne)

Outcome

Students will perform arched phrases showing understanding of tension and release.

Visual Strategy

Teacher gives students a page of the conductor's score and ask them to draw arched shapes above phrases in various selected passages, marking a * at the high point of each phrase.

**CHORAL
TEACHING PLAN**

Handel, *Hallelujah Chorus*

Outcome

Students will describe polyphony, homophony, and monophony.

Visual Strategy

Teacher draws icons on the board to illustrate each texture. Discuss how well each icon represents the sound of the various textures.

monophony

homophony

polyphony

STRATEGIES

Mozart, *Eine Kleine Nachtmusik* (I. Allegro)

Outcome

Students will describe *sonata-allegro* form.

Visual Strategy

Students create their own graphic design of *sonata-allegro* form with the standard parts of the form labeled.

Auditory Learners

Auditory learners learn best when they hear information. Playing an interval will be more meaningful to a auditory learner than writing it on the staff. Likewise, reading handouts or directions aloud will ensure that students hear the information for which you hold them accountable.

Holst, *First Suite for Military Band* (I. Chaconne)

Outcome

Students will recognize and describe the chaconne form.

Auditory Strategy

The teacher will play a recording of a Holst chaconne several times and students will listen with a specific question in mind each time:

- How many times is the chaconne melody repeated? (16 including the first statement).
- Are any of the chaconne melodies altered? (Yes, several are inverted or transposed to a minor mode).

STRATEGIES

**CHORAL
TEACHING PLAN**

Handel, *Hallelujah Chorus*

Outcome

Students will perform with rhythmic vitality.

Auditory Strategy

Because Handel is using voices like instruments, have the students listen to a recording of the piece and assign a neutral syllable to each section that imitates an instrumental sound. For example:

- The opening "Hallelujah" could be sung on "tah" or "pah"
- The quicker fanfare rhythm could be "tah-kak tah tah" (imitating brass)
- The longer notes of "The kingdom of this world" could be sung on "lah" to imitate strings playing long bowed notes
- The fugal sections (e.g. mm. 41-51) could be sung on "bum" with a belltone feeling

By removing the technical problems of the text, the rhythmic vitality of the lines is highlighted. When the original text is restored, ask students to retain the rhythmic vitality of singing as "instruments."

**ORCHESTRAL
TEACHING PLAN**

Mozart, *Eine Kleine Nachtmusik*
(I. Allegro)

Outcome

Students will perform Classical period bowing styles (*spiccato, legato,* etc).

Auditory Strategy

As students are mastering off-the-string bowings, record them. Listen as a group to the recordings and discuss the results. Then, listen to a professional recording to compare and discuss.

Kinesthetic Learners

For many ensemble directors, kinesthetic activities conjure visions of classroom management nightmares. Including kinesthetic strategies in your class need not feel so dangerous. Consider the following verbs: clap, bow, shape, step, and describe. The last verb, describe, tends to be thought of as verbal, but can be kinesthetic if you ask students to physically demonstrate the shape of a phrase or a major scale.

BAND TEACHING PLAN

Holst, *First Suite for Military Band* (I. Chaconne)

Outcome

Students will perform arched phrases, showing understanding of tension and release.

Kinesthetic Strategy

Students pair up, and while standing, join right hands. Teacher plays a recording that demonstrates rising and falling of musical energy. Students pull apart on rising tension and relax when the phrase relaxes. Pairs of students do the same thing with the Holst with one student on the stand playing and the other "pulling."

CHORAL TEACHING PLAN

Handel, *Hallelujah Chorus*

Outcome

Students will perform with rhythmic vitality.

Kinesthetic Strategy

To create a sense of the driving eighth note rhythm, have students rest the heel of their right hand on the shoulder of the singer to their right and tap eighth notes with their fingers while singing. Repeat until students feel like the ensemble's sense of rhythm has improved.

STRATEGIES

★

Mozart, *Eine Kleine Nachtmusik*
(I. Allegro)

Outcome

Students will examine Mozart's compositional devices (unison, motives, sequence, appoggiaturas, motor rhythms, cadence, fanfare, pedal point, repetition, contrast) and the role of these devices in the overall affect of the piece.

Kinesthetic Strategy

Students break into small groups of two or three and are assigned a phrase of the piece to "choreograph." This is not a dance, but rather physical movement that captures the essence of the phrase, how it moves, where its goals are, how it is articulated, where the musical emphasis is, etc. When finished, th groups form one large circle, standing in the order of the piece, and each group "performs" its phrase with a recording while the other students observe. After the performance, the entire ensemble discusses what they observed and how well the movements represented the composition.

Student-Centered Strategies

Effective teachers realize the importance of student-centered teaching where students come first, even ahead of the music. In the student-centered classroom, students share in decision making and take charge of their education, which leads them to become more independent and confident musicians. Student-centered rehearsals are the antithesis of the way most of us have participated in ensembles. The traditional rehearsal model is patterned after the professional symphony rehearsal, where the "maestro" dictates how the music will sound and the players reproduce this specific interpretation. According to this model, individuals subjugate their opinions and interpretations to the needs and wishes of the conductor.

In contrast, imagine a rehearsal where a student warms-up the ensemble while another reads the day's musical goals he has determined based on the previous rehearsal. Next, the students split into student-led sectionals and return with a performance and critique of what they learned and what still challenges them. After the teacher then rehearses the ensemble for a period of time, small groups of students volunteer to sit out, listen, critique, compliment, and offer suggestions for the next rehearsal. Within this model, students are engaging in a variety of musical behaviors, all of which complement and improve their performing with understanding. It is this highly productive student-centered model CMP seeks to promote.

Consider trying the following student-centered rehearsal strategies:

- Invite students to interpret the music's text (not for singers only!).
- Give students short writing moments (in journals, portfolios, 3x5 cards, etc.) asking for suggestions, rehearsal strategies, evaluations of musical moments, etc. These could be shared with the entire class or in small groups.
- Allow students to lead warm-ups.
- Invite student opinions on an artistic decision (e.g. where the *crescendo* should begin, which vowel color suits the piece's mood, which bowing sounds most appropriate for the style).
- Ask students to conduct a phrase, a refrain, a movement.
- Let students lead sectional rehearsals.
- Establish listening-squads, where a small group of students sit out and listen to the rehearsal and offer constructive comments.
- Give students opportunities to evaluate both rehearsals and performances through written comments, small group meetings, and entire class discussions.
- Organize a choir/band/orchestra council or officers to meet and discuss issues from the students' perspective, to act as advocates, and to plan events and group activities.

Moving toward a student-centered rehearsal can be challenging or intimidating. To ensure success, begin with a simple strategy and provide students with clear boundaries and lots of positive reinforcement for their "daring new behaviors." As often as possible, solicit input from students because you will quickly find that they have great opinions and wonderful musical ideas (remember, most of these students have been studying music since the first grade). Sophisticated student responses take time to develop, so listen carefully to what they say and act on as many *reasonable* suggestions as possible. Remember to balance new student-centered strategies with more familiar traditional strategies, and make sure your expectations for an interactive classroom are age and performance-level appropriate. As a result, you will quickly cultivate creative and introspective students.

Example: Student-Centered Strategies

**BAND
TEACHING PLAN**

Holst, *First Suite for Military Band* (I. Chaconne)

Outcome

Students will perform arched phrases showing understanding of tension and release.

Student-centered Strategy

Give the students a copy of the chaconne melody on manuscript paper and then have them play and sing it in unison. After a group discussion about the concept of line and peak of the phrase, have student conductors take turns conducting and showing their concept of the peak of the phrase and how to "set it up." After experiencing a variety of examples, have students discuss and decide as a group how they will shape the phrase.

**CHORAL
TEACHING PLAN**

Handel, *Hallelujah Chorus*

Outcome

Students will explore their own responses to the piece, as well as concepts of popularity, durability, and the "masterpiece."

Student-centered Strategy

After a brief discussion of Handel's *Messiah* and the traditions

**CHORAL TEACHING
PLAN CONT'D.**

surrounding the *Hallelujah Chorus*, have students interview family members and friends about their experiences with the *Hallelujah Chorus*. Ask students to keep these interviews in a journal. Then ask students to write a journal entry exploring why the *Hallelujah Chorus* has become so famous. Have students share these interviews and personal explorations in small groups, asking them to focus on the concepts of popularity, durability, and the "masterpiece."

**ORCHESTRAL
TEACHING PLAN**

Mozart, *Eine Kleine Nachtmusik* (I. Allegro)

Outcome

Students will perform classical bowing styles (*spiccato, legato,* etc.)

Student-centered Strategy

Partner-up students who are working on *spiccato* bowing style. Ask one partner to play a scale using spiccato bowing while the other partner carefully observes. Ask the observer to give feedback to their partner about bow placement, height of the rebound off of the string, bow grip, etc. Ask students to switch roles and repeat the activity.

Using Creative Teaching Stategies

In this section, you will learn numerous creative ways to design and use teaching strategies throughout your entire rehearsal. Remember, you can use every moment of the rehearsal to teach students how to perform with understanding.

Warm-ups

When planning warm-ups, start with your outcomes in mind. Warm-ups should prepare your students to achieve the outcomes. If you make this connection, the students will quickly perceive that warm-ups are more than mundane exercises, but rather strategies that lead them to a better musical understanding.

STRATEGIES

Examples of Outcome-Related Warm Ups

**BAND
TEACHING PLAN**

Holst, *First Suite for Military Band* (I. Chaconne)

Outcome

Students will perform arched phrases showing understanding of tension and release.

Related Warm-ups

- Have students write simple, diatonic melodies (similar to the chaconne melody) on manuscript paper. Make copies for the entire band and use them for warm-ups to practice creating line and arching phrases.

- Warm-up E-flat major or C-minor scales or arpeggios are performed with a conscious effort to create a line that peaks in a consistent place.

**CHORAL
TEACHING PLAN**

Handel, *Hallelujah Chorus*

Outcome

Students will perform with rhythmic vitality.

Related Warm-ups

- As part of a breath and vitality warm-up, students hiss rhythms from the piece in an energized style.

- Students sing the fugue subject, "And He shall reign forever and ever" in various keys, ascending by half-steps, with a different focus each time.

  1. To practice rhythmic and energized releases, snap fingers together on final releases.

  2. To work on intonation, sing on neutral syllables.

  3. For a better sense of the internal rhythm, sing every note *staccato* and/or with subdivided eighth-notes.

  4. For height in vowel formation, sing with palms of hands rhythmically stroking cheeks in a vertical direction.

Mozart, *Eine Kleine Nachtmusik* (I. Allegro)

Outcome

Students will perform classical bowing styles (*spiccato, legato,* etc.)

Related Warm-up

- Students play a warm-up scale four times in the following cycle:

  1. *Detaché,* moderate bow speed (quarter-notes)
  2. *Spiccato* (eighth-notes)
  3. *Molto legato* (quarter-notes)
  4. A down bow (quarter-note) followed by two *spiccato* up bows (eighth-notes)

Take Out the Piece . . .

One of the most engaging, creative, and easy strategies CMP teachers use is the "take out the piece . . ." strategy. If you ask students to, take out *Eine Kleine Nachtmusik,* they will do it, needing only the skill to identify the title of the piece. Notice the difference when you ask them to take out the piece...

1. ...by Wolfgang Amadeus Mozart
2. ...in Sonata Allegro form
3. ...written during the Classical period
4. ...that means "a little night music"
5. ...in G major
6. ...that uses this rhythmic motif (teacher claps, plays, or sings the main rhythmic motif)
7. ...that "I conduct like this" (conduct the beginning measures)

As students solve these puzzles, they are reviewing what they have learned about the music. Do not be alarmed if students consult with each other because these conversations will be productive and sometimes lead to further discussion or discovery about the piece. For example, you may ask the students to take the piece out with a "G" home tone, knowing they have two such pieces. This challenges them to figure out the difference between the two pieces before they can ask which one (one is in G-major and the other is in G mixolydian).

Different Ways to Refer to a Piece of Music

Articulation

Composer

Compositional devices

Contemporary of the composer

Form

Genre

Historical background

Instrumentation

Key signature

Language

Meter

Modulations

Rhythmic motif

Scale type

Solos

Style period

Texture

Tonality

Example: Many Ways to Refer to the Music

**BAND
TEACHING PLAN**

Holst, *First Suite for Military Band* (I. Chaconne)

- Take out the piece in variation form.
- Take out the piece by a British composer.
- Take out the piece that inverts the melody.
- Take out the piece with the alto sax solo.
- Take out the piece in triple meter.
- Take out the piece in E-flat major.
- Take out the piece by a composer who was a contemporary of John Philip Sousa and Ralph Vaughan Williams.

**CHORAL
TEACHING PLAN**

Handel, *Hallelujah Chorus*

- Take out the piece with pedal tones in the soprano part.
- Take out the piece from an oratorio.
- Take out the piece with a text from the Book of Revelation.
- Take out the piece with varying textures
- Take out the piece that premiered in Dublin, Ireland
- Take out the piece with a fugue
- Take out the piece with orchestral accompaniment

STRATEGIES

Introducing a New Piece of Music

Instead of just opening a new piece of music and beginning to rehearse, take the opportunity to formally introduce it in a creative manner that is consistent with your outcomes and the nature of the music. Remember that first impressions are lasting. If students have a bad first experience with music, they may resist learning it, which will make rehearsals cumbersome and tedious. By creatively introducing the music, you create the atmosphere for performing with understanding and you have the opportunity to "hook" students immediately, which will lead to motivating and thoughtful rehearsals.

The best place to begin strategizing creative ways to introduce a piece is the heart. Usually, what you find to be the heart of the piece is the reason you chose to have your ensemble learn it. If you design an activity that leads students to discover the heart, they will discover the attractive elements of the music and be excited about learning it. Conversely, starting with a musical obstacle can be equally effective, because you position students to enjoy overcoming the challenge.

Sometimes musical characteristics or technical aspects of a piece of music might appear as challenges that keep students from making an immediate connection. Difficult rhythms, unappealing harmonies, confusing polyphony, or difficult poetry can sometimes challenge students to the extent that they resist learning it. By anticipating them, you can turn obstacles into learning opportunities and creatively teach tricky, difficult, or potentially unappealing parts of the music.

> ### Example: Randall Thompson's *Alleluia* may present a challenge because it uses only one word.
>
> *Strategy* – Have students describe the qualities a word would need to have if it was going to be the only word in a song (interesting, variable, meaningful). Next, ask them to list single words that could be used as a song (usually they'll come around to "amen" and "hallelujah." Point out obvious flaws in words like "pizza"!). After they have discussed word options, ask them to list compositional devices they would use to make this song interesting (vary texture, dynamics, keys, etc.) Having listed as many elements of music and compositional devices as possible, play a recording of Randall Thompson's *Alleluia* and have students jot down the musical gestures he uses, noting ones not mentioned by an ensemble member. After the form and other elements have been identified, have ensemble members speculate as to why Thompson wrote his composition like he did. What was he trying to communicate by using only one word and the musical elements he did? What is the story of this one-word song?

Example: Pachelbel's *Canon in D* may seem boring because of its repetition.

Strategy – Have students learn and perform the bass line to the canon. Once they are comfortable with this, tell them that they are going to improvise several melodies over the bass line. Ask them to start with the simplest melody they can think of and have the entire ensemble learn it. Then let the improvisations become more complex. After the ensemble has composed several variations, have them listen to a recording of Pachelbel's *Canon in D* and compare his melodic embellishments with their improvisations. The students will now have an appreciation for the development of the theme in the canon.

Example: Murray Schafer's *Miniwanka* uses nontraditional notation that can either intrigue or frighten ensemble members.

Strategy – Have students choose a phrase of music from one of the pieces they are studying. Then ask them to create a new notation system that uses symbols other than musical notes. They can use shapes, colors, lines, pictures—they are limited only by their imagination. Using their new musical language, have students "notate" their chosen phrase on a large sheet of paper and make sure they include a "key" for interpreting the notation. Share these notated phrases either in small groups or with the entire class. Have students "read" the notation and then perform the phrase. When they open Schafer's score they will be intrigued and eager to figure out his nontraditional notation.

For choral or instrumental music based on poetry or songs, the text is often the best place to begin because that is where the composer probably began. Print the text alone in an easily readable format and start by having a student read it to the ensemble. Discuss the text in terms of its meaning and what students would expect the music to sound like given the time period and composer. This strategy works best if the text is critical to understanding the piece (e.g. Romantic German songs, 20th-century poems, etc.). It does not work as well with Latin liturgical texts (since the heart of those pieces is usually the music, more than the text itself).

Examples of Musical Obstacles

Complex harmony
Contemporary harmonies
Difficult foreign languages
Many changing meters
Multiple accidentals
Nontraditional keys
Non-traditional sounds and
   notation
Ostinato
Rapid scale-like passages
Rhythmic layering
Shifting (string players)
Singing in an instrumental
   composition
Slow, soft music
Technical challenges
Thin scoring
Too much new material throughout

Sometimes, listening to a good recording of the piece is an excellent way to get students to invest quickly in the music. Hearing the bigger picture as well as a polished product may be more motivating than a painful sight-reading episode. If you play a recording, however, always have a focus for the listening.

- Give students a puzzle, a problem, or a chance to share their opinion on what they heard.
- Create a mood of focused listening by waiting until the room is absolutely still before beginning.
- Keep initial listening experiences brief.

- Plan carefully the technical aspects such as having a remote control with your CD player or pre-taped excerpts so that you do not break the mood or waste time searching for musical tracks.

This strategy works best when the piece is difficult and sensational. Fast, technically challenging, non-Western, contemporary, or dissonant music make a much better impression when introduced this way (e.g. Britten's *This Little Babe*, Ives' *Unanswered Question*, or Duffy's *Snakes!*).

More Strategies

- Tell an interesting anecdote about the piece (if there is one).
- Be a storyteller and tell the story of the piece, or the story of its text (if it is interesting). Much of our job as teachers can involve drama and acting.
- Talk about the composer. Is there something inherently interesting about the composer, or about his or her relationship to the piece at hand? (e.g. Orlando di Lasso being kidnapped as a child because of his beautiful voice).
- Use a short writing assignment, which is then shared with the group.
- Focus on the historical milieu of the piece and its composer.
- Read a letter (that you create) from the composer about her intentions for the piece.
- Play the important themes of the piece before the first read-through.
- Give students the title of the piece only and ask them, "How do you think it will sound?" Engage their imaginations before they even see the notes.
- Teach folksongs, spirituals and arrangements of folk melodies by ear first. This places the emphasis on the beauty of the melody and students will make beautiful music immediately. Try teaching the entire piece by rote and discuss the lessons you learn as you focus on the music making experience as opposed to the note reading. This method reinforces development of aural skills.
- Tell a personal story that relates to the music.

STRATEGIES

Example Introductions

**BAND
TEACHING PLAN**

Holst, *First Suite for Military Band* (I. Chaconne)

Write the chaconne melody on the board or have individual copies
for each student transposed for their instrument. After students
play and are familiar with the melody ask them, "If you were
a composer and had to create 15 variations all built on this
eight-measure melody, how would you come up with enough
variations to keep it interesting?" Have students individually jot
down ideas and then share them in a giant brainstorming list on
the blackboard. Students may come up with ideas such as change
dynamics, vary instrumentation, use different keys, etc. After the
discussion, play a recording of the piece for students, giving them
an assignment to listen for how many of their ideas the composer
used. Listen and then discuss what they heard.

**CHORAL
TEACHING PLAN**

Handel, *Hallelujah Chorus*

Before passing out the music, ask the students what they think is
the most well known and most often performed piece of choral
music in the Western world. After this debate, pass out the music
and ask them to share their experiences with and any information
they know about the *Hallelujah Chorus.*

> **ORCHESTRAL TEACHING PLAN**
>
> **Mozart, *Eine Kleine Nachtmusik* (I. Allegro)**
> Ask students the following questions: What kind of music do people want at parties? Should the music be background music or should it challenge the listener's ear to pay attention? What kind of party music do you think people listened to in the 18th century?

Strategies That Go Beyond the Classroom

Great teaching strategies are not limited to the classroom. With careful planning and lots of encouragement, you can motivate students to make becoming a musician a lifetime commitment rather than merely a school experience. Consider the following suggestions:

- Encourage your students to make meaningful interdisciplinary connections with other subjects they are studying.

Example: Possible Interdisciplinary Connections

> **BAND TEACHING PLAN**
>
> **Holst, *First Suite for Military Band* (I. Chaconne)**
> Discuss the concept of the "unifying theme" and give examples of how it is used in an essay, a poem, a sermon, a painting, a work of architecture, or an interior design.

**CHORAL
TEACHING PLAN**

Handel, *Hallelujah Chorus*

Compare the style of Handel's oratorios to Baroque art. Compare the art forms in terms of emphasis on the dramatic, on extreme contrast, and on exaggeration and repetition.

**ORCHESTRAL
TEACHING PLAN**

Mozart, *Eine Kleine Nachtmusik* (I. Allegro)

Discuss daily life of the wealthy class in late 18th-century Vienna and Europe in general. Compare it with the daily life of a working class person or peasant. How would Vienna's poor have heard *Eine Kleine Nachtmusik*? Would they have known who Mozart was?

- Encourage students to do related reading or research. This can be as involved as doing a research paper, or as simple as asking a student to check the Internet for information about a composer, or to look up terms in the dictionary.

Example: Interesting Research Topics
(Remember the Vast Internet Resources)

**BAND
TEACHING PLAN**

Holst, *First Suite for Military Band* (I. Chaconne)

Research the history of the British military band, especially leading up to the 20th-century. Discuss when and where they were used, what kind of music they played, their typical instrumentation, the role of women, and how this tradition influenced the rise of band music in America. How was Holst's *First Suite* a departure from this old tradition? How did British military bands compare with American bands? Compare and contrast bands from the early and the late 20th century.

**CHORAL
TEACHING PLAN**

Handel, *Hallelujah Chorus*

There are many stories and legends surrounding the composition and early performance history of Handel's *Messiah*. Research the history of its creation and discuss the creation of some of these longstanding myths versus more recent discoveries that may contradict them. How do these myths begin and why do people keep them alive?

**ORCHESTRAL
TEACHING PLAN**

Mozart, *Eine Kleine Nachtmusik* (I. Allegro)

In preparation for a Mozart birthday party on or near January 27th, have students research the life and times of Mozart and then use their information and imaginations to find or create an appropriate and logical birthday gift for Mozart. Students do not write research reports, but rather keep notes in their journals as they discover historical, cultural, or biographical details about Mozart's life and cultural setting. On the day of the party, students present their gift, explaining to the class what they learned and why they brought the gift they did. Keep a checklist on the chalkboard of ideas about Mozart's life and times as they emerge from the class activity. Celebrate with cake and music.

• Encourage students to listen to music that enhances what they are learning in class. Provide students with listening tapes and discographies, and alert them to local performances.

Example: Possible Listening Assignment

**BAND
TEACHING PLAN**

Holst, *First Suite for Military Band* (I. Chaconne)

Play a recording for students of Pachelbel's *Canon in D* preceded by the question, "What does this piece have in common with Holst's chaconne?" (It is a set of variations on a ground bass). When students are familiar with the ground bass melody and can play it, use the melody as a class warm-up. Students can also improvise along with the recording. Invite students to bring recordings of popular music to class that use ground bass or *ostinato* (*Stand By Me,* for example).

**CHORAL
TEACHING PLAN**

Handel, *Hallelujah Chorus*

Play recordings of many different musical examples of various musical textures and ask students to identify which texture they are hearing. Each day have a different recording playing as students enter the room and begin class with a brief discussion of the texture.

**ORCHESTRAL
TEACHING PLAN**

Mozart, *Eine Kleine Nachtmusik* **(I. Allegro)**

Play a recording of Mozart's Symphony No. 40 in G minor (Movement I) and guide students to discover the structure points of the *sonata-allegro* form (Exposition, first theme, second theme, Development, and Recapitulation). They should be able to identify these points by listening. Encourage students to find other recorded examples of *sonata-allegro* form and discuss the prevalence of this form in so many Classical era pieces.

STRATEGIES

Summary

Writing effective teaching strategies is gratifying, energizing and creative. By writing strategies that account for the variety of ways your students learn and that create opportunities for students to be actively involved in decision making, you guarantee interesting and exciting rehearsals. Additionally, by making sure that your strategies are motivated by your outcomes, you ensure a process by which your students are learning and performing with understanding.

Assessment

As an ensemble director, you spend much of your rehearsal time engaged in assessment. You assess the ensemble's intonation, phrasing, tone production, and musicality. Directors use this information to choose a course of action both in the moment and over time. As a profession, we are good at assessing performing skills on a daily basis. Where we have fallen short is in providing students with systematic feedback, involving students in assessing their own learning, and developing meaningful criteria for grades. For example, many ensemble directors grade students primarily on attendance, attitude, and behavior. This practice conveys to parents, administrators, and students that what is important in performing ensembles is attendance and good attitudes. More appropriate criteria for grades would place emphasis on gaining musical knowledge, growing as a performer, and performing with understanding.

In today's educational climate of accountability and high-stakes testing it is more important than ever to demonstrate to parents, administrators, and students that profound learning takes place in performance ensembles. Assessment can serve as a means of advocacy and is imperative for recruitment of life-long musicians. It provides the opportunity to show parents and administrators that music teaches concepts, skills, attitudes, and appreciation for a basic form of human interaction. Assessment also demonstrates to students that they are growing as musicians and that they possess the skills and knowledge to develop musically throughout their lives.

In this chapter, assessment is presented as a natural, ongoing, and meaningful part of the teaching and learning process. Collecting evidence of what students have learned strengthens the rehearsal and educational process. The CMP planning model asks teachers to develop a systematic method for assessing the effectiveness of teaching strategies in addition to students' musical growth. This chapter provides numerous designs for collecting evidence of learning such as paper-and-pencil tests, checklists, rating scales, rubrics, and journal assignments. It also discusses how to organize this information into a student portfolio.

Assessment and Evaluation

Assessment and evaluation is a process used to determine both how well students have learned the material presented and the effectiveness of instruction. *Assessment* refers to the act of gathering data about learning (such as tests, journal entries, performance reviews) and *evaluation* is the process of analyzing or interpreting data in order to make judgements about what the data means. For example, you ask each of your trumpet players to perform a difficult four-bar phrase to ensure that they can all play it well (*assessment*). In your mind, you have determined an acceptable standard for what counts as good playing. As each student plays the phrase, you determine how well he or she can perform it according to your standard (*evaluation*). After hearing them play and making a judgment about how well they did (*musical growth*), you then determine what to do with this information (*effectiveness of instruction*). If the students played poorly, perhaps you would decide to adjust your teaching strategies to be more remedial. Maybe you would decide the students need additional practice and assign homework, you might even consider whether this piece of music is too difficult. If the students played well, your next step might be to apply these skills to other musical passages or move on and teach the next level of skills. Lastly, you might assign a grade to their performance to let them know how well they are doing compared to the level of playing you find acceptable.

Process of Assessment and Evaluation

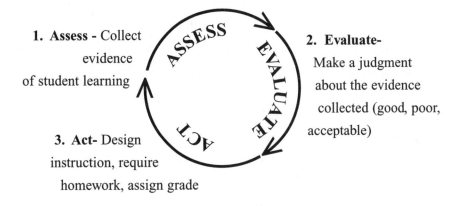

1. Assess - Collect evidence of student learning

2. Evaluate- Make a judgment about the evidence collected (good, poor, acceptable)

3. Act- Design instruction, require homework, assign grade

Assessment happens on an informal as well as formal level. Informal assessment is what teachers do in their heads as they listen and react throughout rehearsals. Formal assessment is taking time to document and record student learning in printed or electronic formats. This documentation results in tangible evidence (written comments, tests, journal entries, rubrics) that reflects how much a student knows or can demonstrate at a given moment.

Often the evaluation of information gained through assessment must be converted to some sort of grade. Grading has posed

---

Some Purposes of Assessment

To make instructional decisions about:
- Where to begin with instruction
- What has been learned
- What has to be taught or re-taught
- Individualizing instruction

To collect evidence for students about:
- Strengths
- Weaknesses
- Interests
- Learning styles

To collect evidence for teachers regarding:
- The effectiveness of instruction
- The effectiveness of curriculum

To collect evidence for stakeholders about:
- Achievement of stated standards
- Innovation or reform
- The effectiveness of curriculum

ASSESSMENT

many problems for ensemble directors. It has not been part of the culture of ensembles to collect *evidence of learning* but rather to collect *evidence of participation* as mentioned in the opening of this chapter. By conducting formal assessments throughout a grading period you not only provide your students with systematic feedback but you also build sound criteria for grading.

However, not all formal assessments will be graded—some will be used to provide explicit feedback about how a student is doing. The evaluation may be in the form of comments; numbers (e.g. 1-5 with 5 being the best); or √, √+, √-. Because letter grades can seem weighty and formidable, sometimes using a more casual system of feedback is less threatening and yields a better learning process.

In the CMP teaching philosophy the domain of assessment and grade assignment does not belong solely to the teacher—students engage in continuous assessment and evaluation also. Just as student-centered teaching strategies encourage musical independence and critical thinking skills, so too does student self-assessment. It is musically productive and educationally desirable to engage students in assessing their own performances as well as that of the entire ensembles, and in the latter part of this chapter we will show you a number of ways to initiate this process.

Where to Begin

Once again, you must return to the outcomes. The assessments you design are generated directly from your designated outcomes and teaching strategies. As a review, the outcomes state what you want students to know, the strategies state how you will teach to the outcome, and likewise, the assessment will tell you if the outcomes have been achieved and if the strategies were effective. If done well, the assessment will also tell you what additional knowledge students gained as they worked toward achieving the outcome. For example, you ask students to perform a scale, checking for good intonation, and notice that most were using better posture and more diaphragmatic breathing. While it was not your intention to assess these additional skills, it becomes apparent that students equate playing in tune with good posture and strong breath support. Learning is always multifarious and teachers cannot account nor plan for all that will happen in an effective rehearsal. Likewise, assessment can often tell teachers more about the learning event or the learner than anticipated because meaningful assessment is itself a meaningful learning experience. The following example demonstrates how these three steps work together:

Outcome

Students will differentiate between polyphony, homophony, and monophony.

Strategies

Teacher draws three icons on the board that represent a different texture. The students discuss these icons, how well they represent the sound of the various textures, and what the textures actually look like in notated form.

Assessment

Students are given six excerpts of choral scores they have never seen before (eight to 12 measures) that represent all three textures. They must identify each of them as polyphonic, homophonic, or monophonic.

There are numerous ways to gather evidence of musical achievement. The remainder of this chapter will review various techniques including pencil-and-paper tests, checklists, rating scales, rubrics, and journal assignments.

Pencil-and-Paper Tests

Generally, music teachers do not think of ensembles as a place for paper-and-pencil tests. However, these tests are often the most efficient tool for quickly assessing how much students know, especially as you ask them to gain substantive knowledge about music. There are two ways of collecting this information: through *selected response* items and *created response* items. Selected response items require students to select a correct response from a list of possible answers. Multiple choice, true-false, matching answers, and fill-in-the-blank are all selected response type questions. Conversely, the created response format requires students to generate a response in their own words as in an essay or short answer questions. Because music students are not used to taking written tests, make sure your first ones are well designed and straightforward to ensure confidence and success.

Consider the following examples from the three compositions that we are studying:

**BAND
TEACHING PLAN**

Holst, *First Suite for Military Band* (I. Chaconne)

Outcome

Students will explore the idea of unity versus variety and how composers sustain our imagination and interest over time in a composition.

Assessment Tool

(Essay Question)

Composers face a challenge of how to use unity versus variety when creating a piece of music. What are the problems with too much of one or the other? How does Holst achieve unity? Variety? Use specific examples from your music and refer to measure numbers or variation numbers.

**CHORAL
TEACHING PLAN**

Handel, *Hallelujah Chorus*

Outcome

Students will describe polyphony, homophony, and monophony

Assessment Tool

(Multiple Choice Quiz)

Circle as many as apply:

1. The texture of the opening "Hallelujah" is

   a. homophonic   b. polyphonic

   c. monophonic   d. unison

2. The "And He shall reign forever" section is an example of a

   a. chorale   b. fugue

   c. homophonic texture   d. monophonic texture

3. An example of monophonic texture is

   a. the closing measures of the chorus   b. Gregorian chant

   c. "For the Lord God omnipotent reigneth"   d. a fugue

4. "The kingdom of this world is become…" is a good example of

   a. polyphonic texture   b. chorale style

   c. homophonic texture   d. a fugue

5. In a polyphonic choral texture, the vocal line that is most
   important is usually

   a. the women's parts   b. the men's parts

   c. all parts   d. whichever part has the theme

ASSESSMENT

Mozart, *Eine Kleine Nachtmusik* (I. Allegro)

Outcome

Students will examine Mozart's compositional devices (unison, motives, sequence, appoggiaturas, motor rhythms, cadence, fanfare, pedal point, repetition, contrast, chromaticism) and their role in the overall affect of the piece.

Assessment Tool

(Matching Answers)

Match the following terms with their definitions or examples:

1. Cadence

2. Sequence

3. Pedal point

4. Motor rhythm

5. Appoggiatura

6. Motif or motive

7. Unison

8. *Spiccato*

9. *Legato*

10. Chromaticism

___Bounced bow

___A short musical idea in repeated segments at higher or lower pitch levels

___A harmonic, melodic or rhythmic figure which closes a phrase or section

___Created through repeated eighth notes

___Use of half-steps which are outside the normal key to add harmonic color

___Smoothly

___Several voices or instruments playing a note or melody at the same pitch or in octaves

___An accented grace note

___A long-held note sounding with changing harmonies in other parts

___A short characteristic melodic figure that recurs throughout the piece as a unifying element.

Observational and Performance Assessments

Most of the learning in performing ensembles is not easily captured by pencil-and-paper tests because students are performing physical and aesthetic tasks. To evaluate if students are growing musically, you want to assess them while performing tasks of a musician. This might include warming-up in tune, playing with correct bowing, singing a phrase with the correct shape and appropriate amount of breath, etc. Assessing students performing these tasks is referred to as *authentic* assessment, because you are assessing them within an *authentic* musical context. This method can be challenging because the assessment design must allow you both to observe and to log musical behaviors.

As with other forms of assessment, a primary concern in observational assessment is the accuracy and consistency of the information gathered. The assessment design needs to be based on well-defined criteria to provide greater validity and reliability. Checklists, rating scales, or rubrics are simple yet effective tools to help you define evaluation criteria.

Observational and Performance Assessment Ideas

Drawing form of piece

Listening and describing

Music-skill computer programs

Playing parts on the piano

Quartet and solo performance

Recording and evaluating rehearsals, sectionals, individual practice

Recording individual students— Etudes, excerpts, scales, folk tunes, original compositions, improvisations

Rhythmic, melodic, intervallic dictation

Sightreading alone

Verbally analyzing octavos

Videotaping and analyzing rehearsals

ASSESSMENT

Checklists

A checklist states the specific criteria necessary for a successful performance. The teacher observes a student's performance and marks whether or not each element was present. For example:

Example Checklist for *Eine Kleine Nachtmusik* (1st. Mvt.—Allegro)

Outcome: Students will perform Classical period bowing styles
(*spiccato, legato,* etc.)
Assessment Tool:
Excerpt Performance
Criteria

	mm. 1-14	mm. 28-39	mm. 61-76
1. Part marked correctly	_____	_____	_____
2. Correct bowing executed	_____	_____	_____
3. Proper bow hold	_____	_____	_____
4. Full use of bow	_____	_____	_____
5. Even/rhythmic *spiccato* stroke	_____	_____	_____
6. Effective *legato* style	_____	_____	_____

The advantage of a checklist is that it lists and therefore highlights some important aspects of performance. With this list, both students and teachers understand where to focus. The total task may be complex (playing a scale well), but the checklist conveniently breaks down the components of the task into simpler and smaller ones. Similarly, the checklist highlights specific elements of a student's performance that are or are not present.

The primary disadvantage of a checklist is that it does not allow the teacher or student to provide feedback on the *quality* of the student's performance. It does not tell you how proper the posture was or how good the breath control. Rather, it indicates that a student accomplished a skill,

ASSESSMENT

but not to what degree. Another challenge in using the checklist lies in making an overall judgement about the performance. For example, how many checks equal a passing grade, and how will the students know? A checklist is a good generic tool for holding students accountable for exhibiting certain skills, and can be filled-out by either the teacher or students. It is useful early in the assessment process when teachers are reticent to grade students but want to offer feedback or create some form of accountability.

Rating Scales

Rating scales are like checklists in that they list the specific criteria for good performances. However, rating scales allow teachers and students to record judgements about the quality of each variable. Three types of rating scales—numeric, graphic, and specific—are commonly used, and the following demonstrates each one:

Numeric Rating Scales

Outcome: Students will perform Classical period bowing styles
     (*spiccato, legato,* etc.)

Criteria

1. Part marked properly	1	2	3	4	5
2. Correct bowing executed	1	2	3	4	5
3. Proper bow hold	1	2	3	4	5
4. Full use of bow	1	2	3	4	5
5. Even/rhythmic *spiccato* stroke	1	2	3	4	5
6. Effective *legato* style	1	2	3	4	5

Graphic Rating Scales

Outcome: Students will perform Classical period bowing styles
    (*spiccato, legato,* etc.)

Criteria

1. Part marked properly   I----------I----------I--------I
                                     Poor   Fair   Good   Great

2. Correct bowing executed   I----------I----------I--------I
                                       Poor   Fair   Good   Great

3. Proper bow hold   I----------I----------I--------I
                                       Poor   Fair   Good   Great

4. Full use of bow   I----------I----------I--------I
                                       Poor   Fair   Good   Great

5. Even/rhythmic *spiccato* stroke   I----------I----------I--------I
                                       Poor   Fair   Good   Great

6. Effective *legato* style   I----------I----------I--------I
                                       Poor   Fair   Good   Great

Descriptive Rating Scale

Outcome: Students will perform Classical period bowing styles
    (*spiccato, legato,* etc.)

Criteria   Rating

1. Good tone quality   I--------------------I--------------------I
                      Unclear, fuzzy   Clear but   Clear, strong
                       Low energy   weak   Full

2. Proper use of bow   I---------------------I------------------I
                      uneven   fairly even   even
                     short stroke   medium stroke   full stroke

Arriving at a grade for a student's performance is easier using rating scales rather than just checklists. The scores from numeric rating scales can be averaged and easily assigned a grade (5=A, 4=B, 3=C, 2=D, 1=F). You can assign numeric values to graphic and descriptive scales and average them in the same manner. Sometimes, instead of assigning a grade, it is more effective to summarize a student's performance in a couple of sentences that describe the overall performance and steps for improvement. Using dialogue as a response focuses students on improving skills or gaining more knowledge, instead of on simply achieving an "A." Keeping track of these assessments will create a chronological record of student growth, which can eventually be assigned a grade—perhaps one that is determined by both student and teacher.

Rubrics

A rubric is a matrix that defines in detail what a student must demonstrate during a particular performance. These can be filled-in by the teacher or by the student as a self-assessment. Rubrics can be adapted from an existing source, created by the teacher, or designed by the students and teacher together. The following is an example of a rubric:

ASSESSMENT

Example Rubric: Vocal Audition–Wisconsin School Music Association

TONE	7	6 5	4 3	2 1
_____ Pts	Outstanding vocal color and quality in all ranges and registers.	Correct vowels, breath support. Register and range are smooth.	Some vowel placement problems. Breath support is not consistently correct. Some register breaks.	Poor vowel placement and inconsistent register breaks. Breath support is not used correctly.
Comments:				
INTONA-TION	7	6 5	4 3	2 1
_____ Pts	All ranges and registers are in tune. Excellent control and listening skills.	Demonstrates minimal intonation difficulties. Control and listening skills are demonstrated most of the time.	Mostly accurate, but includes some intonation difficulties. Listening skills are developing.	Significant intonation problems throughout. Listening skills are not developed.
Comments:				
ACCURACY	7	6 5	4 3	2 1
(Notes and Rhythms)	Outstanding precision throughout. All pitches and rhythms are performed accurately.	Errors infrequent and corrected quickly. Rhythms are correct. A few minor problems in technical passages.	Inconsistent performance of notes and rhythmic patters throughout the piece.	Numerous inaccurate notes and rhythmic passages. Technical passages are weak.
_____Pts				
Comments:				
DICTION	7	6 5	4 3	2 1
_____Pts	Exceptional diction and consistently correct pronunciation.	Mostly accurate vowels and language is pronounced correctly.	Some incorrect vowels and/or consonants. Some problems with words.	Inappropriate vowels, consonants, words not easily understood, and/or pronunciation is not correct.
Comments:				
INTERPRE-TATION	7	6 5	4 3	2 1
_____Pts	Stylistically accurate. Extremely musical, sensitive performance. Expression is natural and highly effective. Outstanding dynamic range and accurate tempos.	Some passages lack interpretation. Style and tempo are accurate most of the time. Very good use of dynamics.	Style is evident but becomes rigid and mechanical at times. Tempo is accurate some of the time. Style and dynamics are inconsistent.	Style is underdeveloped. Mostly mechanical and non-musical performance. Tempos are not maintained and dynamics are not controlled.
Comments:				

ASSESSMENT

When using a rubric, a teacher can more easily and consistently assign scores to a student's work. Also, students can use the rubrics to evaluate their own work or that of other students. It is important to note that including comments with scores is extremely beneficial and lets students understand why they received a particular score, and how they can improve their scores in the future. Likewise, when students complete the rubrics, their comments will help you understand why they assigned themselves the scores they did and where they are on the learning continuum. For example, a student may assign a high score because of a sense of accomplishment rather than because the performance was accurate. Discrepancies in scores between students and teachers will lead to productive dialogue, which is important for nurturing musical understanding and further growth.

Checklists, rating scales, and rubrics are effective tools to help you more accurately and consistently assess student performance, practice, or projects. These systems are the most accurate when they meet the following conditions:

- The specific details that constitute a good performance are identified, delineated, and made clear to students.
- Each variable is clearly described.
- The setting in which the performance will take place is described.
- The performance is evaluated using predetermined criteria.

ASSESSMENT

ASSESSMENT ★

Journal Assignments

In addition to paper-and-pencil tests and performance assessments, journal assignments are a useful method for students to more freely express their musical knowledge and personal growth. Because these questions will more likely be open-ended, students will have more breadth to explore their thoughts and feelings than they would in a rubric or rating scale that focuses on specific skills or outcomes.

Journal assignments can range from personal reflections to reporting practice hours to ensemble critiques. Because students in ensembles are not used to writing, start with short, fun-to-answer questions, such as, "Describe your favorite part of today's rehearsal." (How to use journals is explored more fully in the second part of the book. See chapter seven.)

Brainstorming Journal Entries

- Create stories or endings to music
- Description of what was accomplished during their individual practice time
- Group goals
- Interviews
- Listening activities
- Musical activities outside of classroom
- Opinions about rehearsal issues
- Outside concert reviews/critiques
- Personal goals for the quarter
- Research
- Self evaluations
- Self grading with explanations
- Weekly evaluations

With the first journal assignment, it is imperative that you respond in writing to what each student wrote. Students will be encouraged by this personalized acknowledgement and excited to write again.

At some point you may find that you do not have time to read each journal response. Another way of using the journals is to have students share their responses in small groups or you read a few aloud each day during rehearsal over several weeks. When students believe that their thoughts are being validated their enthusiasm for journaling will increase exponentially and the dialogue between you and the student will deepen profoundly.

Portfolios

Once you have a collection of evidence demonstrating musical learning, CMP teachers recommend organizing it into a portfolio. Teachers of many academic subjects are becoming increasingly familiar with portfolio assessment. This form of assessment was first used by visual artists, where students would select their best work and organize it for review or presentation. The use of portfolio assessment in public schools has become more widespread, but is not yet common. In some schools, portfolios are compiled for each student and comprise work samples from all academic disciplines. In other settings, individual teachers use portfolios for their subject area, such as language arts or math.

In the early 1980s, researchers at Harvard Project Zero demonstrated successful and enticing ways to use portfolios in arts classes, including music. Within the design of Project Zero, a portfolio refers to a collection of student work, and portfolios can play at least two different roles: the Process and the Product portfolio. The Process Portfolio is an ongoing collection of student work. As students complete assignments, assessments, and journal entries they place them in their portfolios. Periodically, students and teachers review the materials to reflect upon or evaluate progress as demonstrated in this developmental record.

The Process Portfolio is similar to the visual arts model, where students select a collection of their most representative work and thereby construct a picture of who they are as a learner or musician, depending on the portfolio goal. The Product Portfolio is a hybrid of the Process Portfolio, in that the latter provides the materials for the former. Constructing a Product Portfolio is a valuable exercise, because students must reflect upon their experiences as they review and select items that represent their learning. Often, a written statement in which the student defends what has been included in the portfolio accompanies the Product Portfolio. The act of reflection creates independent, thoughtful musicians and students.

The following is a table of contents for a portfolio based on the activities designed for Handel's *Hallelujah Chorus*:

Portfolio Table of Contents for *Hallelujah Chorus* Unit of Study

Texture	Homophonic	Fugue
Polyphonic	Monophonic	Chorale

1. Student created glossary of terms:
2. Multiple choice quiz
3. Rehearsal tape of performing fugue part with student who sings another part
4. Interview with parent and friend about personal experiences with the *Hallelujah Chorus*
5. Student essay speculating on why the *Hallelujah Chorus* is so famous
6. Post-concert reflection
7. Post-concert performance critique (based on tape of concert)
8. Student summary of musical growth based on evidence in the portfolio

---

By having parents review the portfolios, these documents become an effective advocacy tool because they clearly demonstrate the variety and depth of learning that takes place during ensemble rehearsals. The following is a letter addressed to parents explaining the portfolio and asking for specific input:

Central Middle School Bands
Parent Portfolio Review

Dear Parents: March 22

In this music portfolio are samples of your son/daughter's work from the entire school year. This work shows some of the things we have done over the course of this year. It shows some of what we do in band rehearsals. You should find notes, individual and group evaluations, listening and composition activities, goals, and rehearsal critiques. All material is listed on the portfolio checklist.

Why do we use portfolios in band? For many reasons! This collection of work shows what we do and how we learn music—

ASSESSMENT

musical understanding. These projects center not on one right answer, but focus on each student's ability to identify problems, use higher-order thinking skills, think creatively and critically, and demonstrate self-expression. When we complete a written exercise or project, EVERY student has a chance to respond. In rehearsal, our groups are so large that not every student has an opportunity to contribute to a class discussion. With a portfolio, every student's voice is heard.

Please take a few moments to review your child's portfolio. I suggest asking for explanations from your child regarding the various items in the portfolio. Please take the time to discuss their work as I think you will be quite pleased with your student's musical vocabulary and depth of understanding. If you have any questions, please call me at the Central Music Office, 555-1111.

ASSESSMENT

YES—I HAVE REVIEWED MY SON/DAUGHTER'S PORTFOLIO

Student Name_____

Date_____

Parent Name _____

1. What did you see in your child's portfolio?

_____

2. Was the material well organized?

_____

3. What would you like to see included in this portfolio?

_____

_____

4. What did you learn about the band program and your child's experience at Central as a result of reading this portfolio?

_____

_____

Extra credit: What are the elements of music?

_____

Portfolio Management

In utilizing portfolios, practical matters arise such as frequency of use, contents, frequency of review (as well as who reviews them), assigning a grade, and storage. The individual teacher, the one responsible for the events that take place in the performing ensemble, best resolves these issues. If you plan to have peers or parents review a portfolio, make sure students are aware of and agree to this before they complete assignments, as they may want to craft responses accordingly. Each teacher will also need to determine the manner in which portfolios are evaluated: letter grade, numerical score, check-off system, or a combination of the above.

It can seem overwhelming to grade 300 portfolios several times during a term, therefore, the use of student self-evaluation, peer evaluation, or parent evaluation can reduce the workload as well as produce creative and effective input. As mentioned previously, when reviewed by parents, the portfolio becomes an excellent advocacy tool for your program. As with any new idea, the application and use of portfolios will be most effective if first implemented on a small scale. Pilot the project with one ensemble, then when you more fully understand the process, expand to include all of your ensembles. Also, make sure that portfolios have an appropriate balance of performance assessments and written reflections. Remember that an ensemble rehearsal is not a writing class, and therefore, writing should be done in small but highly effective doses.

The following example (see pg. 90) demonstrates how you can design a notebook for each student that will include a number of the assessments for the quarter. This notebook then becomes the portfolio to review as you and your students assess what was learned during the quarter.

Top Ten Reasons to Use Portfolios

10. Documents the student's musical journey

9. Opens up another avenue of communication between the student and teacher

8. Documents reflective thinking

7. Helps students become accountable for their learning

6. Paints a richer picture of individual student learning

5. Allows for greater accountability to parents and administrators

4. Plans and re-directs instruction

3. Helps students develop organizational skills

2. Assists help with teacher evaluation

1. Helps students get in touch with their musical understandings through writing

ASSESSMENT

Name_____

Kohler Public Schools

Concert Band

1st Quarter

Keep this notebook in your folder. Bring it to every rehearsal.
To be handed in at the end of the quarter
as part of your portfolio.

This notebook is for:

Goal Setting

Mid-Quarter Self Evaluations

Practice Log

Scale and Key Signature Guide

Musical Development

Weekly Lesson Requirements

Ensemble Rehearsal Critiques

Concert Critique

Standard I Projects

Student/Teacher Evaluations

ASSESSMENT

1st Quarter—Concert Band

Music Goal

Is my goal realistic? Is it measurable? Is it a 9-week goal?

_____

_____

_____

Steps to achieve this goal:

1._____

2._____

3._____

Progress Log

Progress made or obstacles encountered:

Date_____ Progress_____

Date_____ Progress_____

Date_____ Progress_____

Date_____ Progress_____

I ACHIEVED MY GOAL!!!

Date _____

What I've learned from striving toward this goal:

This is my best work.

_____

(Student Signature)

ASSESSMENT

Mid-Quarter Evaluation

Please be detailed and use complete sentences.

What is your favorite piece of music we are rehearsing and why?
Selection: _____

_____

Things you need to improve on before the end of the quarter:

1._____

2. _____

3. _____

Evaluate your performance during rehearsals. CIRCLE ONE:
    poor   fair   very good   excellent

Explain_____

_____

Evaluate your performance during lessons: CIRCLE ONE:
    poor   fair   very good   excellent

Explain_____

_____

_____

What is your favorite part of band this quarter and why?

_____

_____

What are some things the teacher could do better?

_____

_____

How are you doing on your Quarter Goals & Ensemble
Rehearsal Critiques?

_____

_____

Musical Development Rating Scale - Student Evaluation

Quality of Work:

(circle the highest level of achievement)

The student projects and instrumental lessons...

5   were prepared and completed to the student's highest ability or standard.

4   were prepared and completed to a high standard, but left room for improvement.

3   were prepared and completed to an average standard; needs improvement.

2   were sometimes prepared and completed; demonstrations of musical development were not up to students ability.

1 .   was of poor quality.

Practice:

(circle the highest level of achievement)

The student practices at home or at school...

4   four times or more a week for approximately 20 minutes.

3   three times a week for approximately 20 minutes.

2   two times a week for approximately 20 minutes.

1   one to zero times a week.

Work Ethic, Attitude
Rehearsal Contribution:

(check those attributes demonstrated)

In regards to work ethic, attitude, and rehearsal contribution, the student...

_____   demonstrates a mature work ethic and uses time efficiently (e.g. sectional or solo and ensemble practice time).

_____   demonstrates a positive and productive approach in rehearsals.

_____   is consistently prepared with instruments, music, equipment, etc.

_____   maintains focus and attention during rehearsal (e.g. no talking).

_____   demonstrates quality reflection and insight within journal entries.

_____   is a positive leader and/or positive influence within the ensemble.

_____   is consistently prepared with lessons and projects on time.

(   ) Total Points

ASSESSMENT

ASSESSMENT ★

Musical Development Rating Scale -
Teacher Evaluation

Quality of Work:

(circle the highest level of achievement)

The student projects and instrumental lessons...

5 were prepared and completed to the student's highest ability or standard.

4 were prepared and completed to a high standard, but left room for improvement.

3 were prepared and completed to an average standard; needs improvement.

2 were sometimes prepared and completed; demonstrations of musical development were not up to students ability.

1 were of poor quality.

Practice:

(circle the highest level of achievement)

The student practices at home or at school...

4 four times or more a week.

3 three times a week.

2 two times a week.

1 one to zero times a week.

Work Ethic, Attitude
Rehearsal Contribution:

(check those attributes demonstrated)

In regards to work ethic, attitude, and rehearsal contribution, the student...

___ demonstrates a mature work ethic and uses time efficiently (e.g. sectional or solo and ensemble practice time).

___ demonstrates a positive and productive approach in rehearsals.

___ is consistently prepared with instruments, music, equipment, etc.

___ maintains focus and attention during rehearsal (e.g. no talking).

___ demonstrates quality reflection and insight within journal entries.

___ is a positive leader and/or positive influence within the ensemble.

___ is consistently prepared with lessons and projects on time.

(_____) Total Points

Rehearsal Critique No. _____

Piece of music: _____

Composer: _____

BE SPECIFIC Location Parameter or Section		**COMMENTS** My Performance	**PRACTICE PLAN** For Myself

BE SPECIFIC Location Parameter or Section		**COMMENTS** My Performance	**PRACTICE PLAN** For Myself

Parameters:

Notes	Intonation	Tone Quality
Rhythms	Dynamics	Balance
Phrasing	Tempo	Style

Articulation (attacks/releases)

This is my best work._____

(Student Signature)

ASSESSMENT

Scale & Key Signature Worksheet
Concert Band

Name _____

Follow all directions and complete the exercises below.

1. Write an ascending one-octave **Concert B-flat** scale in whole notes. Put in the clef sign of your instrument. Darken in the notes of the arpeggio.

_____
=======================================
=======================================
_____

2. Write an ascending one octave **Concert G** minor scale in whole   notes. Put in the clef sign of your instrument. Darken in the notes of the arpeggio.

_____
=======================================
=======================================
_____

3. The instrument you play is called the _____.

4. It is a member of the _____ family.

5. Given any concert pitch, how do you determine what note to play on your instrument?

_____

_____

_____

_____

ASSESSMENT

Concert Band - Practice Log

Week	Date	Assignment / Goal	Sun.	Mon.	Tue.	Wed.	Thu.
1	Sept. 2						
2	Sept. 9						
3	Sept. 16						
4	Sept. 23						
5	Sept. 30						
6	Oct. 7						
7	Oct. 14						
8	Oct. 21						
9							
10							
11							

The practice record should be filled in daily. Rehearsal time and lesson time do not apply on the practice log. Skipping some days of practice and making it up on others is an acceptable although not quite as effective method. If days are skipped, these days should be crossed out with an X.

Student signature_____

TACKLING THE PRACTICING MONSTER
(Winton Marsalis)

1. **Set goals for yourself.** When you practice, what are you trying to accomplish?
2. **Write out a schedule.** Time management is important to develop, especially if you are an involved KHS student.
3. **Seek out instruction.** If you have a question about the music or problem practicing something, ask the music teacher for help. The music teachers are always available before school, noon hour, and after school for advice or suggestions.
4. **Concentrate.** Fifteen minutes of concentrated or focused practice is much better than one hour of frivolous playing.
5. **Don't show off.** Nobody likes a show off. Practice to fix mistakes and learn. Learn from your mistakes.
6. **Practice slowly.** Practice the difficult sections slowly. You cannot run if you cannot walk. Be disciplined enough to take small steps.
7. **Be optimistic.** Nobody likes a pessimist. Practice with energy and passion or it will be boring.
8. **Look for connections.** Why do scales? Why practice articulation? Is there a connection with the skills you're developing while practicing and the music you are rehearsing in band? They are there—you have to find them.
9. **Practice Healthy Habits.** Start with stretching or some physical warm-up. Remember to practice for 30-minute intervals and then get up a move around.
10. **Use a mirror.** This will help you develop good posture, hand positions, and embouchures.

GOOF-UP CERTIFICATE

Everyone makes mistakes. Therefore, you will now be able to use this waiver to help cover up some of your mistakes. If you forget a lesson time, left your instrument at home, or were not prepared, you now have a second chance to make up for your mistake.

This certificate allows for
One unexcused lesson to be reassigned.

It is only good for band music or method book lessons.
Students are only allowed one goof-up per semester.

Certificates will only be issued to middle school band members
at the beginning of the first and third quarter.

Student Name _____

Date of goof-up _____

Excuse/goof-up _____

Reschedule lesson date _____

Summary

There are a variety of ways to collect evidence of musical growth and the effectiveness of your teaching. Moreover, these data gathering moments need not be an interruption in learning, but rather one more strategy that moves the learning process forward while providing tangible evidence as to what learning has taken place. Assessment is most useful when both teacher and students participate in evaluative measures. By encouraging students to assess, evaluate, and reflect upon their performances, you are teaching them to think like a teacher and thus take more responsibility for their learning, a practice that nurtures independent and confident musicians.

Consider the Following Questions as You Design Assessment Tools:

- Who is it for (teacher, student, parents, administrators)?
- What is the purpose of the assessment and how will it be evaluated?
- Are the criteria for success clear to students and parents?
- Who will design and evaluate the assessment? Students? Teacher?
- Do students get clear and honest feedback according to the criteria?
- Will there be well-organized records?
- Are the assessments (tests, rubrics, checklists) well designed?
- Does a grade have to be assigned?

ASSESSMENT

By not assessing musical achievement, you lose a valuable opportunity to demonstrate significant learning and advocate for your program to the students, to their parents, and to school administrators. When students perform a successful concert, they realize that they have learned the music well; however, little attention typically is given to all the other learning that took place. Having students reflect upon and assess their performances can enrich the concert experience. Assessment tools highlight the process of learning and instill in students a valuing and comprehensive understanding of music and the process of becoming a musician. Perhaps it is this knowledge and confidence that creates life-long musicians.

Music
Selection

One of the most frequently heard laments in music education today is the cry for better music. Teachers dedicated to quality repertoire bemoan the lack of commitment from publishers or retailers to maintain a high standard of compositional integrity in the music they put forth. Publishers and retailers in turn counter with, "Well, that's what the teachers are buying!"

The solution for what seems like a chicken-versus-egg conflict falls squarely on the shoulders of music teachers. Teachers of performing groups have a unique opportunity, unlike their colleagues in academic areas, to choose the "curriculum" and "textbooks" for their ensembles. This freedom to choose can be both liberating and intimidating because teachers must select with great care. Therefore, we need to be vigilant in examining the music we choose to study and challenge ourselves to seek out the best music we can find.

"Any great work of art is great because it creates a special world of its own. It revives and readapts time and space, and the measure of its success is the extent to which it allows you in and lets you breathe its strange, special air."

—Leonard Bernstein

So, how does one know if a piece of music is worthy of in-depth study or not? Let us look at the three examples we have been using in these chapters (the Holst, Handel, and Mozart). We know from the outset that these are great pieces of music because they are all considered "classics," a safe category within which to work when looking for quality literature. However, it is also apparent that these are great compositions because they have withstood the "test" of the CMP model.

In other words, they each resulted in a rich analysis that led to numerous concepts to teach which provided substantial and diverse outcomes. Not every composition fairs as well when studied through the CMP model. In fact, many reveal themselves as superficial and trite by the time you are part way through the analysis. Consequently, the CMP model provides a method not only for teaching music, but also for evaluating it.

As you write more and more CMP lesson plans you will eventually evaluate music more quickly because you will immediately analyze it for diverse teaching concepts as well as a rich historical, cultural, or social context. With time and experience your "radar" will sharpen and become more accurate. To help you move quickly to that point, consider the following characteristics of well-written music:

Uniqueness

A good composition has something ingenious that holds our attention and makes us remember it vividly. There is something novel in the piece that is innovative or unusual and sets it apart. Questions to consider are, "What does this piece say better (or at least differently) than any other piece similar to it?" "Does it stand alone as a unique artistic expression?" "What is inventive or new about the piece?" "Does it avoid cliché and triviality?" and "Does it contain evidence of beauty and craft?"

Form

Good form usually means the proper balance between the two key principles, repetition and contrast. Too much repetition of the same ideas creates monotony, whereas too much contrast gives the ear nothing to latch on to, recall, or identify. Both are needed, but either in extreme creates formlessness.

Design

Good compositions reflect the conscious design of their composer. All good pieces are a series of carefully planned events. In other words, good design means that the high point of the piece makes sense and that it doesn't come too early or too late. It means that the composer uses effective and logical transitions to connect musical events, and that all the musical events are paced skillfully.

Unpredictability

A good piece of music has enough surprises, harmonic twists, melodic variation, or rhythmic development to keep the listener sufficiently interested. If a musical idea is repeated twice, the third time should delight the ear with the unexpected. A good composition reveals a striving toward a musical goal and the best pieces have unusual musical goals that are reached in a somewhat indirect way. A predictable musical goal reached by the quickest, most obvious, or most direct route will not hold lasting interest for students, teachers, or listeners.

Depth

Quality music bears repeated hearings because it challenges the ear to probe and understand its layers of meaning. These meanings can be musical puzzles as is offered by Classical music or social/contextual offered by folk or popular music. This does not mean that the music must be more difficult or complex. A solo melody like Bach's *Bist du bei mir* continually reveals the genius of its construction and the force of its expressive power, though it can be sung by children.

Consistency

A good piece of music sounds like everything belongs together and all sections are consistent in quality. Profound moments are not followed by trivial ones.

Orchestration/Voicing

In quality compositions, composers demonstrate the ability to use colors and textures effectively and a good knowledge of voicings or instruments. They handle parts in a skillful manner and use unusual musical gestures based upon an artistic concept.

Text

Composers choose a worthy text for a good composition. It should provoke discussion or insight apart from the music setting. The composer should also demonstrate a good understanding of text by being sensitive to its structure, poetic devices, and overall meaning.

Transcendence

A truly great piece of music changes for the better all who come in contact with it and provides the opportunity for all to grow in some way. Great music encourages you to think in new ways, feel new or deeper emotions, or embrace new cultures.

Music selection has been placed at the end of the model because by the time you walk a composition through the model, you know whether it is worth performing and whether meaningful outcomes can be taught with this piece of music. However, music selection is usually where conductors begin. Often teachers are attracted to certain pieces of music and then scrutinize it according to several different criteria—whether it meets the interests, needs, and desires of the ensemble; whether it is age- and skill-appropriate; whether it meets criteria for performing (as listed above); and whether it fits into the concert program and overall unit of study for the grading period.

To ensure a comprehensive music education repertoire, choices should always reflect a diversity of styles, historical periods, and genres as well as levels of difficulty, especially over the course of a year. It is equally important to design a comprehensive three- to six-year music curriculum during which students learn about and perform an even larger diversity of musical genres, forms, composers, etc.

To help guide your musical choices and ensure that your ensemble program is comprehensive, consider the following checklists. Reflect on whether or not your current seniors have experienced most of the following:

Checklist for a Three-Six year
Comprehensive Band Program

Historical Periods

☐ Renaissance

☐ Baroque

☐ Classical

☐ 19th Century

☐ 20th Century/Avant Garde

Musical Genres

☐ Marches

☐ Overtures

☐ Symphonies (movements)

☐ Film Music

☐ Folksong Arrangements

☐ Concerto

☐ Programmatic Music

☐ Jazz

☐ Musical Theater

Musical Forms

☐ Theme and Variation

☐ Rondo

☐ Sonata

☐ Prelude and Fugue

☐ Suite

☐ Canon

☐ Minuet and Trio

☐ 12 Bar Blues

☐ ABA

☐ Through Composed

Varied Use of Ensemble

☐ Full Band

☐ Wind Ensemble

☐ Chamber Ensemble

MUSIC SELECTION

Checklist for a 3-6 year
Comprehensive Choral Program

Historical Periods

☐ Medieval

☐ Renaissance

☐ Baroque

☐ Classical

☐ 19th Century

☐ 20th Century/Avant Garde

Languages

☐ Romance Languages

☐ German Languages

☐ Baltic, Slavic, and Celtic

☐ Afro-Asiatic–Hebrew, Arabic

☐ Sino-Tibetian–Chinese,
Tahitian, and Russian

☐ Niga-Cong–Middle and
South African

Music Genres

A. Madrigal

☐ German

☐ French

☐ Italian

☐ English

☐ Folk Songs

B. World Music

☐ Asian

☐ African

☐ Middle Eastern

☐ Central American

☐ South American

☐ Australian

☐ Eastern European

☐ Celtic

C. Other

☐ Motet

☐ Partsongs

☐ Chant

☐ Canata

☐ Oratorio

☐ Opera Chorus

☐ Mass

☐ Musical Theater

☐ Vocal Jazz

☐ Gospel

☐ New Commissions

Varied Use of the Ensemble

☐ A Cappella

☐ Full Choir

☐ Chamber Choir

☐ Quartets

☐ Accompanied Music
(using various instruments
as well as full orchestra)

MUSIC SELECTION

Checklist for a 3-6 year
Comprehensive Orchestra Program

Historical Periods

☐ Renaissance

☐ Baroque

☐ Classical

☐ 19th Century

☐ 20th Century/Avant Garde

Musical Genres

☐ Concert Overtures

☐ Symphonies (movements)

☐ Film Music

☐ Folk (e.g. fiddling, blue

grass, etc)

☐ Folk Song Arrangements

☐ Concerto

☐ Suite

☐ Programmatic Music

☐ Jazz

☐ Musical Theater

Musical Forms

☐ Theme and Variation

☐ Rondo

☐ Sonata

☐ Prelude and Fugue

☐ Suite

☐ Fugue

☐ Canon

☐ Minuet and Trio

☐ 12 Bar Blues

☐ ABA

☐ Through-Composed

Varied Use of Ensemble

☐ Full Orchestra

☐ String Orchestra

☐ Chamber Orchestra

☐ Chamber Ensemble

(duets, trios, quartets)

☐ Chorus with Orchestra

MUSIC SELECTION

Part II

**The Practical Realities of Teaching
Comprehensive Musicianship
through Performance**

CHAPTER 6

Becoming a Different Kind of Ensemble Director

Although there is a certain comfort in staying with familiar past practice, CMP asks you to teach students how to perform with understanding, which means teaching musical skills but also comprehensive musicianship. It invites you to enrich your teaching on two levels. First, you are encouraged to dig deep and find your inspired inner musician—to remember the reasons why you became a music teacher. It probably had something to do with an intense and powerful passion for music, a desire to be an inspiring leader, and/or a quest to reproduce life-changing musical experiences or emulate inspiring role models. Let these memories, experiences, and wishes guide your repertoire choices, and motivate you both to analyze your music and to prepare well for rehearsal so you have a depth of understanding to share.

In addition to finding your inner musician, you are also asked to become a consummate music educator who motivates students to fully engage in musical learning. You must embrace the belief that concerts will be profoundly better if students perform with understanding and that rehearsal time spent studying, debating, and exploring composers' intent, style periods, and students' personal relationships to music can be efficient and balanced with improving performing skills. Further, you must believe that your students will become better and life-long musicians if they actively take charge of their learning by analyzing music, designing strategies, and assessing their own knowledge.

The key to change is becoming a risk-taker and enjoying the thrill of reinventing yourself as you discover new ways of teaching your ensemble. Teaching is deeply personal and as varied as snowflakes. CMP is intentionally a teaching model, as opposed to a method or a curriculum, so that you can shape the ideas to fit your style, strengths, and personality. Once you have experienced success with your first new strategy or assessment, you will have opened the door of change and be in for incredible experiences. What you have to look forward to are great musical conversations with your students, students taking initiative and being fully engaged in learning, and affective experiences during which you and your students will see a variety of human conditions and, as a result, grow in your humanity.

You may be thinking, "This sounds great, in theory, but I have 300 students. How do I start and what are realistic expectations?" The best way to start is with one piece of music for one ensemble. Write a CMP Unit Plan, which means doing an analysis, writing outcomes, designing appropriate strategies, and assessing the effectiveness of your outcomes. As you proceed to designing daily teaching plans, make sure you think completely through your initial activities. Consider the following process:

- Think through what you are going to say and do.
- Imagine all possible responses students may give, including the worst-case scenario, and how you will respond.
- Put yourself in the shoes of your students and ask if you would enjoy doing this activity if you were their age.
- Make sure all materials needed for the activity are available and ready to use. For example, if you are using a recording or a video clip, cue it to the part you want your students to hear or see.

To ensure success and entice student interest, keep your initial activities short (five-ten minutes). It is best to try only one new activity per week until you are used to this new teaching style. If you try too many activities at once, students may feel anxious about learning the music and lose enthusiasm for this new way of learning. Also, be reasonable in your expectations. Do not think that a strategy was unsuccessful because the outcome was completely different than you anticipated. See each new step and the various responses (however surprising) as grounds for reflection for both you and your students, and paths to new kinds of learning. For example, imagine the following scenario:

> You have programmed Schumann's *Zigeunerleben*, which is about the Gypsy lifestyle, and decide to introduce the piece by creating a context for your students to explore what it means to be a Gypsy. You ask the students to sit in a circle on the floor and pretend they are sitting around a campfire on a damp night (the setting for part of the song). You dim the lights as you ask students to imagine a gigantic bonfire in the middle of the circle. As the lights dim the students start to giggle. You ask students to warm their hands and feet as they watch the fire leap and crackle, and to enjoy the company of their comrades. You now notice some students getting silly, over-exaggerating movements, and pulling the focus of class members. After asking those particular students to behave, you ask the class to tell you what they know about Gypsies and their lifestyles. Unfortunately, the ensemble is too distracted and all they can do is giggle. Out of frustration you ask students to return to their seats, give them a brief lecture about maturity, ask them to take out a different piece of music, and begin pounding notes.

How do you recover from an activity like this one? Take a deep breath and think about the lessons your students could learn. The next class period, you could start with a conversation about why your students enjoy making music in an ensemble. Perhaps they will say things like, it is a creative outlet during the school day, it is an opportunity to express themselves, and that it is fun. You could then choose one of these and probe further. For example, if this is their creative outlet, how do students find themselves being creative during rehearsals? Generally students will discover, once they examine what they do during a rehearsal, that there is little

A DIFFERENT KIND

about a typical ensemble rehearsal that allows them to express their creativity—everything pretty much is determined by the director. You could then ask them why it is important for them to be creatively engaged in a rehearsal. The students will gleefully tell you why their ideas and individuality are important and how much more fun rehearsals are when they have a chance to offer their creative input. Preparing to "rope them in," you could point out that yesterday's activity was an opportunity for them to creatively engage with music, but something went wrong. If you ask students how this process could be a productive and useful activity, they will have all sorts of opinions and ideas to share with you. A productive way to conclude this discussion to prepare for future lessons would be to ask students what is needed from them in terms of effort and behavior as they engage in new learning strategies. As students answer, they will realize why they should not repeat the behavior pattern from the previous day.

By using the problem as a springboard and being willing to talk with students about difficult moments, you lead students to see ensemble rehearsals as a place where their opinions matter and where they can actively engage in learning. This trusting and honest relationship will reward both you and ensemble members with greater opportunities for performing with understanding.

Make a Commitment to Continue

The best way to become comfortable teaching comprehensive musicianship is to make a commitment to continue doing CMP with one piece of music for each concert. It just stands to reason that the more CMP lesson plans you write, the more adept you will become at writing them. The added bonus is that your knowledge about music will accumulate and eventually you will look at new scores and immediately have musical insights because of time and effort previously invested in analyzing other scores. The other incentive to continue will be the level of engagement from your students. You will feel the difference between teaching a CMP lesson where you have analyzed and developed goals for teaching on auto-pilot. "Pounding notes" will no longer be satisfying to you or your students. By making a commitment to continue, within a couple of years, teaching comprehensive musicianship will become second nature for you and expected by your students.

Stay in the Zone

Lastly, make sure you work within your comfort zone as you devise new teaching plans. Adapt these ideas to your teaching strengths for optimum success. Pointing out motivic development and other music theory concepts may feel intimidating, but talking about the historical context or style period may be something you do with ease. Start with what you know, and remember that you know more about the score than your students because you have analyzed it and because you have general musical knowledge to share (at least four years of undergraduate music study!).

After you have completed a CMP teaching plan, you will find yourself excited about all the things you have learned about the score. Often, in a fit of zeal, teachers try to share everything they know about the music in one protracted lesson. If you find yourself having this urge, STOP, take a deep breath, and remember that you know students will be overwhelmed and disinterested if you give them too much information at once. There are some general rules of thumb that we all know about good teaching that merit review:

- Teach one concept at a time; anything more is confusing.
- Carefully sequence each learning activity so you are slowly leading students through new ideas.
- *Teach,* don't *tell.* Sometimes the best strategy is to share a good story with the students during which you impart considerable amounts of information. However, most of the time, students will retain information if they discover it for themselves. So, spend your time carefully crafting strategies that invite students to unravel puzzles and discover elements of the music you find important.
- Make sure your students experience success early in the strategy so they will be game for more learning.
- Celebrate each little victory and remember that failures offer opportunities for growth and improvement, and therefore, are little gifts.

A CMP Rehearsal

Because there are few models for what has been described in this book, it may be difficult to envision what CMP rehearsals might look like. The following are descriptions of two CMP rehearsals—one orchestral and one choral. These examples demonstrate how CMP teachers weave teaching about music into daily rehearsals. It is important to remember that CMP rehearsals are as different as the teachers who teach them, so try to use these examples as inspiration and not absolute models. Also, it is difficult to capture an entire rehearsal on paper, so these examples highlight the application of CMP ideas for performing with understanding. Therefore, you will read about discussions the ensembles have regarding musical ideas. Remember that these discussions are balanced with practicing and performing the music throughout a week of rehearsals.

Looking In on a CMP Instrumental Rehearsal

Orchestra members saunter in, some with purpose, others chatting casually with their friends. Over the next few minutes, cases are emptied and seats are filled. The air starts to hum with open strings and snatches of familiar tunes. The bell rings and Jessica, the concertmaster, leaves her chair and stands before the group. The warm-up noodling whimpers to a halt.

Warm-ups

Jessica faces the bass section, which listens carefully to her "A" and painstakingly attempts to match it, adjusting their "A," down and up, down and up. Austin, the freshman, takes a little longer than the rest of the section and when he is done, his "A" is still not really high enough. Brett, the senior next to him, leans over with a "little bit higher" sign and Austin tries again. The rest of the orchestra sits quietly, also listening. Jessica then faces the cello section and repeats the process, just focusing on their "A" string. Next is violas and violins. Players are mostly tuning carefully, trying to play only as loud as they need to in order to hear themselves.

I have been watching from the side. I notice a couple kids who don't really appear to be listening, only going through the motions. It's time to teach.

Uncharacteristically, I step on the podium in the middle of the tuning process. The students know something is up. "Stacia, please play your 'A.' Everyone else listen." Stacia does. "Everyone, please give me a thumb sign: too high, too low, just right." They do, some stealing glances around them to compare answers. "OK, back to tuning. Remember, this is kind of a sacred moment, kind of like prayer," I remind them, "So invest in it like it's important." I step back off the podium, and they continue with the "A" until Jessica sits down. Now everyone begins tuning their instruments, top to bottom. I don't think it's just my imagination—they really do seem to be listening and working more carefully.

I jump back on the podium, baton poised. "D major, two octaves, half notes." A "D" scale ascends and comes back to rest. "If I said the words bell tones how would you play these half-notes?" A few hands go up to reply, but I lift my baton and say, "Try it." They play just an octave and I stop them. "That's great. Keep going and finish the next octave, but I want you to think about what you're doing with the bow and how you would describe it. Really listen to the bell tones you're creating." We finish the octave. "Which ones sound more like bells, the down-bows or the up-bows?" They have no idea, no one ventures a guess. "OK, let's try it again, eyes closed." We do, but I only let them play a few notes. Hands go up and the consensus is "down-bows."

"Why is that?" I ask. A quick discussion ensues about the sharp attack and long decay of a bell tone, and how gravity, the weight of the hand at the frog, and the natural diminuendo of the downbow make it the natural stroke for this effect. "OK, here's the big challenge. Close your eyes and we'll play it again,

117

but see if you can disguise the down-bows and up-bows, so they both sound like bell tones equally well, and we can't tell the difference between them."

They start off diligently, but by the second octave, it's less convincing and I can tell they've both gotten the idea and are tired of it. We reach our last note and they play the tonic chord with which we end our scales. "Great job tuning! You've gotten a lot quicker at centering that chord in the last couple weeks."

Without explanation, I start to snap offbeats and sing for them a syncopated pattern:

"Do, mi, re, fa, sol, fa, mi."

They sing back, feebly. "Hey, I can drown you all out!" I chide them, also with a wink. Still snapping, I sing again, they echo. "Much better!" I'm still snapping. "Now play it—a five-six-seven-eight!" They do. They echo about six little phrases after my lead, all eight beats long, all D major, all within the range of *do* to *sol*. Each one is a little more challenging than the last, and they know what's coming.

"OK, Dylan, take a turn." (I'm still snapping.) Dylan takes my role, but instead of singing the call, he plays it, and the orchestra, listening intently, responds. Without dropping a measure, I've already made eye contact with Lorena, who knows she's next. Right in tempo, she offers her little improv, and the group echos her. I invite about six students to keep the tune going, one by one, including Matt, who adds a "blue note" slide, which gets a few catcalls from the bass section. It seems like a good place to end. "Good job, you all! I'm really impressed with the risks you're taking—I know it's a little scary. Thanks for trying."

Take Out the Piece

"Please take out the piece in D minor." We had determined its key the day before, a laborious process that surprised me by taking longer than I had hoped. Students are pawing through their folders looking at the repertoire inside, trying to remember what D minor looks like, some of them glancing sideways for clues from neighbors. Eventually, they all are looking at the Bach "Contrapunctus" from the *Art of the Fugue.*

"I asked you to prepare a good bowing for the first eight measures. What did you come up with?" No response. Hmm, bad question, I think to myself. "Was it all *detaché*?" They murmur something that sounds like "no." "Where did you have to slur or hook anything?" Sure enough, many had figured out a few places where double upbows made it "feel better." "There's a reason why you instinctively want to do that," I say, "and tomorrow I'm going to ask you why, so think about it." As I'm talking I jot a note to myself on the planning page for tomorrow so I don't forget to ask the question.

"OK, let's try it with the bowing you worked out at home." A quick read-through of the first phrase, all instruments in unison.

With barely time to put their instruments down, I spur them on. "Now try it with bell tones on the half notes." They do, but it's awkward and not together. "Come on, try it again, and don't lose your internal rhythm this time. Stay together."

It's a little better, but still sounds awkward, with half of them working hard at the bell tones and the other half abandoning any concept of beautiful sound, just trying to hold the ensemble together. "OK, one more time. Remember, you have two things to think about: listening hard so you're together, and how you're using your right hand to make the bell tones."

I wouldn't say it's brilliant but it's better. Time to move on.

"Look on the board please." I've taken the same phrase and transcribed it in each of the three clefs they need, with a number under each note. "If this phrase were an arch, where would the high point be, the peak of the phrase, the most important energy moment? Talk to your stand partner and come up with a good answer and a 'why.' "

I give them only about 30 seconds to confer, and then start fielding their ideas. The majority of votes are for either note five or note eight. We play each version, usually twice to give it a fair hearing, and students defend their choices. Answers like "It just sounds better" don't fly and I encourage them to figure out good reasons for their choice. When pressed, they come up with answers like, "It's the highest note, so it naturally sounds the most important," or "It's the longest note," or "It's got those two short notes ahead of it that seem to lead right up into it."

I had hoped they would "see it my way" and decide that the best place to arch the phrase was note five, the lowest note of the phrase. But as we worked, I actually became more persuaded about note eight. I confessed to them my original opinion and how I had changed my mind through our work. Time for a little "sermon."

"See, this is the kind of thinking I want you to do always. Don't just take my interpretation for granted. When you get a new piece of music, ask yourself these questions and figure out for yourself how the phrasing should go. That's the most important thing—to be an independent thinker about your music."

I can see they are intrigued by my sudden fire and passion about something that seems, to them, not that big a deal. I can also see that for my sermon to work, I have to end it right here and move on.

Listening Activity

"Please look over on this side of the board." I had written:

_____ n. a short melodic or rhythmic idea that is used over and over to unify a piece.

"Here's a definition. Anyone know the word that it defines?" Brett says (without raising his hand)

"Motive, or moteef, or somethin' like that?"

A DIFFERENT KIND

"Amazing," I say, "How did you know that?"

"I dunno, heard it somewhere."

"That's exactly right...." (I take on a new nonchalant pose and an understated monotone.) "Wow... senior leadership."

"Can anyone name the most famous motive in history?" Many hands. Stacia is bubbling over. "Stacia?" She sings it, the first four notes of Beethoven's Fifth Symphony.

"You're right. What's the piece?"

Gabe: "Beethoven something, like fifth symphony maybe... I dunno."

"Exactly right. OK, you're going to make a whole piece out of these four notes. What can you do with them to make the piece interesting?"

They sit there, looking at me. "Think like a composer. How many things can you do with those notes?" With marker in hand, I step to the board and write "1." They're thinking, "Oh, he's serious. It's going to be one of his lists."

Within two minutes our list includes:

1) Start on a different note.

2) Make it go up instead of down.

3) Change it from minor to major, or vice versa.

4) Change one of the notes.

5) Change registers or have different instruments play it.

6) Slow it down or speed it up (I know they mean augmentation or diminution, but there's no time to introduce those words today.)

"Grab a piece of scratch paper. I'm going to play just the first 45 seconds of Beethoven five—what a treat, huh?—a great piece like this in our orchestra room!—and I want you to tally how many times you hear the motive, in any way, shape, or form."

As I'm walking to the sound cabinet: "I'm warning you, there are a lot and they go by very, very fast. Fasten your seat

A DIFFERENT KIND

121

belts!" My hand poised on the CD player, I look up at them one last time, as if to say "Great moment about to happen—everyone with me?" I press "play" and they begin ticking off, some with eyes closed, some squinting to hear better. A big dramatic caesura from the orchestra, dramatic horn solo about to happen and I push "stop." A groan from the class as all that pent up energy is suddenly aborted.

Before I can ask the question, they are shouting things like, "Dude, I got like 48!" I point to our list, and ask, "How many of these things did Beethoven actually do?" We tick them off, and they realize they did a pretty good job of predicting how a motive can be used.

It feels good to be in the presence of Beethoven, and hearing the whipcrack of that symphony raises the energy level in the room. But I notice I've only got five minutes left before the bell. Time to "bring it home."

"I wanted you to be prepared for a piece that we're going to start tomorrow." (Pause for effect—they are listening intently and all eyes are on me.) "It's almost as famous as Beethoven five and it's also built on a short motive, even shorter than Beethoven's. Here it is." I point to the corner of the board that we haven't used, and sure enough, there it is. The three note motive (G, F-sharp, G), I wrote before class and no one had noticed yet.

"This little motive is the brick that a very famous composer used to construct a giant cathedral of sound. Tomorrow I'm going to take you inside that cathedral and we're going to stand in the middle of it, and look up at the beautiful ceiling and look around at the majestic walls, and we're going to go, 'Ahhh…'" (I'm laying it on thick and they're looking at me with a mixture of "He's weird—he's scary—we like him anyway—when does the bell ring?") "It's an amazing piece and I can't wait to share it with you."

Wrap-up

Another pause for effect.

"OK, let's do some funk." A few whoops as they take out the blues/funk tune *Skylife* (Turtle Island String Quartet) from their folders. They're moving fast now, and I can tell they're eager to play.

"I've asked you to do a lot of thinking today and we haven't had a chance to play through much. I'm gonna start you up and just let you play from B to E. You'll have to stay together on your own, so listen around you like a good string quartet."

Two minutes to go.

I start my characteristic off-beat snapping while they lay bows on strings.

"A one...two...a one, two, three, four!" They're off, enjoying the pleasure of the intricate cross rhythms and counterpoint. We're just approaching E when the bell rings. Most students stop playing and gather their things quickly, others keep playing past E. I'm hoping that they're trying to make the music last as long as possible.

Finally, it's over and the last student is packing up. The bell has rung, and now it's the hallway which brims with noise and motion. But my class hasn't quite ended.

"Is it *Eine Kleine Nachtmusik*?" Nathan asks.

"Excuse me?"

"The new piece. Is it?"

"Well, can you hear that motive in *Eine Kleine Nachtmusik*?" He leaves a little dejected, trying to hum what he remembers of the Mozart, but already knowing the answer to his question.

"I bet it's Bach," I hear some girls saying as they pick up their backpacks and leave. "I think I know what it is."

I'm pretty sure that none of them have played Brandenburg Three, and most have probably never yet heard it. That will make tomorrow a great day. I'm already looking forward to it. I have a hunch at least a few of my students are, too.

A DIFFERENT KIND

Looking In on a CMP Choral Rehearsal

The class bell rings and the choir room fills with sounds of hissing. Sixty sophomore students stand in front of their choir chairs and begin various stretching exercises. Although some of them interact with facial expressions, most students focus on limbering their bodies after a long day of sitting and thinking.

Student-Centered Warm-ups

"Please look at the notation on the board. Take a minute to figure it out and then we'll perform it together."

All eyes stare at the board as students quickly run through the rhythms to themselves. A few students check a measure or two with their neighbor just to be sure. "Ready? Let's just read it straight through and go ahead and repeat it as indicated. Jim, will you please give us a tempo."

Jim smirks at his power to create a tempo for success or for failure. "I guess I'm feeling nice today. How about one, two, ready go!"

The class jumps in with enthusiasm and those who miss a few rhythms the first time easily correct it the second time through the exercise.

"Great job! Let's do it as a canon. Mary, what order should the voices come in?"

"Let's do it by rows instead of sections today." Students grin at her changing the system by not splitting the choir according to voice type. "Fourth row first, then third, second and first. Ready go!" She counts the students off and everyone reads steadily through the canon twice.

"How did we do?" I ask. The students know that this question means they need to do something better. A general "good" drones through the choir. "Do you feel like you really warmed-up your breath?"

"Nooo" the choir drones back.

"Then what do we need to do?"

"I think we could probably use more energy," a soprano suggests.

"Great idea. Try and use enough energy to blow the chalk off of the blackboard!" As the choir repeats the exercise the energy level in the room doubles. As they finish I start making siren noises and students join in. Some of them copy the hand movement I use as I circle my hand above my head to indicate the height and freedom of the sound. Other students create their own gestures, and a few more timid students use no gestures at all.

Next I start singing a five-tone scale and students join in. The choir moves the exercise up by half steps, correcting tone quality and intonation as I point out the problems. When we have gone through several different vowels and keys, I ask, "Who would like to suggest the next warm-up? Think about how your body feels and what you would like to sing next to feel warmed-up."

David, a thoughtful bass, replies, "I need to go lower and work on brightness. I feel like my voice is sticking in the back of my throat. Could we sing..." David sings down a five tone scale on kee-koh-kee. Halfway through the exercise most of the students join him. As they continue to take the exercise lower I remind them to brighten the sound on the bottom by pulling it forward into the nasal cavities. Some students add gestures as they sing to help pull the sound forward.

"How's that, David? Feeling a little more connected to your lower range?" I ask,

"Actually, I'd like to go a little lower if we could and can we do that thing where we sing it nasally?"

"Of course. In your best nasal voices..." The choir continues through the warm-up until no one can reach the lowest pitch and everyone giggles at those macho enough to try!

Take Out the Piece

"Can you please take out the piece that is full of metaphors about relationships?" The students pick up their folders and start thumbing through the music. Most of them know right away that I am referring to Zanenilli's *The Water Is Wide*, because we have spent time exploring several of the textual metaphors such as life being like a wide body of water through which to navigate the currents and tides of falling in and out of love. Once they all have the score in their hand, I begin to play the accompaniment and the students sing through the entire piece. I know this quick run-through will refresh their memories and prepare them for today's lesson.

"Who can tell me what the texture is for the first two verses?" Students thumb through their score and a few hands go up in the air. "Amy, what do you think?"

"They are homophonic because all the voices have the same rhythm."

"Excellent!" I reply, "Can you tell what the texture is for the third verse?"

"I think it would be polyphonic, but it's sort of homophonic also?"

"Nope, it's polyphonic," Jason blurts out. "The men's voices look homophonic and so do the women's, but when you put it together then you get polyphony."

"Does everyone agree?" Across the room heads move up and down in agreement. Homophony and polyphony are terms this choir learned as freshman, so they are very familiar with the concept. "OK, the million dollar question then is…what compositional device did the composer use to create polyphony?" I pause in anticipation of a bit of a struggle from students as they sort out what "compositional device" means.

"That's easy," blurts out an alto and before I could ask her to hold on for a minute while everyone wrestles with the puzzle.

"He uses a canon or a round."

There are noises of realization and recognition as students figure out what she is saying.

"If that was so easy, let's try the billion dollar question...why did Zanninelli use a canon for the third verse?" The room is once again silent and students avert their eyes when I look around the room so that I won't call on them. Finally I just call on Jim.

"Well, maybe he used it because it would be too boring to do the same thing he had done in the first two verses?" Everyone laughs at the frankness of his answer.

"OK, we know that sometimes composers change texture to create contrast. But is that all he was doing here? This is such a poetic and metaphorical text, do you think he was trying to create a musical metaphor or 'text painting' by using a canon?"

The students are quiet. Even though we have spent time talking about the poetic metaphors, the idea of a musical metaphor seems like a bit of a stretch. I decide to take a different tact and to move them quickly along. I write a summary of the text on the board.

Verse 1.

Life is sometimes hard and difficult, but if you have someone to go with you through it, life can be more enjoyable.
Verse 2.

I found someone to go through life with. I put a lot of time and trust in that person and they wound up breaking my heart. Now life is even more difficult.
Verse 3.

I know that love can feel wonderful and exciting, but I also know that love can hurt and fade away, leaving you feeling empty and lonely.

"Would you agree with this summary of the text?" They all

nod in agreement. "Which verse is the climax of the song?" There is silence as students ponder the text in front of them. "Does the arranger give you any hints when you look at the dynamics?" As the students thumb through the score perusing the dynamic markings, several of them point out that they are the same for all three verses, so the arranger does not indicate through dynamics what the climax is.

Finally, a bright-eyed soprano offers an opinion. "I may be going out on a limb here, but I think he was trying to reflect on love by using the voices to sound like reflection. So the guys make a statement and then the girls sing it back as if they are reflecting. The canon helps listeners reflect on love because they hear each statement sung twice."

The class, astounded by her insight and courage to share, applauds this interpretation as the soprano blushes. "Wow! That's tremendous. Can we sing the verse and incorporate the idea of reflection?"

As I play the two-bar introduction to the third verse, students scoot to the edge of their seats. The guys begin to sing with a sense of thoughtfulness and the girls reflect their sentiments by singing a dynamic softer. It is quite beautiful and I can hear and see that they are moved by their collective interpretation. As they cut off before the coda, I stop them and see smiles dawning across the choir.

"Pretty cool? So why did the arranger use a canon at this point?"

Several students offer interpretations with the main idea being that he wanted listeners to reflect on the ups and downs of going through life with a loved one, and the canon wound-up being the perfect compositional device for doing so.

"I would like to make one more request. When we get to the climax of the verse, which is one measure after F, notice that Zanninelli indicates a dynamic level of *mezzo-forte*. Could you try singing piano instead as you ascend that line, and then let the piece get softer and softer as you end?"

I begin the accompaniment, the men come in, and the women echo with much tenderness. When they arrive at the words, "But love grows old," they *decrescendo,* and I can feel a significant mood shift in the choir and the tenderness increases 100 fold. Again I cut them off before the coda, asking, "What did you think?"

I see several nods of enthusiasm, a few dissenters, and many who have not made up their minds yet. "Let's sing it one more time to get the feel of *decrescendoing* at the climax."

Journal Assignment

After the students finish singing, I ask them to take out their notebooks and use the last eight minutes in class to form an opinion about how they would like the choir to sing the phrase. I ask them to create a musical, poetic, and personal defense (in other words—what felt good to sing) for either *crescendoing* or *decrescendoing* at letter F.

As the class bell rings, the students are still eagerly writing about their interpretations. I encourage them to finish their thoughts for homework and let them know that we will share these ideas in class tomorrow. I listen to snippets of conversations in which students compare their opinions as they walk out the door and find myself curious about what they wrote and how that will change or solidify our interpretation tomorrow.

A Support System

Please know that the CMP master teachers are prepared to help you brainstorm ideas and construct effective lesson plans. We are happy to hold your hands through the process or listen to stories of triumphs. If you want to get in contact with a CMP teacher please go to http://www.wmea.com/cmp/ and select a teacher to write to. We guarantee that we will respond to your email quickly.

CMP Master Teachers

Band

- Glen Hayes, UW-Whitewater
- Dave Mueller, Eleva-Strum High School
- Patty Schlafer, Mount Horeb Middle School
- Laura Sindberg, Graduate Student Northwestern University
- Richard Tengowski, Kohler High School
- Jan Tweed, Wisconsin School Music Association

Choir

- Rick Bjella, Lawrence University
- Margaret Jenks, Butler Middle School
- Susan McAllister, Prebel High School
- Mary Schmidt, Sun Prairie High School
- Heather Thorpe, Badger Ridge Middle School
- Rebecca Winnie, Homestead High School
- Patti O'Toole, Wisconsin School Music Association

Orchestra

- Wendy Beuhl, LaFollette High School
- Katherine Punwar, Ray Sennett Middle Schools
- Leyla Sanyer, Oregon High School
- Randy Swiggum, Wisconsin School Music Association
- Gary Wolfman, Appleton North High School

A DIFFERENT KIND

Effectively Using Journals

One challenge ensemble directors face is engaging every student as a thinker and a musician. Because ensembles have a large membership and are primarily a group effort, it is easy for students to be quiet, disengaged participants. Journal assignments are an effective tool to individualize the ensemble experience as well as encourage thoughtful and personal interactions with the music. If introduced carefully, most ensemble members enjoy journaling, because they recognize the opportunity for their ideas and opinions to affect and shape their music-making. CMP teachers have used journals in ensemble rehearsals for decades and in this chapter, offer the wisdom of their experience and effective, practical examples.

There are numerous reasons for and ways of using journals in ensembles. This chapter highlights four different types of assignments geared towards assessing different aspects of the rehearsal—getting to know ensemble members, clarifying the ensemble's purpose or focus, assessing skill development for both individuals and the entire ensemble, and better understanding the repertoire.

Assessment of Individual Skills or Ensemble Progress

It is educational to have students write about their individual or the ensemble's skill development. These journal exercises are useful throughout a grading period, but especially pertinent when evaluating a concert or an individual's accomplishment for the quarter. Listed below are numerous examples used by CMP teachers:

Combo Review

Using your best essay writing skills, explain something unique about the performance or rehearsal of the bluegrass tunes in your combo. Considering that this was most likely a new experience for you, discuss the ways you grew as a musician and what you think you learned from the time spent in the bluegrass combo.

Concert Reflections and Critique

Use some of the following questions as a starting point. Please write neatly and use your best writing skills (as you would with any writing assignment). You should include an introduction and a conclusion. Your reflections should be at lease one page in your portfolio notebook pages.

- How did you feel before the concert?
- Which compositions do you think your choir performed best and why?
- Which pieces performed by other ensembles did you especially enjoy or did you think were effective?
- Which composition did you personally perform the best?
- How did you feel during the performance?
- Do you feel that you were prepared for the performance? Is there anything you would do differently?
- Did you receive any comments from family members or other audience members?
- Which piece was the most emotionally satisfying to you and why?
- From what piece did you learn the most—why and how?
- What pieces demanded the most from you intellectually, emotionally, and technically—why was that so?

USING JOURNALS

Post-concert Journal

Please share a comment you heard from an audience member (please keep the audience members anonymous). It can be a positive or negative comment. Then explore why you think someone would make this comment about our performance.

Listening Critique of Pieces Performed in a Concert

When discussing what you hear, please include the elements of music (rhythm, harmony, melody, form, texture, timbre, and expression) because it will make your argument more substantial.

Listen for and comment on specific technical aspects that we have worked on—phrasing, diction, vowel uniformity, tone, word stress, intonation.

In your opinion, did our performance of the piece express the emotional content or the composer's intent?

Examing Your Favorite

Write the name of one piece your ensemble performed that made a particular impression on you during the last concert. Then, using your best essay-writing skills, explain something unique about the performance or rehearsal of this particular piece and how it affected your musical response at the time. Use at least one paragraph, complete sentences, appropriate terminology, and original ideas.

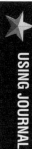

USING JOURNALS

END OF THE QUARTER SELF-EVALUATION

Write your Quarter Self-Evaluation in your Portfolio notebook pages.

APPROACH TO CLASS WORK

Discuss your attitude and effort in regards to your ensemble participation and your development of productive rehearsal techniques. Then, give yourself a grade for both on a scale of 1-10.

- Attitude and Effort in Participation: Leadership by example; A positive spirit of cooperation; A sense of ensemble; A consistent energy, willingness to contribute, participate, and share; Respectful of entire community of learners.
- Rehearsal Technique: Ready to rehearse when class begins; Has folder, portfolio, and pencil; Marks score in rehearsal; Focuses and listens; Does not talk out of turn; Helps neighbor to concentrate and focus by not being a distraction.

SKILL DEVELOPMENT

In what ways have your vocal skills developed? What improvements have you made? Vocal skills: posture, vowel formation and clarity, intonation, agility, articulation, breath, ease of range, and expressiveness

MUSICAL KNOWLEDGE/UNDERSTANDING

Consider how your understanding of music increased this quarter in light of studying the following:

- Theory and sight-singing
- The elements of music
- Music history and cultural connections
- Personal and artistic expression

GOALS

How have you achieved or worked toward your personal goal this quarter? Make a new personal goal for the next quarter.

CODA

Include any other accomplishments, improvements, contributions, extra credit work, suggestions, observations, or comments.

Often, you will be amazed at the insights and awareness students have about their performance during a concert and during a quarter. Generally speaking, they will pinpoint problems and notice the need for improvement in areas you would identify. However, do not be alarmed if a student occasionally has a different opinion than yours. You will know immediately if the student just is not engaging in the activity and you will have an appropriate course of action. Otherwise, this discrepancy may be a sign that the student has not learned a concept fully or that he measures success differently than you. Again, these self-assessments will increase your knowledge of individual ensemble member's self-esteem and learning modes, which will in-turn help you plan better rehearsals.

Student Examples

Explain something unique about our performance or rehearsal of Beethoven's Fifth Symphony—Movement One and how it affected your musical response at the time.

Beethoven's 5th Symphony was the piece that I think we played the best. There were some technical things that could have been better, but the feeling was definitely there. Usually when other sections really start getting intense I play even better which also inspired someone else to get into the music more. I think there was a lot of that happening when we played this piece. I think the performance was the best we had ever played the Beethoven.

The most unique attribute of this piece was how it relied on secondary instruments. They often led the orchestra and set the tempo. Another thing that amazed me was how much concentration mattered when playing this piece.-Jennifer

USING JOURNALS

Thinking about where you are at now, list three areas for improvement:

1. I would like to have better bowing and always be bowing in the right direction
2. I would like to concentrate on asking more questions in class.
3. I think I have to learn my scales better and know how to identify them all.-Tim

1. I would really like to work on music theory more.
2. I would like to work on composition.
3. I would like to work on improvisation.-John

What piece from our fall concert was the most moving to you personally? In your essay response please comment on the technical, musical, and contextual aspects of the piece and how each contributed to your personal experience.

"Sed Diabolus" was my favorite selection that we performed at the Choral Festival. Although it isn't a difficult selection note-wise, it was difficult technically and musically. We also spent a lot of time looking at and discussing the context of the piece. We spent a lot of time working on the technical aspects of this piece. We concentrated on using breath support and control; to make the piece seem circular. We also worked on control of our vibratos since the style of the piece demanded little or no vibrato. Releases were key....we had to build a real sense of ensemble because the releases of phrases are not marked in; we had to feel them as an ensemble....As mentioned above, the piece is in unison so vocal blend was essential. We had to strive to match vocal quality among all four sections so we would sound as one...we concentrated on phrasing and word and syllabic stress to produce the high points and emotion of the piece.

"Sed Diabolus" is very different from any piece we've sung so far this year. It is so ancient — a chant written in the 11th century. Music was so different then compared to what our ears are used to. It was written in neumes (symbols rather than notes) and harmony was almost unheard of. I liked the experimentation we did with the tenors singing a perfect fifth or perfect fourth higher than the basses. It created an empty, somewhat mysterious aspect to the piece. The fact that this piece was written by a woman, Hildegard of Bingen, is fascinating to me. What's more interesting is that the piece has survived from such an ancient time. I loved hearing about her, her accomplishments, and the respect she earned from great persons.

-Francis

USING JOURNALS

REVIEW OF AMERICAN RIVERSONGS

(A concert review written in the form of a poem by a middle school band student)

A new piece before us
American Riversongs
"Oh no," I thought
Not another changing time signature song

The first time we played it
What a horrible sound
We weren't at all together
It sounded more like a round

Rhythms were wrong and so were some notes
For this song no longer
Did I have high hopes

We took each song
Glendy Burk, Shenandoah, Down the River
Took it apart piece by piece
And soon produced a sweet tone to make you quiver

But practice it took
And lots of hard work
On all three songs, but especially 196 in Glendy Burk

So many things going on
Different with each instrument
But each day before the concert was closed with a little
more improvement

The night had finally come
Five months crammed
Into a three minute piece
Played by the Concert 8 Band

I was excited to begin,
Anxious to play
American Riversongs
Yet many songs are played before I have my way

This is it, no more practice
The conductor raises her hands
We play the piece with our heart and soul
And sound like one of the state's better bands

There's a round of applause
That makes me feel good
I played from within
And it was the best that I could

-Tracy

Questions for Better Understanding the Repertoire

Journals can also encourage students to understand more deeply artistic expression and to make connections between the music and their own experiences. Students find these assignments motivating and answer them with enthusiasm. This type of exercise also encourages creativity and imagination. Listed below are examples of music-related journal questions developed by CMP teachers.

Folksong: *Every Night When the Sun Goes In* (arr. Suzanne Hunt Paterson)

Text: *Every night when the sun goes in, I hang my head and mournful cry. True love don't weep or morn for me, I'm goin' away to marble town. I wish to the Lord that train would come to take me back where I come from.*

The text and melody of this song are obviously mournful and full of emotion, but the story is not really present in this arrangement. Write a letter to your true love as if he or she were the person to whom you are speaking in this text. Decide in what context you might utter these words, where you "come from," and what would make you want to return.

USING JOURNALS

Three Songs about Longing

Folksong: *Shenandoah* (arr. Erb SSATTB arrangement), Palestrina: *Sicut Cervus*, Brahms: *O süsser Mai*

Write a journal entry on whether you think Shenandoah is about longing for a person or a place, and why. (Do this prior to giving students historical information about the song.)

Discuss how Palestrina expresses the longing of the soul through imitative sections.

The Romantic composers often chose texts that were about nature and longing to be free. Discuss how this text and Brahms' compositional devices create that feeling in *O süsser Mai*.

Show how these three songs connect thematically and then write about one of your profound longings. (Please remember that this may be shared with the rest of the choir).

Listening Assignment

Using the remaining space on this page and the back, write down your musical thoughts about the following piece. [Nicolai Rimsky-Korsakov *Capriccio Espagnol*—performed by Chicago Pro Musica (1985)] Listen first and then write. Think about instrumentation, style, thin and thick texture, how the composer uses contrast, and repetition.

Compare and Contrast

Listen to these two pieces of music by Baroque composers from different countries and then compare and contrast their styles.

Vivaldi, *Spring (Four Seasons)*

Bach, Double Concerto in D Minor

Modern Translations

Rewriting texts into modern or teenage language can be a fun and useful exercise. The following are good texts for this translation exercise: King Henry VII: *Pastime with Good Company*, Brahms: *Neue Liebeslieder* (one movement at a time, of course), Debussy: *1. Dieu! qu'il la fait bon regarder!* (from Trois Chansons).

USING JOURNALS

Inquiring Minds

List your top three favorite songs played on the radio and discuss whether or not you think they'll be listened to in twenty years. Give specific reasons for your answer.

Student Examples

How do the two marches we read this week compare to one another? Tell me about the style, texture, and your perception of melody and harmony.

I like both of them, but they are different from each other. Amparita Roca is a Spanish march and Black Watch is not. I guess Black Watch is a military march because the kids that did the research on it said that it was a group of soldiers that patrolled the Scottish Highlands. I think the Spanish March is more exciting to play. I like the trombone and baritone parts in Amparita Roca a lot more than the low parts of Black Watch. The melody of Amparita is in minor and Black Watch in major. I like minor better. I don't know why, but it sounds better to me. I like both pieces though and I really like band this year! -Sam

We've talked about how composers use compositional devises to evoke certain feelings. How does *Esprit De Corps* by Yager make you feel? (this was a journal topic given on 9/10/01 to be turned in on 9/14/01)

I think I may have answered this question differently a week ago. This has been a horrible week and I don't even want to talk about it anymore because it makes me mad and scared at the same time. At a time like this it forces all of us to look more seriously at what we have that's really important. I think that is what's happening and I hear music everywhere. Patriotic music seems to be cool and comforting to a lot of people who didn't care before. I think music is able to make people feel sad, happy, or right now good about being an American.-Marty

Write down your musical thoughts about the following piece. [Nicolai Rimsky-Korsakov—Capriccio Espagnole—Chicago Pro Musica (1985)]. Think about instrumentation, style, texture, and how the composer uses contrast and repetition.

It starts very upbeat and lively with almost the whole group bringing out a full melody. It moves into a slower section which starts with very few instruments playing and gradually fills out while switching melody and accompaniment between section. After the slower "romantic" section it moves into an Allegro section which seems almost Baroque. Then it has a short section that has a definite "mariachi" feel to it... I wanted to dance. It was mostly horns and brass. It has definite contrast between all the sections of the group. Then there is a violin/flute dominated section which is slightly slower and more drawn out. It switches between a thin sound with few instruments and a full thick sound with full instrumentation. The piece ends with a full symphony orchestra sound. Very cool piece!

The powerful violin solo gives substance and variety to the forthcoming section. It then incurs some very low, slow undertones while the higher instruments work in contrast. It is a nice piece with some catchy melodies and some smart contrasts. This piece almost seems like it jumps from musical culture to musical culture. It seems to go from European to Hispanic to Greek to German music components.-Marie

Write about your thoughts and experiences as we studied *Vita de la mia vita* by William Hawley. Some of these may be used as program notes.

USING JOURNALS

I have gained an appreciation for life and the importance of all that it entails . . . It truly is a magnificent piece.

When we first translated this piece in class, I was skeptical that it was a love song. [The poet] calls his love a pale olive and a faded rose. Those are not flattering images. [My interpretation now is that] his love is dying—she is ill, and is wasting away. The song is a tragedy, because she is beautiful and will soon be gone and she has been the 'love of his life.'

This song has taught me how as singers, we can make a song music instead of notes. Although it is in a different language, you can understand the emotions that are being expressed. This song is one that people can relate to and it comes alive when it means something to you. -Paul

Getting to Know Individual Ensemble Members

These are good exercises to start the journaling process because the questions ask students to share their opinions and to write about themselves—two things students love to do! These assignments are generally brief, fun, and easy to answer.

- What was your favorite part of rehearsal this week and why?
- How do you feel about being in this ensemble?
- If you had one wish for this ensemble, what would it be?
- What is your favorite piece of music and why?
- Tell me something you would like me to know about you.
- Why have you chosen to participate in music?
- Describe something you wish we could do more often.
- In your opinion, what makes an exciting musical experience?

The responses to these assignments will help you understand your students' motivations, desires, and needs as ensemble participants and, in turn, help you plan more effective rehearsals. Students will often share very personal information, so be prepared to take your relationship with students to a deeper level after reading their journal entries.

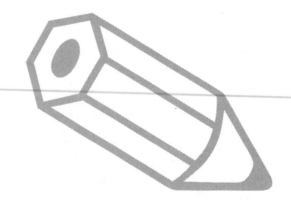

USING JOURNALS

Student Examples

Tell me how you felt when you found out that you were assigned to the Women's Choir.

When I first was assigned to the Women's Choir I was really disappointed. Since I think the first time I heard about Concert Choir I wanted to be in it more than almost anything else. To the point where I sacrificed my art education as well as computers. I had this idea that if I was in Concert Choir, I'd be a better person or something. It started out ok. I was consistently in the elite groups of talented singers like triple trio, etc. in grade school. But on arriving at high school the dreaded Concert Choir audition loomed closer. I guess I started fearing failure more and cared more what everyone else thought of my voice, and so on the day when I discovered that I hadn't gotten into concert choir, I was crushed. My audition had been terrible. I was sick and scared and sounded like someone who had never sung before instead of someone who had been studying music all her life. I felt, on reading the list of accepted people, like I'd wasted my time and hard work. People I had often helped figure out music, people who constantly talked during choir, had made it into Concert choir. And it wasn't fair. They had been hypocritical in the Sophomore Choir saying that everyone should work harder and then they'd go back to braiding each other's hair.

Maybe it isn't totally fair. Some people did deserve to be in concert choir and I'm glad for them. I guess I felt like the pot of gold at the end of the rainbow had been stolen. I know I'll still get to be in there next year, but all the people I used to sing with and who used to get me to help them, moved up and left me behind. Maybe they have less stage fright than me, maybe they have better voices than me, but I tried at least as hard as they did and when I read the sign I felt like it was all for nothing.

What is something you have learned this week, in orchestra or anywhere, that is important to you?

 I have learned not to be afraid or embarrassed playing by myself.-Mark

Tomorrow is not promised to everyone. (Week of 9/11/01)-Sara

I learned that starting off the school year in a positive way really helps.-Jane

I learned that once you go to college no one really cares what your GPA was. I also learned some improv.-Mike

I learned that when I play volleyball, the lower I am the easier it is to get a good pass.-Tim

Clarifying the Ensemble's Purpose or Focus

During the school year, the ensemble may experience periods of frustration due to varying levels of self-discipline, varying motivations for participating, and varying opinions about the repertoire. This is a good time to journal because it will help everyone express their feelings and identify a clear focus for rehearsals. By emphasizing the functioning of the ensemble, the director can often regain the efficient and effective pace felt just prior to concerts. The following journal assignments are designed to elicit responses that help focus the ensemble:

Journal Assignments

- If you were director of this group, what ONE change would you make and how do you think that change would benefit you or the group?
- Write a letter to me and tell me how things are going for you in this class.
- Describe something you could do to make rehearsals more productive.
- Describe your attitude in rehearsals and give reasons for your attitude.
- How could the ensemble learn their music more quickly?
- Rehearsals have felt slow and tedious lately. Name one thing you could do to make them better. Name something I could do to make them more interesting.
- Why does everyone need to try her or his hardest every day?
- Is it possible to try your hardest every day? Why or why not?
- What does it mean to have a good attitude in this ensemble?
- What is causing this ensemble to have the "blues?"

USING JOURNALS

You may be surprised that most students understand the issue and have many good suggestions for how rehearsals can improve and be more focused. If you implement student ideas, the ensemble's work ethic will grow stronger, because participants will recognize that their ideas are important and as a result take more ownership of the learning process

At the same time, be prepared for honest answers that may offer you constructive criticism. You may learn that a student is trying her hardest with little recognition because your focus is on the majority of ensemble members who are not working to the best of their abilities. Or, perhaps you have created tense rehearsals because you are anxious about the nearing concert. Remember, these critiques indicate a commitment to and concern for making the ensemble better. However, be sure to introduce a policy of "honesty with care" so students learn to express their feelings and concerns in appropriate ways.

Student Example

Student teachers asked the choir members to tell them how it was going and to make any suggestions for improving rehearsals.

Well, you know what you guys need to ease up. Chill out cause I am always in a great mood before I get to this class. I liked this class before you guys came in here. I liked it cause the teacher joked around a lot and hardly ever got mad. I mean, he got mad at me a couple of times but not for a really bad reason, but then the next day everything was ok with me and him.

But, you guys are taking things too seriously. You make this class a living *ell for me. Now I dread coming to this class. You guys are mean to me. I feel you hate me so that is why I want to drop out of this class.

And if you think that I don't care about this class, why would I be writing this to you. I ♥ this class, (well not anymore).-Lisa

---

Getting Started

Because students are not accustomed to writing during ensemble rehearsals you must insure success with your first assignment. Here are tips to guarantee success:

- Make the first exercise short and fun.
- Be sure to respond to the first entry or else students will feel that the exercise is mere busy work. Your response should include more

than just a check-mark. It should acknowledge what they have written and encourage them to continue to think deeper and express themselves more fully.

- Use a 3x5 card instead of a blank sheet of paper. An entire sheet of paper may intimidate students not used to writing during ensemble rehearsals.

- Give students a small amount of time in class to answer the question. Psychologically, it will feel more manageable if they have five minutes instead of 15 to write the first time they journal (although it may well take 15 minutes). It is good to leave them wanting more. You can increase the time as they become more experienced with journals. Eventually the exercises may become homework assignments.

- Be enthusiastic about their writing and thank students for their efforts, even if

Trying Something New: One Teacher's Journey…

Background—I had just returned from an intense CMP training weekend and I was FIRED UP about CMP and all my new ideas. I decided to try a journaling activity with my advanced choir. We had recently audio taped a rehearsal and I planned to use a snippet of one of the taped selections for assessing our progress. The assignment, I thought, was simple: listen to the excerpt and write one thing that you thought was good and one thing that you thought could be improved. I collected the assignment as the bell rang for dismissal. Well, within five minutes my phone rang. It was the Business Education teacher who also happened to be a choir mom. Her son, a star tenor, had gone right to her after class complaining about our new activity. She stated that, everyone is going to drop choir! I was shocked— the class had apparently held court in the hall and expressed displeasure. I immediately called Mike George, one of my trainers from my recent CMP weekend, related my story to him and said, "Thanks for nothing!" He patiently replied

USING JOURNALS

149

that change takes time and generally tried to simmer me down. But I was crushed—I was so excited about trying some new activities and my students seemed to feel that all they wanted to do in choir was sing.

The next day was business as usual—I did not bring up the previous day's activity nor did anyone else.

Toward the end of the week there was a controversial decision made by the principal. "Can we journal about it?" someone teases. "No," I reply.

About two weeks later, we performed the Gloria by John Rutter. The day after the concert I asked the students to respond in writing to two items—share your scariest moment and your most joyous moment of the performance.

Well, I laughed and cried and cried and laughed as I read the responses.

you were disappointed in the quality of their response. As students feel encouraged they will write with more passion and insight.

Once students have written a journal response, you have important decisions to make regarding what will be done with that response. You must take great care with the students' writings if they have taken the risk of sharing feelings and opinions. If the exercise required a personal response, you may want to be the only one to read it. However, if the question is based on opinion or exploring the music, there are several ways to use the information. Perhaps you will use peer reviews and have other ensemble members respond in writing. You may want to send the entry home for parents to review and comment. These responses can also be used as a basis for class discussions either in small groups or with the entire ensemble. By taking a moment to have all students write down their thoughts before entering into a class discussion, you will have 100% participation.

In summary, journals can play an important role in ensemble

rehearsals. They serve as a means for better understanding individuals, as tools for self-assessment, as creative ways to explore and make connections with the music, and as a basis for good class discussions. By starting with short, fun questions, you will quickly entice your students into becoming more thoughtful musicians and thus making them more capable of performing with understanding.

They were poignant, thoughtful, funny, and very accurate. No one complained and all completed the assignment.

My students now think nothing of writing several times a year on various topics. In retrospect, I realize that no matter how or when I introduce a new activity, there will always be some complaining. I was simply unprepared for the mutiny that ensued, but the fuss was short-lived. Just be prepared for the response, "I didn't take choir to write—I just want to sing." Of course we still sing—but this teacher is trying to help kids see that there can be so much more.

CHAPTER 8

Homework and Listening Assignments

Because shaping sound musicians entails exposing students to numerous ideas including (compositional techniques, music history, improvisation, repertoire, recordings of excellent ensembles, etc.), you may occasionally want to assign homework in order to accomplish all of your outcomes. Homework assignments must be well designed, connected to classroom activities, enjoyable and enhance ensemble development. Some good reasons for assigning homework include:

- Students need more time to think about an exercise than what is available during class.
- It is an enrichment activity to enhance and extend class work such as attending a performance of music the ensemble is learning and writing a paragraph comparing and contrasting the concert to the class' performance.
- The assignment requires resources not available during rehearsal time such as the Internet.
- A parent is needed to help complete the activity.
- Students need to practice in addition to playing during rehearsals.

It is important that homework assignments do not feel like busy work. Make sure your assignments are directly applicable to the music being studied and that information gathered will be discussed or used during the ensemble rehearsals. Showing students an immediate connection between homework and class work guarantees a stronger investment in and an enthusiastic attitude towards homework. A "sneaky" way to get students thinking about their music beyond the classroom is to ask for volunteers to look up information and then have them share the information with the rest of the class while you praise their initiative and ingenuity. Eventually, these requests may become homework assignments students complete with enthusiasm.

Examples of Effective Homework Assignments

These are examples of homework assignments used by CMP teachers that have been popular with students.

HOMEWORK

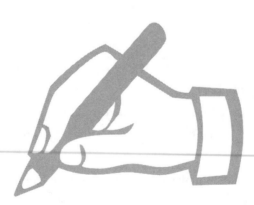

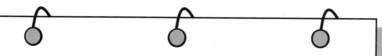

Using the Internet

While studying Baroque music in orchestra, the students were given a variety of topics to research on the Web. These topics included composers (Bach, Vivaldi, Corelli, Purcell), fugue, counterpoint, polyphony, concerto grosso, trio sonata, two-part invention, harpsichord, Stradivarius, violin bows, etc. The students then gave a three minute presentation to the ensemble during which they talked about their findings and played a short excerpt from a recording of Baroque music found on the Web. Students then handed in a one-page paper about their topic and these papers were turned into a booklet on the Baroque period.

While preparing a concerto grosso by Corelli, a student researched Baroque bows and printed pictures for the class to view. A discussion followed on how Baroque musicians held the bows, and how these positions and bows affected the tone and performance of the music, and how that information informs a contemporary performance of Corelli.

While learning an arrangement of George Gershwin's *I've Got Rhythm,* a student volunteered to research the piece on the Internet and found a recording of Gershwin playing the tune on the piano. This excerpt was played for the class and used to discuss style, tempo, and dynamics.

HOMEWORK

Self Assessments

By doing these at home, students have more time to think before they respond.

Quarter 1
Self Assessment and Evaluation

Take some time to study the following categories and assess your progress since last spring in orchestra. You will be graded on both the fact that you complete the assignment and the depth of thought which you put into completing it.

A = Serious approach to assessment
    Complete all sections
    Writing in complete sentences
      and thoughts
    Clear and neat copy of
      assessment

B = Finish assessment
    Complete all sections
    Writing mostly clear and easily
      understood
    Copy clarity adequate

C = Assessment partial
    Most sections complete
    Writing needs work to be clear
    Copy of work unclear in places

D = Incomplete work
    Few sections complete
    Writing unclear when done
    Copy of work not legible

F = Assessment not turned in

Based on your past work and your own standards assess yourself in the following areas (circle one):

1. Technical improvement

Tone:	Excellent	Very good	Improving	Fair
Intonation:	Excellent	Very good	Improving	Fair
Bowing:	Excellent	Very good	Improving	Fair

Comments:

2. Practice time outside class (at home or during school)

      Excellent   Very good   Improving   Fair

Comments:

HOMEWORK

3. Concentration during rehearsals (focus and contributions)

Focus:	Excellent	Very good	Improving	Fair
Contribution:	Excellent	Very good	Improving	Fair

Comments:

4. Musical and theory knowledge (understand keys and scales)

Excellent   Very good   Improving   Fair

Comments:

5. Contribution to class discussions (ask questions and share ideas)

Excellent   Very good   Improving   Fair

Comments:

6. Extra solo and ensemble study

Yes   No

Comments:

7. Study of secondary instrument or voice

Excellent   Very good   Good   Fair

Comments:

8. Composition, improvisation, or extra musical projects

Yes   No

Comments:

9. Self-motivation to learn more about music

Excellent   Very good   Improving   Fair

Comments:

10. Self-motivation to learn more about your instrument

Excellent   Very good   Improving   Fair

Comments:

11. Listening to many different types of music and musical styles

Yes   No

Comments:

HOMEWORK

Mozart's Birthday Party

While learning Mozart's Requiem, students were given invitations to Mozart's birthday party. They were each asked to bring a gift that would be appropriate for and appreciated by Mozart. This meant that students (either individually or in small groups) had to learn something about his life and career and then find or construct a suitable gift. On the day of Mozart's birthday, students were greeted with an elaborate birthday cake and after singing Happy Birthday, proceeded to share their historically informed gifts.

Project: Motif Composition

Objective: Compose and record an original melody in a distinct style of your choice.

You can compose and perform either as soloist or within a group. The melody must be eight or more measures. Sketch out your melody in standard notation. See the teacher for suggestions or help. Notation and recording must be handed in together.

Title:

Finale Project

Objective: Using Finale Notepad, compose an original eight measure melody in a distinct style of your choice, or transcribe your last motif composition.

If you would like your own copy of Finale Notepad, you can download the software for free. Go to www.codamusic.com/coda/ for the free download. If you do not have Internet acess, the teacher has one copy on CD.

See teacher for suggestions or help. Notation must be printed and handed in or emailed to the teacher

Finale Notepad Project Rating Scale

4 pts— melody demonstrates imagination and creativity.

3 pts— melody is "singable" and contains accurate key, note values, expressive markings, and dynamics.

2 pts — melody contains missing note values or inaccuracies.

1 pt— melody is not recognizable

HOMEWORK

Scavenger Hunt

Classify the following into their correct categories.

Bach	Bizet	Mozart	Sparke
Beethoven	Riverdance	Ragtime	Gillespie
Jadin	Ellington	Debussy	Copland
L'Orfeo	Messiah	Gliere	Nutcracker Suite
Jazz/Blues	Rite of Spring	Vivaldi	Phantom of the Opera

| Music Era | Genre | | |
	Composer	Title	Type of Music
Baroque			
Classical			
Romantic			
20th Century			

Classify by genre and style (and by historical period, composer, and title) a varied body high-quality and characteristic musical works and explain the characteristics that cause each work to be exemplary.

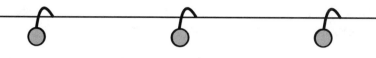

Concert Review

Each student must attend one live concert of your choice each quarter. You must write a review of the concert and discuss the elements of music in your writing. Write the critique as a concert review for your local newspaper.

Using Listening Examples

Many times you will use recordings during rehearsals to teach musical concepts, to inspire a higher level of performance, to demonstrate the overall effect of a piece of music, or to offer comparable or contrasting examples. CMP teachers have found that directing the students' listening results in a more educational and focused process.

In other words, if you just play a recording and ask students to listen quietly they may not pay attention or they may focus on an unimportant aspect of the music. Therefore, you should always have a reason for students to listen to a recording, focus their attention on that aspect, and then discuss what they heard. The following lists things for which you can have your students listen:

1. Pick one. This piece sounds: a. very old b. sort of old c. not very old
2. In what century do you think this piece may have been written?
3. What language is being sung? How do you know?
4. How large is the group that's performing?
5. What kind of a choir is singing, boys, girls, women, men, mixed? How old are they?
6. Give me an expressive word to describe the mood of this piece.
7. What instruments get to play the melody in this piece?
8. How many times do you hear the motif? Keep a tally of them as you hear them.
9. Given the mood of the piece, what might the text of this foreign language piece be about?
10. Is this piece homophonic or polyphonic?
11. Who might be a possible composer for this piece? Why?
12. Does this piece sound like a Classical or a Romantic piece?

HOMEWORK

13. Are the strings in this example playing on or off the string? How can you tell?

14. Is the texture relatively thin or relatively thick?

15. Which section is playing/singing the most out-of-tune in this excerpt?

16. What's the unusual instrument that plays the solo in this piece?

17. What is the meter of this piece?

18. Listen with your eyes closed. Every time you hear the main theme, in any form, raise your hand.

19. Listen for the places where the orchestra on this recording adds rubato and mark them in your part.

20. Which of these musical elements do you think is most important in this piece: melody, harmony, or rhythm?

Another useful tool for listening examples is the Venn diagram, which looks like the following:

Venn Diagram

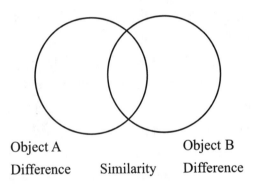

Object A   Object B

Difference   Similarity   Difference

HOMEWORK

The Venn diagram is a useful tool to organize listening and discussion activities that compare and contrast two different things, such as two different recordings of the same piece of music, two different pieces that use the same form (ABA for example), two different interpretations of music (one art music, one folk music for example), and so on. Begin by having the students write notes while listening to the excerpt (you may want to play it twice so that students can be more thorough). After the recording has finished, ask students to share their written ideas as you or one of the students place the comments in the appropriate category on the diagram (difference or similarity). After the class discusses how the ideas on the board relate to one another and what they learned about the composition from this exercise, play the example one last time so that students can listen with "informed" ears. Notice how the performance of the music changes as students play with a deeper understanding of the composition.

Here is an example of a Venn diagram completed by a middle school band student as he compared two different performances of *Danny Boy*— one performed by a brass band and one performed by a saxophone ensemble.

Danny Boy

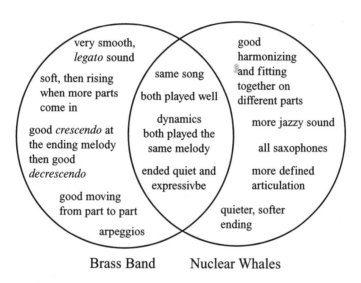

very smooth, *legato* sound

soft, then rising when more parts come in

good *crescendo* at the ending melody then good *decrescendo*

good moving from part to part

arpeggios

same song

both played well

dynamics both played the same melody

ended quiet and expressivbe

good harmonizing and fitting together on different parts

more jazzy sound

all saxophones

more defined articulation

quieter, softer ending

Brass Band   Nuclear Whales

Summary

Homework can be useful in a CMP classroom because it gives students more time to think through a question or problem. However, homework should be assigned judiciously and only when it will directly impact classroom learning. Listening can also be used to enhance learning, just remember to help students by providing a point of focus for listening.

163

CHAPTER 9

Concerts That Teach

This chapter applies the concept of comprehensive musicianship through performance to concert programming. CMP teachers have found that as they create long-term goals for their ensemble, they program entire concerts so that the repertoire is connected and teaches to those goals. This can be an exciting way to choose repertoire because it provides a clear educational focus, and it has the potential to teach the audience if you take the time to share your curriculum through program notes or through talking about the music during the concert.

This chapter contains the following concerts: "The Birth of the Symphony," "Imagine That!," "Music Honoring the Civil Rights Movement," "What's Opera?," "The Bach Project," "Westminster Abbey," "A Romeo and Juliet Evening," "Celestial Suite," and "Commissions and Programming a New Work." In this chapter, these concerts are described by the teacher who designed and performed them. The teachers share with you CMP strategies they used to implement these study units as well as insights regarding student participation. As each concert is listed, it indicates for what type of ensemble it was designed: high school orchestra, middle school band, etc.; however, each concert idea could be adapted and designed for any type or level of ensemble. Each concert is a unit of study on a particular topic that could be studied by all types of ensembles by merely inserting different repertoire. Therefore, take time to browse each concert as you are sure to glean ideas for your own concerts.

CONCERTS

High School Orchestra Concert:
THE BIRTH OF THE SYMPHONY

The long-term outcome for this unit was to study the development of the symphony orchestra and of string/symphonic music. The students study how the orchestra grew from:

- Solitary string player
- Two violins, cello, harpsichord
- *Concerto grosso*- a *concertino* (small group of instruments usually the same as the trio-sonata) against a the full orchestra (usually a string orchestra) called *concerto*, *tutti* or *ripieno*
- Chamber orchestra plus a few winds
- Chamber orchestra plus more winds and percussion
- Full orchestra
- Full orchestra plus technology to enhance the sounds
  Repertoire was chosen to represent each developmental phase of the orchestra:

Program

First Suite for Unaccompanied Cello . . . . .J. S. Bach
Trio Sonata . . . . .Tartini
Christmas Concerto Opus 6 #8 . . . . .Corelli
Eine Kleine Nachtmuzik . . . . .Mozart
Symphony No. 104 in D major, 1st mvt. . . .Haydn
Symphony No. 5, Finale . . . . .Beethoven
Marche Slave . . . . .Tschaikowsky/Herseth
Selections from Phantom of the Opera . . . .Webber/Custer

The following CMP script was written by orchestra students while studying this unit. Their intention was to share what they had learned with audience members so that listeners would more fully appreciate the concert. The story is organized around a single, old cello built in 1600. The play is told through the eyes of that cello, which kept getting new owners as the orchestra grew and changed.

CONCERTS

Script for "Birth of a Symphony," as told by an old cello!

OPENING

(Cello sits on its side on center of stage with spotlight)

Cello Voice (off stage): I remember so much over my 300 years of music making. Music has really changed over time. I remember when it was just the two of us, my owner and myself, and no one else was around to intrude on my beautiful music. Of course, my owner was poor, but we were very content making music for the public.

SCENE ONE

(A few lights come up on stage. A chair and stand sit center stage. A cellist walks in wearing a hat. She puts her hat down in front of her chair, picks up the cello, and plays *Prelude* from *Bach's First Suite for Unaccompanied Cello*. People begin to walk by dropping coins in the hat.)

SCENE TWO

(Two violinists walk by carrying cases and folding stands.)

Cellist: Hi! Would you like to play with me? We could make more money if we combine our talents. Plus, I have this great piece that my friend Tartini composed.

Other two violinists: Let's look at it.

(Violinists come closer to cellist and stand around her while the three musicians play *Trio-Sonata* by Tartini. More people enter from sides and drop coins into the hat. A wealthy stranger enters and listens attentively until the end of the piece.)

SCENE THREE

Stranger: You three sound marvelous as a group! I would like to invite you to perform at a dinner party that I am having at my castle this Friday evening in honor of the Baroness. (*As the man hands the musicians his card the musicians nod with excitement.*) Only one problem— there will be many people attending the party and I am not sure that we

CONCERTS

will be able to hear you very well. Do you know of any other musicians who could join you? You could perform music written by my court composer, Mozart.

Cellist (nods in agreement with the others): That would be wonderful. We will be there early on Friday.

SCENE FOUR

(Curtain goes up and Chamber Orchestra assembles on stage. The cellist and the two violinists join the orchestra and lead the beginning of *Eine Kleine Nachtmusik*).

(After the performance the Baroness enters applauding).

Baroness: That was a lovely performance! You have impressed my guests and I would love to have you play for another party I'm having in London. I am throwing a celebration for the holidays and we will be raising money for charity. I would like you to play with some of the new wind instruments we are hearing so much about these days.

(With much agreement from the orchestra, the Baroness turns to the stranger)

Baroness: We must begin setting up the concert hall!

(The Conductor's podium and more chairs are set up for a performance of the Haydn Symphony. Flutes, oboes, clarinets, bassoons, horns, and trumpet come through the audience and onto the stage. Orchestra performs).

SCENE FIVE

(Stage lights go down and the spotlight goes back on the cello).

Cello Voice (off stage): I have played in many concerts, quite a few that I have forgotten about. Yet, there was one concert somewhere in Germany that I will never forget. This crazy composer Ludwig decided to bring loud outdoor instruments inside. They used to be called sackbutts, but now they are known as trombones. This piece was one of the firsts that allowed those loud, obnoxious instruments to join the fun! Listen to how it sounds!

168

(Trombones walk through the audience and enter the stage. Orchestra performs the finale to Beethoven's Fifth Symphony).

SCENE SIX

(Spotlight back on cello).

Cello Voice (off stage): So far I have lived in Austria, England, and Germany, with those sackbutts. Soon after that concert I was sold to a wild Russian musician who was vacationing at a famous spa in Germany. My new owner played in a large orchestra that used pots and pans as instruments. They were called percussion instruments, but to me they were just loud! They covered up my beautiful soft, gorgeous, plaintive, loving, warm, fertile sound.

(Sigh—pause) Well, you decide what you think. The audience loved it!

(Percussion players come through the audience playing on the cymbals, snare and bass drum. Full Orchestra plays *Marche Slave*).

SCENE SEVEN

(Spotlight back to the cello).

Cello Voice (off stage): Well, after the Cold War ended, my Russian owner died of old age. After many years sitting in a dusty, old attic, I was finally sold to an Englishman. The gentleman was researching old opera houses. I was taken back to merry old England and found myself playing very unusual music. There were people on the stage above us singing and dancing. I did not like it because I had to sound soft most of the time. Plus, the singers wore strange costumes. In one scene they were all wearing masks on their faces. I can still hear the music now.

(Orchestra plays *Phantom of the Opera*).

CONCLUSION

(Spotlight on the cello).

Cello Voice (off stage): I have been played for hundreds of years, and have never gotten tired of creating wonderful sounds in many differ-

CONCERTS

ent styles. The orchestras that I have played in kept getting larger and larger. Always remember to… (Cello plays the song, "Think of me, think of me fondly...")

END OF CONCERT

Middle School Band Concert: IMAGINE THAT!

This concert, presented by middle school bands, is intended to engage the audience as active listeners who creatively imagine the music as they hear it, as opposed to passively letting it roll over them. Because each piece of music is descriptive, the listeners have the opportunity to engage their imaginations as well as their ears. It is also a good program to show parents that their students are having more than fun in band. They are learning about how music is constructed and how it functions.

In preparing for this concert, the students participated in a number of interesting activities to explore descriptive images. They wrote formula poetry describing some of the programmatic music, which was then read in the concert. They listened to recordings of Aaron Copland's music and discussed how the open fifths painted the image of the open prairie. In *Train Heading West*, they studied the role of the snare drum used to create the image of a moving train, in addition to other images created by the composer. In *The Red Balloon*, they traced the movement of the floating balloon melody through the flute (while also teaching the flutists a B-natural) to the clarinet to the trumpet; and in *Aquarium*, students identified the motif for each fish by listening to a recording and studying the score. In addition, students learned the concept of augmentation and diminution by altering one of the motifs from *Aquarium* to be longer and shorter than originally written.

CONCERTS

Program

Music is melody and harmony and rhythm. It tells a story, evokes an emotion. It soothes, it inspires, it is essential, it is etenal.
—Nancy Landon Kassebaum, U.S. Senator

Music has been called the universal language. While you may or may not agree with that statement, one thing is undeniably true—music has the power to ignite our imagination. Whether you are listening (and possibly watching) the music and story of *The Sorcerer's Apprentice* or the pure sounds of a Beethoven Symphony, music can tell stories and take us to new places.

Tonight's concert celebrates two things. First, the work of the young musicians before you, which represents hours and weeks of study and practice, with one common goal in mind: musical excellence. Second, the creation of living art, which, on this occasion, is music that tells a story or paints a picture with melody, rhythm, harmony, expression, timbre, and texture. From the celebratory opening of *Declaration and Dance* to the dramatic conclusion of *Aquarium*, your imaginations will be engaged and your spirit warmed.

Grade 7 Concert Band

Declaration and Dance . . . . Larry Clark
Declaration—a manifesto; an announcement; a solemn statement. Dance—to move rhythmically in a pattern of steps; a piece of music suited to dancing.—Larry Clark

The Red Balloon . . . . .Ann McGinty
The Red Balloon is an original composition based on a painting the composer saw just once. The painting showed a small child and a grandfather, facing away. The two people in the background were done in white on white. The only color in the painting was the red balloon, held by the child. The music depicts the balloon floating in the air. —Ann McGinty

Train Heading West and
Other Outdoor Scenes . . . . .Timothy Broege

    I. Prairie Ritual

    II. Rain on the Mountain

III. Train Heading West

The evocation of the great outdoors has been a tradition in 20th century American music, with perhaps the best examples found in the music of Aaron Copland. The use of open intervals and powerful elemental tunes has become familiar in concert music as well as film scoring. —Timothy Broege

Ancient Voices .Michael Sweeney

This composition is suggestive of the moods and sounds of early civilizations. This piece may conjure thoughts of early peoples of this continent. Or it may bring to mind even earlier populations who used the bones of mammoths and other animals as musical instruments tens of thousands of years ago. —Michael Sweeny

Grade 8: Concert Winds and Percussion

Royal Coronation Dances . . . . .Claude Gervaise
arr. Bob Margolis

I. Arrival of the Court

This movement depicts the guests, both noble and common, flanked by flag and banner bearers, arriving at the palace to view the majestic event, flags swirling in the air, cloaks brightly colored.

Snakes! . . . . .Thomas Duffy

Snakes! is a short piece of program music that explores different sounds which one might associate with different snakes. Big snakes, little snakes, cute snakes, writhing piles of snakes, swaying cobras and dangerous snakes are all represented throughout. After an introduction, which hints of hissing and the dangerous potential of snakes, the "rattlers" in the percussion are joined by an overlay of melodies. —Tom Duffy

Down a Country Lane . . . . .Aaron Copland
trans. Merlin Patterson

While not intended as a strictly programmatic work, this piece evokes images of a peaceful walk, perhaps at the turn of the previous century. The mood and colors are unmistakably Copland in this gentle work, originally commissioned by *Life Magazine* in 1962.

The Headless Horseman . . . . .Timothy Broege
This short piece compresses a fair amount into a brief time span. The introduction sets the stage for the entry and journey of the Headless Horseman. Some audience members have been frightened by the opening bars of the piece. There is drama and excitement in this brief musical ride, so let the faint-hearted pass it by. —Timothy Broege

Aquarium . . . . .Johann DeMeij
    I. Allegretto Grazioso
    II. Andante/Adagio
    III. Finale: Allegro Giocoso
The suite, Aquarium, features six tropical fishes, each of them represented by a motif, and surfacing in several forms. The composition consists of three movements of which the second and third merge uninterruptedly into each other. —Johann DeMeij

High School Choral Concert:
MUSIC HONORING THE CIVIL RIGHTS MOVEMENT

This concert introduced singers to a variety of musical genres within the African American vocal tradition—Classical music, spirituals, freedom songs, contemporary/pop, and traditional and contemporary gospel music. The choir also studied the role music played in the civil rights movement and discovered the power of music to move bodies, change minds, and stir the soul.

The choir arranged the freedom songs, a feat that was quite challenging as choirs rarely attempt such an activity. They also studied the life, speeches and poetry of Martin Luther King, Jr., and Langston Hughes.

The most significant component of this concert was partnering with a local African American gospel church choir. The school choir of predominantly Euro-Americans had a transforming experience when they performed during a church service. As the congregation engaged with the music, the students learned that music could be a dialogue, that music

requires an active, full-bodied participation, and that singers must believe in and be emotionally connected to what they sing in order to affect listeners.

The gospel choir performed on the concert with the school choir and offered more lessons in how to transform the often sterile atmosphere of concert halls into a lively and meaningful space.

This concert offered the singers and listeners the opportunity to broaden their conception of African American music (it's more than just spirituals and gospel music), to learn about significant historical events and people, to connect with and appreciate a different culture, to arrange and improvise music, and to have a transforming cultural experience. One student summed up the concert by saying he could never have learned all of that from a textbook.

Program

One of the main cultural expressions of the civil rights movement was collective singing. As the nonviolent struggle against segregation spread from lunch counters to swimming pools from movie theaters to public schools and from public accommodations to voter registration, and as the movement itself spread from state to state in the south and then to the north and west, collective singing spread with it. The sources of the songs were mainly—but not exclusively—from the African American tradition. Hymns and spirituals took on an added depth of meaning within the context of the contemporary struggle.

—George Brandon, excerpt from *Singing in the African American Tradition*

We Are . . . . Ysae Maria Barnwell
Sweet Honey in the Rock
Sweet Honey in the Rock is a group of five African-American women who have inspired audiences around the world with music ranging from traditional African to contemporary blues, jazz, and

gospel. In this selection, Dr. Barnwell combines elements from traditional African music such as a chant-like melody and the use of *ostinato* accompaniment with contemporary harmonies to create a beautiful, meditative tone. Her text draws upon traditional African beliefs that our ancestors are a significant part of who we are, and that we are all "seekers of truth, and lovers of life, we are one." The gesture that the choir is performing is sign-language (which is always a part of Sweet Honey in the Rock performances), for we are one.

I'm Gonna Sing till the Spirit Moves
in My Heart . . . . .Moses Hogan

Moses Hogan has earned a reputation for his outstanding contemporary settings of spirituals. This spirited selection is fairly traditional until the final section, where he introduces a more contemplative tone exemplified by the upper voices' ending "moan."

The Cloths of Heaven . . . . .Adolphus Hailstork

Adolphus Hailstork is a contemporary African American composer who is known for his orchestral and choral works. In this selection he blends 20th-century compositional techniques with extended chords from the jazz idiom. These chords give depth and color to the bitter-sweet text, "I have spread my dreams under your feet. Tread softly because you tread on my dreams."

"I have a dream that one day this nation will rise up and live out the true meaning of its creed: 'We hold these truths to be self-evident; that all men are created equal." —Martin Luther King, Jr.

Three Freedom Songs . . . . .Traditional

Arranged by the Chorus

Freedom songs had several functions in the civil rights movement. They were songs of protest and persuasion. They were used to solicit and arouse outside support and to reinforce values in individuals supporting the movement. There were also psychological factors involved. The power of a mass of human voices is remarkable. It sends out a wall of sound in advance of the singers which is almost palpable; a physical force which is clearly felt within the group as well as outside of it. This was particularly important in a nonviolent struggle in which protestors had no weapons or other means of physical self-defense.

CONCERTS

We're Marching On to Freedom Land
> *We're marching on to freedom land,*
> *We're marching on to freedom land,*
> *God's our strength from day to day,*
> *As we travel the narrow way,*
> *We're going forward, we're going forward,*
> *One day we're gonna be free.*

Dog, Dog
> *Dog, dog, d-dog a dig-a-dog dog*
> *Dog, dog, d-dog a dig-a-dog dog*
> *Dog, dog, d-dog a dig-a-dog dog*
> *Dog, dog, d-dog a dig-a-dog dog*
> *My dog love your dog and your dog love my dog*
> *And my dog love your dog and your dog love my dog then*
> *Why can't we sit under the apple tree.*

Ain't Gonna Let Nobody
> *Ain't gonna let nobody turn me round,*
> *Turn me round, turn me round*
> *Ain't gonna let nobody*
> *Turn me round, keep on a-walkin', keep on a-talkin'*
> *Walkin' up to freedom lan'*

His Eye Is on the Sparrow . . . . . Words by Civilla D. Martin
Music by Charles H. Gabriel
This song is popular in the African American church. With the text, "I sing because I'm happy. I sing because I'm free" it is especially well suited for our civil rights program.

Stand . . . . John P. Key
John P. Key is a popular gospel artist who combines contemporary musical elements with a traditional choral sound. He is known for his powerful and soulful singing and is well represented by our soloist, Maurice Jackson.
> *"You ought to believe something in life, believe that thing so fervently that you will stand up with it till the end of your days."*
> —*Martin Luther King, Jr.*

CONCERTS

176

MLK . . . . .Words and music by U2

Arr. Bob Chilcott

The King's Singers made this version of U2's (Irish rock band) tribute to Martin Luther King, Jr. popular. Martin Luther King, Jr. had hoped to be a Baptist preacher in a Southern city. Instead, by the time he was assassinated in 1968 at the age of 39, he had been awarded the Nobel Peace Prize and had led millions of people in a nonviolent movement that shattered forever the Southern system of segregation of the races. He asked to be remembered as a "drum major for justice," and he is. (Coretta Scott King, *The Words of Martin Luther King, Jr.*)

Melodies from Heaven . . . . .Kirk Franklin

Kirk Franklin is one of the most popular contemporary gospel artists. He was an overnight success and his recordings have crossed over to secular radio.

Revelations 19:1 . . . . .Jeffrey LaValley

Scored by Thomas. W. Jefferson

This soulful hymn is a tradition in the African American church. It is frequently sung at Martin Luther King, Jr. celebrations. If you know this song you are welcome to sing along.

"Love is the most durable power in the world. This creative force, so beautifully exemplified in the life of Christ, is the most potent instrument available in mankind's quest for peace and security."
—*Martin Luther King, Jr.*

Get Excited . . . . .Miami Mass Choir

Within the gospel tradition, there are a number of mass choirs that consist of the best gospel singers from the community's choirs, in this case Miami Florida. With its use of a B-3 organ and tambourine, this piece hearkens back to a more traditional gospel sound.

"And when this happens, and when we allow freedom to ring from every village and every hamlet, from every state and every city, we will be able to speed up that day when all of God's children, black men and white men, Jews and Gentiles, Protestants and Catholics, will be able to join hands and sing in the last worlds of that old Negro spiritual, 'Free at last! Free at Last! Thank God almighty, we are free at last!'" —*Martin Luther King, Jr.*

CONCERTS

High School Choral Concert:
WHAT'S OPERA?

This choral concert, featuring Bizet's *Carmen*, was the culmination of a semester-long study of opera forms and conventions. *Carmen* is in many ways an ideal "first" opera for high school students with little exposure to the genre. Its music is tuneful and exciting, and its choruses and ensembles are scored in such a way as to make them performable by young singers. Its plot is fast-moving, action-packed, and credible to contemporary youth, who are already familiar through popular entertainment, with issues of violence, crimes of passion, love triangles, jealousy, and revenge.

The final performance was a concert version of *Carmen* that told the story of the opera in 30 minutes, using four choirs, a narrator, student soloists, guest professional soloists, and a small ensemble of instrumentalists and piano. The professional singers sang the roles of Carmen and Escamillo; student soloists covered the smaller roles of Mercedes, Frasquita, Zuniga, and other minor characters. Narration linked the separate numbers and was usually underscored by a small orchestra that included a piano (providing the body of the accompaniment), a few brass and woodwind players for color, several string players, and percussion.

Each of the choirs sang a "feature" number from the score and all the choirs combined for the finale, the famous "March with Chorus" that opens the final act. The program included:

Program

The Chorus of Cigarette Girls
sung by the Women's Choir, an intermediate level group

The Habanera
sung by the advanced Concert Choir, with the part of
Carmen sung by a professional mezzo soprano

The Chanson du Toreador
sung by the extra-curricular Men's Choir, with the role of
Escamillo sung by a professional baritone; incidental solos

> *in the refrain were sung by students*
> The Smugglers' Chorus
> *sung by the advanced Concert with student soloists*
> The Chorus of Street Vendors
> *a short, relatively easy piece, sung by the beginning, entry-level choir*
> The March with Chorus/Finale
> *sung by combined choirs, with professional soloists*

The learning process began three months before the concert, at an annual weekend choir retreat, where the choirs learned their parts in an English singing translation. Rehearsals were interspersed with viewings of the 1984 Francesco Rosi film version of *Carmen*, starring Julia Migenes-Johnson and Placido Domingo. This is an excellent film for opera neophytes: the acting is believable, the stars charismatic, and the cinematography stunning. Students were never bored, and each segment offered plenty of ideas for discussion. It was this weekend immersion experience of *Carmen* that "hooked" students completely, in some cases to obsession. (The traditional choir retreat talent show even featured such acts as "Beastie Boys sing *Carmen*" and "Kung Fu Toreador!")

During the following weeks, the choirs continued to polish their *Carmen* choruses, and gradually the original French text was learned to replace the English. By this time, students had memorized the English, so the general sense of the choruses was clear to them. They were happy, however, to learn the French, since by this time they were immersed enough in the opera to realize that singing in English wouldn't "feel quite right."

Throughout the rehearsal process (which incidentally included a wide variety of other repertoire besides *Carmen*), the choirs were gradually exposed to vocabulary and concepts related to the culture of opera, including the aria, recitative, libretto, ensembles, overture, entr'actes and scene change music, underscoring, the relationship of composer to

CONCERTS

librettist, and the use of the orchestra (particularly exciting in *Carmen* and very interesting to choral students with little exposure to instrumental techniques).

Other, more complex issues were also explored:

- the differences between opera and spoken theatre in terms of amount of text, amount of action, and the role of music in telling parts of the story.

- the differences between plot-driven theatre (and television) and lyric theatre, which takes more time to dwell on emotional reactions and the characters' interior lives.

- the difference between an opera film (like the Rosi) and a filmed version of a staged opera. Students watched excerpts from several Metropolitan opera versions of *Carmen* and compared the filming techniques, acting styles, and advantages of one over the other, for directors, actors, and audience.

The week before the concert, the professional soloists rehearsed with the choirs and discussed with the students their lives as opera singers. By this time, students had enough information and interest to ask good questions.

The semester final exam was a comprehensive written test that included mostly short answer and essay questions and some listening examples of both familiar and new excerpts to discuss (e.g. "Is this an aria or recitative? How do you know?") The exam was designed to give students a chance to demonstrate their understanding of the various terms, ideas, and conventions of opera, as well as reflecting on their own experience of bringing an opera score to life in performance.

The experience of most choral students is too often limited to performing dozens of small pieces each year, without a sense of the historical importance of large choral and stage works. This project was repeated successfully in succeeding school years, focusing on a different opera, oratorio, or extended work, including abbreviated versions of Mendelssohn's *Elijah*, Handel's *Israel in Egypt*, Orff's *Carmina Burana*, Gershwin's *Porgy and Bess*, and Gilbert and Sullivan's *The Mikado*.

CONCERTS

High School Choral Concert:
THE BACH PROJECT

This high school concert featured Bach's Cantata 150: *Nach dir Herr, verlanget mich*, performed by combined choirs and a chamber orchestra of nine string players and harpsichord. This piece works well as an introduction to Bach, to the cantata genre, and to Baroque style in general. It is practically a compendium of Bach's stylistic markers and 17th-century compositional techniques. It is one of the least difficult Bach cantatas for young singers to master, and can be performed in its entirety by choirs, without using soloists. The movements are relatively short and not too taxing, the melismatic choral writing is reasonable in range, length, and technical demands. The accompaniment is spare: two violins and continuo (although for our performance we tripled the violins and bass instruments to better balance the choral forces).

Program

Cantata 150: Nach dir Herr . . . . .J. S. Bach
(Each movement of the cantata offers many concepts, skills, and vocabulary to teach)

Sinfonia (orchestra): *basso continuo*, chromatic scale, the "longing" motive.

Nach dir Herr (SATB): Text painting, musical symbolism, number symbolism, imitation, suspension, diminished chords, chromatic scale, the "longing" motive, homophony versus polyphony, fugue, melisma.

Doch bin und bleibe ich (Soprano aria): (Although this would have been performed originally by a boy soloist, it works equally well sung by the entire soprano section of an advanced choir). Text painting, musical tone painting, Baroque ornamentation, diminished intervals.

CONCERTS

Leite mich (SATB): Scale, text painting, musical symbolism, melisma, homophony versus polyphony, imitation, motive.

Zedern müssen (ATB): Text and tone painting, symbolism, hemiola, imitation. (This movement can also be sung by the choir, rather than soloists.)

Meine Augen (SATB): Stasis versus motion, text painting, tone painting, harmonic rhythm (slow versus fast), fugue, hemiola, major versus minor, chromaticism, Picardy third.

Meine Tage (SATB): Ground bass, chaconne, variation form, text painting, "longing" motive, Picardy third.

Rehearsals

Rehearsals included a mix of learning to sing the choruses and learning about the music of Bach. Student materials included a vocal score for each student, a side-by-side translation of the German text and its sources, and a listening guide to an extensive listening list that students were responsible to know.

Listening Project

The listening included:

- Cantata 150 in a professional recording
- Bach: Passacaglia and Fugue C minor for organ (to compare chaconnes)
- Brandenburg Concerto No. 1, First Movement
- Minuet and Badinerie from Orchestral Suite No. 2
- *Badinerie* (same as above) sung by Swingle Singers
- Three movements from the B minor Mass
- Prelude and Fugue No. 1
- Three movements from Cantata No. 158, 211, The Coffee Cantata

CONCERTS

- Scenes from the *Saint Matthew Passion*
- Solo Prelude for Lute
- Opening Chorus from the Magnificat in D
- Solo aria "Mein Glaübiges Herze" from Cantata 68
- Last movement of Brahms' Symphony No. 4 (which borrows its chaconne theme from Bach's Cantata 150)

These examples were studied in class over the course of the semester and students had recordings to study at home.

Takin' It Home

Two weeks before the concert, students were given a homework assignment to be completed with their parents. The purpose was for students to teach their parents as much as they could about the cantata, in preparation for the approaching concert. An in-class discussion explored a characteristic of Classical music that sometimes poses a barrier to audience appreciation: the music is too rich and complex to be understood on one hearing. Students were invited to share their frustration with having worked hard on a piece in choir, only to have a parent say after the concert, "That was pretty," or "That was weird," or worse yet, say nothing. Students were well aware that their audiences, (mostly parents and friends, of course) rarely got to experience the piece in the same depth of understanding that they did by spending time with the piece daily over several weeks. This strategy was intended to address that problem, and students were enthusiastic about it because they immediately recognized the benefits. By this time, they were so excited about the cantata they were eager for a forum to share it with their parents.

The homework assignment was essentially a one-page combination listening guide and worksheet to be completed by one or two parents, under the tutelage of their son or daughter. It was due the day of the concert, ensuring that our audience was well prepared to hear the cantata with understanding. The homework looked like this:

CONCERTS

TAKIN' IT HOME

One of the marvels of Bach is in his ability to create music of amazing structural, almost mathematical perfection that is still emotionally moving. Because so much of what he is trying to say is buried in the complexity of his counterpoint, it is almost impossible to grasp it all in one hearing. The wonderful thing, though, is that this music does not get tiresome with repeated hearings. Indeed, it is so rich that there are always new rewards to be discovered for a serious listener. It is an endless stream ("Bach" in German) of ideas and moods and feelings. Hopefully this preview will help you to enjoy our performance of this masterpiece even more.

Sit down together armed with your listening tape and listening guide. Follow the instructions below. If you listen and discuss together, your student will meet the basic requirement and receive one enrichment point. If you actually fill out the worksheet below, you'll get three enrichment points. Add an additional point for including two parents.

I followed the listening guide through the entire cantata with my son/daughter_____, and I feel like I understand the piece a little better than before. (1 point)

_____
(Parent Signature)

We're going for Baroque here. We went through the recording so carefully that I was able to answer the questions below. I am now prepared to understand this piece in performance. Please award three points!

_____
(Parent Signature)

CONCERTS

Before listening, have your student talk briefly and explain the basic meaning of "text painting."

Now begin listening. Stop the tape before each movement, read through the study guide together, listen to the movement, then stop the tape again. Ready to begin?

1. Sinfonia: What mood seems to be created by the opening Sinfonia? If you didn't know what was coming next, what might you guess the cantata will be about?

_____

_____

2. Chorus #1: In mm. 1-20, trace the longing motif as it weaves its way through the voices and orchestra instruments.

Who has the motif in mm. 4-7? (be specific)

_____

_____

3. Soprano Aria: How does Bach text-paint these words?
toben (rage) _____
Höll (hell) _____
ewig (eternally, forever) _____

4. Chorus: Before listening, have your student point out the rising scale in each part. Read the listening guide for this section. Study the two motives at ten until the end (patient and anxious). Who has the "patience" motif at m. 24?

_____

CONCERTS

185

5. Movements Five and Six: Read the texts of these movements carefully and read the listening guide for each one before listening.

6. Final Chorus/Chaconne: Sing the chaconne melody together once through (or at least hum along with the tape) and have your student explain ground bass. Study the text and find examples of text painting, with the help of your student.

Can you find the "longing" motif in this piece? Where?

Answer one or both (if you feel smart!) of these questions:
How many variations are there all together? (Remember that the ground is always exactly four measures long.)

_____

The ground begins on the pitch B, but Bach varies it occasionally by transposing it to start on other pitches. What are they? Draw them on the staff below and indicate in what measure they occur. (There are four altogether, in addition to the original B.)

Which movement was your favorite? Why?

_____

_____

Obviously this assignment was an unusual expectation, but most students approached it cheerfully and were eager to teach their parents about something they had come to value and appreciate. The response from parents was enthusiastic and grateful. Many of them realized, perhaps for the first time, just how much their students were learning in choir beyond getting the concert ready. The students themselves had an unusually confident understanding of this complex music, due mostly to having to teach it to someone else. All of this learning came together the night of the concert.

There was an unusual bond between performers and the audience that night. Rarely had an audience at one of our choral concerts come with such anticipation and such a high level of understanding of the music they were about to hear.

Because the cantata is only about 15 minutes long, I took the opportunity to do a brief "Pre-concert Demonstration." I explained five key spots that would help the audience listen with understanding, and each was played/sung by the performers with whom I had rehearsed these short excerpts beforehand. No one who had been through the "Takin' It Home" worksheet complained about having to sit through another "review"—in fact, many commented on what a pleasure it was to be able to follow the examples and be familiar with them. For other audience members, it provided a chance to "peek" into the piece before hearing it in its entirety.

I had originally intended this entire homework activity to make the concert experience a richer one for parents in our audience, many of whom are not that familiar with Bach, or even art music in general. I was merely hoping for a post-concert reaction from parents to their children that went beyond, "That was nice." In fact, the unexpected rewards were reaped for a long time after the concert. Students carried with them a deeper understanding of this great masterwork that lasted well beyond the fond memories of the concert experience. They had a new bond with their parents and something new to talk about. (Many parents expressed gratitude about how this activity opened some new avenues of dialogue between them and their child.) Perhaps best of all, these parents had a new appreciation, not just for Bach, but also for the kind of work their students were doing in choir. I believe many of these same parents became new advocates for music education that night.

High School Orchestra Concert:
WESTMINSTER ABBY

Many famous composers are buried in or commemorated at Westminster Abby in London, England. This concert sought to focus on the music of the composers buried there, and on the poetry from those commemorated in Poets Corner. Students researched the history of Westminster Abby and presented short reports on the people commemorated in the Abby. Musical selections were chosen to feature one composition by each composer being studied. Other students researched the poets and poetry and selected many poems to be read in class.

During the concert, slides were shown of the different parts of Westminster Abby and a student announcer shared some historical and architectural information with the audience. An explanation of each composer's life and compositional style were shared with the audience before the orchestra performed his composition. Between the musical selections, students presented the background on a famous poet and then read one or two of his poems. Poets and writers researched included: Matthew Arnold, Francis Beaumont, William Blake, Robert Browning, Lord Byron, Geoffrey Chaucer, John Clare, Charles Dickens, Thomas Hardy, George Herbert, Ben Jonson, Rudyard Kipling, William Shakespeare, Robert Southey, Alfred Lord Tennyson, and Oscar Wilde.

Program

Welcome to the music and poetry from the Westminster Abbey in London, England. All the music performed tonight will be of composers who are buried or commemorated in the abbey. In-between music selections, students will read poetry from the poets featured in the famous Poet's Corner found in the abbey.

Freshman Orchestra

Entrance of the Queen of Sheba . . . . .Handel/Fisher
Concerto Grosso Opus 6, No. 2 . . . . .Handel/Dackow
Selections from the Fireworks Music . . . . .Handel/Frost

Symphony Orchestra

English Folk Song Suite . . . . Vaughan Williams

(A choral student will sing each folk song before the orchestra performs each individual movement.)

    1. March—*Seventeen Come Sunday*

    2. Intermezzo—*My Bonnie Boy , Green Bushes*

    3. March—*Blow Away the Morning Dew , High Germany*

Rhosymedre . . . . .Vaughan Williams

Jupiter Bringer of Jollity . . . . .Holst

High School Orchestra Program:
A ROMEO AND JULIET EVENING

The play *Romeo and Juliet* by William Shakespeare has inspired many composers to write music to enhance the plot. This concert was designed to compare and contrast the way composers tried to portray the play through sound. During the nine weeks of study, students discussed and reflected on how each composer used the elements of music to create certain scenes. They studied the compositional devises composers used to create the needed tension and release in the different compositions.

While studying the play students asked if they could act out scenes during the concert. One student asked permission to direct these scenes as a project for her theatre class. She held auditions, cast the roles, and designed and made the scenery. Other students in the orchestra choreographed the Renaissance suite that opened the concert. Another student designed the concert program to look like a scroll with burnt edges.

The concert opened with the orchestra playing neo-Renaissance dances. Two student announcers then introduced the audience to the power of Shakespeare's *Romeo and Juliet* and its influence on musical composition. Three scenes were acted out on the front of the stage. Before each scene ended, the orchestra would start playing the next musical selection so there was no break between the acting and the music. After applause at the end of the musical selection, the next scene was set-up by

CONCERTS

the announcers. The concert ended with *Selections from West Side Story* by Leonard Bernstein arranged by Mason, which brought the themes of *Romeo and Juliet* to modern day society.

Program

Suite for String Orchestra . . . . Peter Warlock
1. Basse Danse
2. Pavane
6. Mattachins (Sword Dance)
      (All three movements danced by student dancers.)

The Montaques and the Capulets . . . . .Prokofieff/Siennicki

The Balcony Scene from *Romeo and Juliet* . . . . .Shakespeare

Love Theme from Romeo and Juliet . . . . .Nino Rota/Gordo
From the film music of *Romeo and Juliet*.

The Apothecary Scene from *Romeo and Juliet* . . . . .Shakespeare

The Death Scene from *Romeo and Juliet* . . . . .Shakespeare

Introduction and Finale . . . . .Tschaikowsky/Mueller
Themes from the *Overture to Romeo and Juliet*.

West Side Story Selections . . . . .Bernstein/Mason

---

Middle School Orchestra Concert
Celestial Suite

Celestial Suite (original composition by middle school orchestra teacher, Kathy Punwar) uses musical effects to create a "picture" in the music. The four movements are I. The Moon; II. Stars; III. Rain Clouds; and IV. The Sun. We began by studying the themes and other compositional devices and explored the images and ideas each movement suggested. After learning and exploring all four movements, students were asked to either create a piece of art or poetry about one or more of the movements. During the concert, the poems were read before the movement, and their artwork was displayed in a slide presentation behind the orchestra as they played.

1. **The Moon** uses an *ostinato* in the cello and bass line. The violas have the melody after the countermelody is first played by the first and second violins. Finally, the countermelody, melody, and *ostinato* combine togeth-

Elise Saffell-Lande

er. The tone of the piece is calming, yet majestic. Students explore the different elements that portray the dignity of the moon. They will eventually compare the first and fourth movements that, although they use the same thematic material, are quite different in effect.

2. **Stars** uses a pentatonic, *pizzicato* melody, first introduced by the cellos and basses. The effect is at first "sparse" and simple (like twilight). Then the cellos and basses start the same melody over, but the violas and vio-

Chuck Kraege

lins layer in. The overlapping melodies create the effect of more stars being visible in the sky. They briefly converge on a little variation of "Twinkle, Twinkle, Little Star." Then brief glimpses of the theme reappear, becoming a bit more sparse again (as in the pre-dawn hours).

3. **Rain Clouds** uses more sound effects than any of the other three move- ments. *Tremolo* is used by the cellos and basses to create the sound of distant rumbling thunder. A *sforzan- do/tremolo* is used by the violas and second violins to create a "flash" of light-

Tami Wiggius
Krysia Magnuson

ening. Later the violins use *collegno* to create rain. It is not a strong and powerful storm, but one of rumbling thunder and a steady rain that eventually dwindles, and with a last quiet rumble, the storm has passed. The theme is shared by both upper and lower strings at two different parts of the movement. Violins and violas have the first theme while cellos and basses have the "thunder" *ostinato.* Later the cellos and basses have the theme while the violins and violas are "raining."

4. **The Sun** uses the same melody as is used in The Moon. But now the accompaniment has more energy— trills and stronger rhythms. The beginning of the movement creates the

Charles Bellenger

image of the sun's rays breaking over the horizon. There are snippets of the theme used in the introduction and coda to tie it all together.

Middle School Band Concert: Commissioning and Programming a New Work

"Wisconsin Landscapes and Other Treasures" was a concert featuring a newly commissioned work for middle school band. The commission was supported by local funding and sought to provide students with an opportunity to get to know a composer and the compositional process, and to support the creation of new music for young students.

By being involved with a professional composer, students were interested and motivated to participate in the creative process of writing a new composition. As a result, I took this opportunity to teach band students how to compose their own music. For this concert I selected compositions which also lent themselves to composition-related activities. Selections included:

1. *Rhythm Machine*, by Timothy Broege—Students completed a study sheet where they analyzed the motivic development and form of the piece.
2. *Gamelan*, by Walter Cummings—Students composed a rhythm

rondo to demonstrate their understanding of how this form is creat-ed. Students also learned about Javanese Gamelan music through listening to a variety of recordings.

3. *Suite in Minor Mode,* arranged by Siekman and Oliver, originally written for piano by Dimitri Kabalevsky. Students compared the original score with the band transcription.

To help students get to know the composer, each student:

- Sent a note or letter of introduction asking questions about the composer, his or her method of composing, and occasionally a request for a solo or "good" part.
- Listened to a tape or a sketch of the piece and reviewed background information about the music and the composer.
- Listened to other works by the composer or music by other composers which may be similar in style to this composer.

A benefit of getting to know our composer in residence was that students were anxious to get to know more of the composers whose music they were playing. Frequently now students will look up and e-mail a composer and then share this information with the band. We also display—these comments in the lobby prior to band concerts so that parents can view them.

During the process of learning "Wisconsin Landscapes," students described their experience of meeting a composer through questionnaires. The following is the questionnaires used to evaluate the project:

CONCERTS

> **MEET THE COMPOSER III**
>
> 1. Describe your performance of "Wisconsin Landscapes."
> 2. Describe the band's performance of "Wisconsin Landscapes."
> 3. How did you feel about having a piece created for your band?
> 4. What makes this a good piece?
> 5. Have your ideas about it changed since you first played it? How?
> 6. Did your ideas about composers change after meeting Mr. LaPlante? How?
> 7. Do you think our school should bring a composer to work with students again?
> 8. If you had a friend who was going to work with a composer next year, what would you tell your friend to expect?
> 9. If someone were to say that working with a composer is not really a serious part of school, what would you say?

The printed program for this concert was carefully designed to provide information about the new piece, the commissioning project, and the program with program notes by students. Here is the concert program:

> # Program
>
> Making music, in fact, is the very best way of learning
> —Richard Baker
>
> **Concert Band**
>
> Renaissance Couplet . . . . .arranged by Elliot delBorgo
> I learned that playing slow can be fun. I love the harmony of this piece. The variation of time signatures, tempos, and dynamics make Renaissance Couplet more interesting.
> —*Erin Tonn, Oboe*

Gamelan . . . . .Wayne Cummings
What makes this a good piece is that it is something different and new
to us. It is a good piece because everyone has a melody.
—*Ryan Dion, Baritone*

Along the Caney Fork. . . . . .John Hosay
arranged by James Hosay
From this piece I learned how to play long, sustained notes. I liked
being able to play the long notes and have the responsibility of
keeping the band together. This is a good piece because it is very
expressive.
—*Charlie Thomson, Trombone*

All Ye Young Sailors . . . . .arranged by Pierre LaPlante
I learned more about 6/8 time. It seems hard to count, but isn't. I
like the piece—it is different from the others because it is in 6/8
time. It is a good piece because it challenges us.
—*Bethany Tierney, Percussion*

Rhythm Machine . . . . .Timothy Broege
I learned about the motive of a piece. The motive is a short musical
idea. Rhythm Machine has many parts and is in rondo form.
—*Chad Murdoch, Trombone*

Concert Winds and Percussion

March de Provencal . . . . .William E. Rhoads
This is a very lively piece. Its form is quite interesting. Marche de
Provencal changes from major to minor a lot, which makes it more
interesting to listen to.
—*Elizabeth Eilliott, Horn*

Sinfonia XVII-The Four Winds . . . . .Timothy Broege
The rhythms make this piece sound mystical and very much like
wind sounds in a storm.
—*Joe Steffes, Percussion*

In this composition, the melody and harmony work together, giving
the songs a mysterious, vague feeling.
—*Vanessa Blackman, Clarinet*

CONCERTS

Ave Verum Corpus . . . . .Wolfgang Amadeus Mozart,

arr. by Barbara Buehlman

This is a song that shows the magnificence in a style that everyone enjoys. Anyone can play loud, not everyone can play soft. We have worked to learn to play soft.

—*Heather Lemm, Oboe*

Suite in Minor Mode . . . . .Dmitri Kabalevsky,

arr. Siekman and Oliver

Each of the movements has its own personality. One may be loud and quite fast, but the next is quiet and slow.

—*Danielle Duranceau, Flute*

Wisconsin Landscapes . . . . .Pierre LaPlante

Between 1940 and 1946, Professor Helene Stratman-Thomas and her assistant crisscrossed the state making field recordings of ordinary folks singing and playing songs and tunes that had been handed down and learned from family and friends from the earliest times on. These songs were intended to be those which "transmitted familiar legends and stories...expressed moods, lifestyles, and varied aspects of culture (untainted) by records, radio, or commercialism." The work of these folk song enthusiasts remained untapped until they were assembled and published in *Folk Songs Out of Wisconsin* (1977) by the State Historical Society of Wisconsin as part of the American Revolution Bicentennial Celebration.

The opening of "Wisconsin Landscapes" is based on the "Pinery Boy," a song collected by Fraz Rickaby in Eau Claire. The song tells of a young girl who seeks her lover, a craftsman, working on the Wisconsin River. She finds out he has perished on the river and is so distraught she dies of a broken heart. Despite the tragic and melodramatic nature of the verse, the tune is broad and expansive (an octave plus three notes). The first movement of "Wisconsin Landscapes" is intended to convey a feeling of grandeur and beauty of Wisconsin long ago.

The second half of "Wisconsin Landscapes" is based on the "Turkey Song." It is believed by some authorities that the tune originated in Kentucky and came to Wisconsin via Kentuckian settlers. The "Turkey Song" appears in various children's song collections including those of Pete Seeger and Jill Trinka.

Unlike the "Pinery Boy," the "Turkey Song" is in the minor tonality and has two distinct sections (AB form). Both songs share common melodic patterns that make them sound like they are related to each other. In the final section (Maestoso), the two themes are brought together before the final coda (Allegro).

The Central Middle School Bands Commissioning Project

Begun in the 1994-95 school year, the Central Middle School Bands Commissioning Project seeks two things: to provide students with an opportunity to meet and get to know a composer as he or she creates an original composition; and to support the creation of new music for young band students. This new music will be available to students around the country. The project will continue as long as funding is available, and preliminary contracts have been reached for the next school year. The announcement for the next school year is made during the spring concert premiering a new work.

Through the Commissioning Project, band students at Central are involved in composing music themselves. The composition work is introductory, but serves to provide students with opportunities to create their own music. This is in accordance with the comprehensive musicianship philosophy of the band program as well as national standards developed by the Music Educators National Conference. Through meeting and getting to know a composer and through the process of composing themselves, students have a much greater understanding of what it is like to create music in a very real way.

Our journey on the path of creating music has just begun, but hopefully wherever they go from here, students will continue to create and perform their own music.

Tonight's premiere was made possible in part through the support of the Wisconsin Sesquicentennial Commission, with funds from individual and corporate contributors and the state of Wisconsin. We thank the Commission and funders for their support!

CONCERTS

CHAPTER **10**

CMP at a Glance

This chapter includes summaries of each point of the model for you to use as a quick reference while writing CMP teaching plans. Each point of the model has been summarized on one or two pages, highlighting the main issues covered in the corresponding chapter. Further, additional reminders or comments appear in the margins to assist you in thinking more broadly and outside of the box.

The chapter also includes templates for writing teaching plans, which come in two varieties—*a unit plan* and *day-to-day teaching plans.* The unit plan is the initial work you do with a piece of music to discover the curriculum within. This includes the full analysis, list of long-range outcomes, creative strategies to incorporate during the unit, and assessment tools for determining to what degree the outcomes were achieved. The unit plan will be fairly long because it is where you explore and do your thinking about the entire piece of music. This plan then becomes the reference for writing daily teaching plans.

The daily teaching plan begins by listing the long-range outcome toward which you are working. By listing this first, your lesson will be focused and move towards achieving your long-term goals. The next step is to list the outcomes for the day (short-term goals), remembering to include knowledge and affective as well as skill outcomes. As you write these goals you may want to review your analysis, so it is a good idea to keep your analysis handy or in the same notebook as the plans. To achieve the outcomes, you will design a variety of teaching strategies, including warm-ups that relate directly to your pieces being rehearsed. The last category on the daily teaching plan is assessment. If your lesson includes a formal assessment of a goal, such as self-assessments, journal

entries, or dictation, you will list these on the plan. However, you probably will not do a formal assessment every class period, so there is a place
for writing your informal assessment of the rehearsal, such as what did or
did not work, what the ensemble needs to do next, etc. These reflections
will guide the design of your next teaching plan.

AT A GLANCE

A thorough analysis of the music is a necessary foundation for significant learning and great performances

ANALYSIS

Broad Description
How would you describe this composition?

Type/Genre
(suite, motet, overture, etc.)

Background Information
- Research the style period this was written for and determine the compositional elements that make it a characteristic or uncharacteristic example of the period.
- Research the composer's life and style characteristics Pay particular attention to those aspects that pertain to your composition and that would interest your students.
- Explore why the composer wrote this piece (e.g. commissioned for a special event or written as part of job) and determine whether it is a good example of her/his work.
- Determine who originally would have performed this piece and in what setting.
- Discuss any traditions that accompany this piece (such as standing for *The Hallelujah Chorus*).

Additional Choral Information
- If the text is in a foreign language, translate it yourself and then compare it to the given translation.
- If the text is written by a famous poet or writer, then research the author and poem to determine its historical/cultural significance.
- What story or mood does the text tell or create?
- Is this edition historically accurate? Can you check it against a more authentic version of the piece in a collected edition?

Additional Instrumental Information
- Describe solo requirements.
- Are the technical challenges appropriate for the target age group or level?
- Describe the quality of the transcription or arrangement.
- Is this the original instrumentation? If not, how has the original been modified for this composition and why might the arranger have made these modifications?

Background information for non-Western, folk, or popular music:
- Find out about the country and musical tradi-

Students can participate in the analysis of a composition

While doing an analysis, you may be reminded of related pieces, which can serve as interesting rehearsal strategies or good programming ideas

The time invested in an analysis is directly related to the depth of student learning

tion from which this composition comes. List style characteristics of the music tradition.

- With what instrumentation would this music be performed in its original country/culture/ or tradition?
- Who would have performed this music and for what reasons?
- What can you find out about the arranger and how well this piece represents the tradition within which it is written? How Westernized is it?
- If your arrangement is based on a folksong, try to find the original tune.
- Translate the text if it is not in English.
- What story or mood does the text tell or create?
- If the text is written by a famous poet or writer, then look up the author and poem to determine its historical/cultural significance.
- Discuss any traditions or rituals that accompany this piece. Would it have been just sung, or might there be dancing and instrumental accompaniment? Think about how these answers might affect your interpretation.

Elements of Music

How are they used and why did the composer make those choices?

Form—What is the structure of this piece? How is the piece organized—e.g. binary, ternary, through-composed? What recognizable devices does it include—e.g. fugue, chorale, trio?

Rhythm—What are the primary motives? What note values are the most common? Is there syncopation or a peculiar time signature? Are there challenging rhythmic devices such as hemiolas and mixed meters?

Melody—What is the shape of the theme? What is the tonality—major, minor, modal, or a combination? Does it progress by step or skip? Is there a melodic motive? Is there even a melody? Are there counter-melodies that are important for the audience to hear?

Harmony—What is the harmonic rhythm? How and when does it modulate and what are the key relationships? Where are there dissonances? Are there any suspensions?

Timbre—What are the colors in the piece? Is it primarily bright or dark and what instrumentation or voicing creates the colors? How does the timbre reflect the text, title, or mood?

Texture—Is this piece primarily homophonic, monophonic, or polyphonic? Is it melody and accompaniment or monody? Does the density of the overall texture change? How does the composer contrast textures and what effect does that create?

Expression—What are the dynamics, phrases, articulations, and tempi for this piece? How and when is each element used and applied?

Additional Considerations

- How does the composer create moments of tension and release?
- How does the composer use and create contrast?
- How does the composer unify the composition?
- How does the composer sustain interest throughout the composition?
- How does the instrumentation contribute to the overall effect of the composition?
- How does the orchestration represent the style period?

The Heart

- What attracted you to this piece of music?
- What maintains your interest in it?
- What gives this music its distinctive qualities?
- What do you learn about yourself through the eyes of this music?
- How has the composer created your response through compositional devices?

Reasons to Perform This Composition

What is the value of the music in relationship to available rehearsal time and student needs?

Things You Could Teach with This Composition

Think specifically about what this composition teaches well or uniquely. Lots of music teaches phrasing or motivic development, but few pieces teach it exquisitely.

AT A GLANCE

OUTCOMES

What do you want your students to learn?

Skill Outcomes

What will students learn about technical facility and performing skills, such as vocal technique, spiccato bowing, double tonguing, playing chromatic scales quickly, and singing long lines in tune?

Knowledge Outcomes

Share your goals with your students

What historical and theoretical ideas will students discover as they study the music?

Affective Outcomes

What internal and subjective aspects of students' musical experiences—attitudes, values, desires, commitments, and tastes—will you focus on while teaching this piece?

Verbs for Writing Skill and Knowledge Outcomes

Bloom's Taxonomy

Remember to think about goals for an entire year as well as for an entire program (3-4 years)

VI. Evaluation

(most complex)

Appraise, compare, critique, criticize, evaluate, support, summarize, judge, consider, recommend, weigh, relate

V. Synthesis

Combine, plan, role-play, invent, compose, revise, design, hypothesize, construct, create, develop, produce, organize, originate

IV. Analysis

Analyze, classify, survey, distinguish, categorize, subdivide, differentiate, infer, separate, select, point out

III. Application

Apply, change, choose, solve, show, sketch, modify, dramatize, classify, discover, produce, prepare, use, paint

Listen to student goals— they may differ from yours

II. Comprehension

Convert, change, transform, rewrite, give examples, express, illustrate, paraphrase, restate, match, infer, relate, extend, explain, defend, predict, distinguish, generalize, summarize, interpret, compare

I. Knowledge

(most simple)

Define, describe, memorize, label, recognize, locate, name, recite, state, identify, select

AT A GLANCE

Terms for Affective Outcomes

Appreciate
Articulate opinions about
Be inspired by
Be motivated to
Be open to
Be sensitive to
Be thoughtful about
Be willing to explore
Develop a personal philosophy
Express feelings about
Make a commitment to
Perceive
Prioritize
Question what you believe
Respond to
Show awareness of
Value

Qualities
of a good
outcome:
- *Interesting*
- *Students learn*
  something
  meaningful as
  opposed to
  obvious
- *Integral to*
  performing
  the music well

Terms Describing Roles of a Musician

Assess
Analyze
Arrange
Bow
Classify
Compose
Conduct
Discuss
Evaluate
Identify
Improvise
Move
Name
Notate
Orchestrate
Play
Read
Reflect
Research
Respond
Sightread
Sing
Write

STRATEGIES
Verbs for Writing Teaching Strategies

How will students learn?

Act	Identify
Analyze	Improvise
Arrange	Interpret
Articulate	Journal
Bow	Listen
Choreograph	Move
Clap	Notate
Classify	Orchestrate
Compose	Play
Conduct	Record
Describe	Reflect
Design	Research
Discuss	Sight-read
Draw	Sing
Evaluate	

Learning Styles

Visual—write on blackboard, use handouts, have students write in music

Auditory—play intervals, read out loud, model parts, and phrasing

Kinesthetic—clapping, bowing, moving, stepping, physically describing

You are designing the creative journey your students will take on the path to performing with greater understanding.

Student-centered Strategies

Students interpret music, conduct sectionals, design rehearsal strategies, lead warm-ups, give opinions, listen and critique, determine shape of phrases, discuss in small groups, give feedback to partners, etc.

Warm-ups

Do things in small doses—a rehearsal is not a theory or history class. It is a workshop in how to perform with understanding.

Start with outcome in mind and then design warm-ups that prepare students for performing with understanding during the rehearsal. You should have both short and long-term goals in mind.

Take Out the Piece

How many different ways can you refer to your piece?

Articulation	Language
Composer	Meter
Compositional devices	Modulations
Contemporary of the composer	Rhythmic motif
	Scale type
Form	Solos
Genre	Style period
Historical background	Texture
Instrumentation	Tonality
Key signature	

Introducing the Piece
You only get one chance to make a good first impression! Start with:

A recording	Telling an anecdote
A short writing assignment	The heart
An obstacle	The historical milieu
Playing important themes	The original folk song
Reading the text	
Talking about the composer	

Practice the art of brainstorming new rehearsal strategies without the censoring voice that says "It'll never work."

Going Beyond the Classroom
• Interdisciplinary Connections
• Internet
• Listening Assignments

ASSESSMENT

Begin with an outcome
Consider the following questions:
• Who is it for (teacher, student, parents, administrators)?
• What is the purpose of the assessment and how will it be utilized?
• Who will design and evaluate the assessment? Students? Teacher?
• Does a grade have to be assigned?

Finding out what your students are or are not learning will change what and how you are teaching

Designing the assessment
Paper-and-pencil tests
• Matching Answers
• Multiple Choice

Ask students to evaluate their own progress.

Observational and performance assessment
• Listening and describing
• Music-skill computer programs
• Quartet and solo performance
• Recording and evaluating sectionals and individual practice
• Rhythmic, melodic, intervallic dictation
• Sight-read alone
• Verballly analying scores
• Videotaping and anlyzing rehearsals

Journal assignments
• Opinions about rehearsal issues
• Outside concert reviews/critiques
• Personal goals for the quarter

AT A GLANCE

- Self-evaluations
- Weekly reviews
    Self evaluations
    Self grading with explanations
    Description of practice hours
    Musical activities outside of classroom
    Listening activities
    Interviews

Share portfolios with parents and administrators to advocate for comprehensive musicianship

Tools for Assessing Observation, Performance, and Journals
    Checklists
    Rating Scales: (numeric, graphic, descriptive)
    Rubrics

Portfolio: organization of information about and documents demonstrating student learning and musical achievement

Evaluation

Of the assessment *design*
- Are the criteria for success clear to students and parents?
- Do students get clear and honest feedback according to the criteria?
- Are the assessments (tests, rubrics, checklists) well designed?

Of the assessment *results*
- Will you use comments, √s, numbers, or letter grades?
- Will there be well-organized records?

Action

What will you do with the information gathered?
- Reflect
- Design instruction
- Require homework
- Assign grade

MUSIC SELECTION

A good composition, regardless of the level of difficulty, has lasting qualities

Determining the Quality of the Composition

Uniqueness	Form
Design	Unpredictability
Depth	Consistency
Text	Transcendence
Orchestration/Voicing	

Everyday Needs to Be Considered

Programming	Level of Difficulty	Personnel
Length	Maturity	Voicing
Audience	Technique	Tessitura
Special Guests	Literacy	Instrumentation
Community	Rehearsal time	Solos
		Accompaniment

Balancing the Curriculum

BAND

What do your students need?

Historical Periods

Renaissance	19th Century
Baroque	20th Century/Avant Garde
Classical	

Musical Genres

Concerto	Musical Theater
Film Music	Overture
Folk Song Arrangements	Programmatic Music
Jazz	Symphony Movements
March	

Is the knowledge gained transferable?

Musical Forms

12 Bar Blues	Sonata
ABA	Suite
Canon	Theme and Variation
Minuet and Trio	Through-composed
Prelude and Fugue	

Varied Use of Ensemble

Full Band	Wind Ensemble
Chamber Ensembles	

CHOIR

Historical Periods

Early Music	Classical
Renaissance	19th Century
Baroque	20th Century/Avant Garde

Varied Use of Ensemble

Folk Choir	Chamber Choir
Quartet	A Capella
Various Accompaniments	

Multiple Music Genres

Cantata	Musical Theater
Chant	Opera Chorus
Folk song	Oratorio
Gospel	Part Song
Madrigal	Vocal Jazz
Mass	World Music
Motet	

ORCHESTRA

Historical Periods

Renaissance	Romantic
Baroque	Impressionistic
Classical	20th Century/Avant Garde

Forms

12 Bar Blues	Minuet and Trio
ABA	Rondo
Canon	Sonata-Allegro
Fugue	Theme and Variation
	Through-composed

Musical Genres

Ballet Music	Jazz
Commissions	Musical Theater
Concert Overture	Opera Selections
Fiddling	Programmatic Music
Folk Song Arrangements	Symphony Movements

Varied Use of Ensemble

Full Orchestra	String Orchestra
Chamber Orchestra	Chorus with Orchestra
Chamber Ensembles	
(duets, trios, quartets)	

CMP UNIT PLAN

This plan may be several pages in length and will serve as a reference for writing daily reaching plans.

Analysis (by the time you gather background information, analyze the elements of music, and determine the heart, this will be at least four pages in length).
Long-range Outcomes
    Knowledge
    Skill
    Affective
Strategies (specific pedagogical ideas for this piece)
    Introduction
    Warm-ups related to challenges in this composition
    Visual, auditory, and kinesthetic
    Student-centered
    Others—interdisciplinary, listening assignments, internet research
Assessments of Long-range Outcomes
    Journals
    Rubrics
    Recordings
    Paper-and-pencil tests
Music Selection
    Part of a comprehensive program
    Demonstrates qualities of a composition

Ideal Format:
1. Outcome
    A. Strategies for outcome
        1.
        2.
        3.
    B. Assessment of outcome

DAILY TEACHING PLAN

Start with the long-range outcome so that your lesson is building toward a larger curricular goal.

Long-range Outcome(s) Pertaining to This Lesson
1.
2.

Today's Outcomes (knowledge, skill, affective)
1.
2.
3.

Strategies (learning styles, student-centered)
Warm-up Strategies
1.
2.
3.

Rehearsal Strategies
1.
2.
3.

Assessment
Formal (may not happen everyday)

Informal (What worked? What did not? What next?)

AT A GLANCE

Part III

Unit Teaching Plans
Written by Randal Swiggum

These plans were created by Randal Swiggum with the contributions of Rebecca Winnie, Patricia O'Toole, Wendy Buehl, Mary Schmidt, Glenn Hayes, Jim Arrowood, Gary Wolfman, Margaret Jenks, Katherine Punwar, Laura Sindberg, and Patty Schlaefer.

Because these plans were written by one teacher and intended to be used by another, they are necessarily long, comprehensive, and dense with instructive detail. When you are writing your own teaching plans, much of the detail will be in your head, and only the "bare bones" of the plan will actually be written down. On the other hand, the more of the plan you commit to paper and the more detailed your approach, especially in the area of analysis, the richer your final teaching plan and the richer your students' experience of the piece.

Sample Teaching Plans

Band

Choir

Orchestra

Middle School Band
Level 2

BALLADAIR
Frank Erickson (1923-1996)
Bourne, Inc. (1958)

Background Information

Balladair is representative of a genre that appeared in the U.S. after World War II—the school band piece written with young bands in mind. Composers like Clare Grundman and John Kinyon created a wealth of these pieces, a genre that had been largely neglected before, but burgeoned because of the expansion of school band programs with young baby boom students after the war.

Frank Erickson came of age in the 1930s studying piano and playing trumpet in his high school band, where he composed the first of more than 400 compositions. During the war, he served in the Army Air Force, where he further honed his musical skills by arranging for army bands. Attending the University of Southern California on the G.I. Bill, he studied composition with Halsey Stevens and Maria Castel, graduating in 1950. After completing a master's degree in 1951, he taught at the University of California-Los Angeles and at San Jose College.

In 1951, the Bourne Company published Erickson's *Little Suite for Band*, which would be the first of a group of pieces that would make Erickson's name familiar to band students around the country. These pieces included *Toccata for Band, Air for Band*, and *Balladair*, published in 1958. Throughout his career, which included more than 250 compositions and arrangements for band as well as the *First Division Band Course* (with Fred Weber), Erickson focused much of his writing on the young band, enriching this repertoire immensely and influencing succeeding generations of composers for band.

In program notes for the piece, Erickson said that *Balladair* was written in a "modern dance style." This is puzzling, in a way, because its very title, "ballad" and "air" both suggest song, not dance. What Erickson had in mind, no doubt, was the popular music form of the day, the 32-bar song form, common to both pop songs and the dances of the big band era.

It is not hard to hear *Balladair* as a very pop song of the 1950s (albeit a very sophisticated one), with its "circle-of-fifths" progressions, its lightly-tinged jazz harmonies, and above all, its sumptuous melody.

Elements of Music

Form

The form of *Balladair* is entirely straightforward, which makes it not only effective musically but accessible for student study. Borrowing the standard 32-bar song form (four phrases of eight measures in an AABA structure), Erickson extends the piece in two ways:

1. He expands the B section by adding yet another new melody of eight bars.
2. He recaps the memorable A strain twice rather than once.

Thus, the overall form becomes AABCAA. Because the relative weight of each section is now identical, however, it might more properly be seen as ABA, and this is the way students are likely to hear it during their preliminary discussions of its form.

Melody

It is the well-crafted melody that distinguishes *Balladair* as a great work of its kind. It is a classically constructed melody that balances upward with downward melodic direction, and large intervallic leaps with stepwise motion.

The first eight-bar phrase presents a good example: the first four bars press upward, first with a leap of a fourth, then an octave, both with the ultimate destination of a high D. The midpoint of the phrase, measure five, is also the melodic peak of the phrase, from which each successive measure descends.

Examining the B melody reveals similar tendencies: structural tones that outline fourths and fifths, with lyrical, stepwise motion to connect them.

The "C" strain (mm. 25-32) is only one that moves strictly stepwise— a very conservative melody that depends on harmonic interest (i.e. suspensions) for its effect. The fact that it is so conservative in its motion is a perfect foil for the return of the A section, whose opening gesture, soaring upward, now feels suddenly new, fresh, and expansive.

These structural relationships within the eight-measure sections create a very satisfying and balanced antecedent/consequent relationship between each pair of four-measure phrases: the first four measures of each section set up a kind of question which is then answered in the second four-bar phrase.

Rhythm

Balladair is not "rhythmic" in the sense that rhythm is an obvious feature. Its liquid, lyrical mood is unbroken by special rhythmic effects or unusual rhythmic patterning. However, a close look reveals that this fluid elegance is the result of careful crafting of rhythmic flow and motivic unity. More than half the measures of the piece contain this characteristic rhythm:

In the first four measures, this motif is the reaction to the preceding half note (in other words, it follows it as part of the flow of the phrase). In the second half of the phrase (mm. 5-8), it shifts to the front side of each measure, where the ear hears it as the same, unifying motif, but with a new, more confident character. It is this motif that also launches the B melody (m. 17).

The incredible sense of forward motion and flow of *Balladair* also depends on the use of eighth notes to pull one phrase into the next. These eighth notes, either alone or in pairs, appear at the end of each two bar or four bar phrase segment. Their rhythmic tugging on the forward direction of the phrase becomes apparent when they are removed:

"Balladair" melody without rhythmic 'tugs'

One syncopation idea is used for dramatic purposes in the last five bars, where various lower voices accentuate offbeats with downbeat rests.

All of the above rhythmic ideas are entirely absent from the C melody, whose more solemn quality depends on the absence of dotted rhythms, syncopations, or moving upbeat rhythms that connect phrases and create flow. Its unique character, however, is shaped by a particular rhythm: the over-the-bar line ties, which connect mm. 25-26 and 29-30. This "tied-over" rhythm was already suggested by similar ties in the B strain, but here the ties are combined with harmonic suspensions, which serve both to emphasize their rhythm and create a more austere, hymn-like mood.

Harmony

The lyrical sweetness of *Balladair's* melody is enhanced by an appropriately conservative harmonic setting which relies strictly on triads and diatonic seventh chords—in other words, the harmonic language of popular music of the 1950s (and today).

Most of the harmonic movement can be analyzed as classic examples of good voice leading or species counterpoint. The A melody, for example is often moving against a bass line which changes direction in counterpoint with it. As it arches up in the first few measures, the bass line is descending.

The second half of the A strain (mm. 7-8) is built on a "circle-of-fifths" progression in the bass line: B-flat-E-flat-A-D-G-C-F-sharp (F natural). Both the B and C strains depend on similar progressions. These "circle-of-fifths" harmonies are the strongest progressions for forward motion and contribute to the sense of flow in *Balladair*.

The lyrical melody of *Balladair* is also given a more "classic," almost reverential quality by the liberal use of suspensions, the first of which appears against the melody in the second measure. Other examples include:

A Section

m. 5	Beat three
m. 10	Beat one
m. 13	Beat three
m. 16	Beat one (an almost "Amen" feeling to close the A section)
m. 47	Beat one (a final "Amen")

B Section

Only one suspension, as part of the melody

mm. 18	Beat three
mm. 23	Beat three.

C Section

Depends on downbeat suspensions for character

mm. 25-26

mm.29-30

One of the sweetest harmonic moments in the piece is the re-transition to the final A section in measure 32. The B/C section has taken us afield harmonically, to G major. The final cadence (m. 32) is on the dominant (D major), where Erickson uses a sustained A in the melody as a common tone to effect an F chord, a new dominant which pulls us back to B-flat and into the recap. It is a simple device, but a refreshing way to approach the concluding A section, and a favorite moment for students.

Texture and Timbre

Balladair relies on a consistent homophonic texture (melody and accompaniment) with brief suggestions of counterpoint in the form of moving inner lines. The scoring is rich and deep (especially if the conductor and players keep the upper voices in check). Upper voices (trumpet, flute, oboe, clarinet) carry the majority of melodic material, as their timbres have the most potential to be heard above the thick harmony provided by horns, saxophones, trombones, and baritones. Middle voices are scored with less motion, and the low brass and woodwind outline the harmonies in long tones or provide moving bass lines.

The overall effect of continuous full band scoring is one of a giant pipe organ with only occasionally a subtle shading of timbre. One such moment is the opening of the B section (m. 17), where the melody is given over completely to the brass, a change of color that creates a momentary noble effect. The brasses are immediately answered by woodwinds, who join them for the rest of the melody.

Typical of young band music of this period is the percussion scoring: only timpani, snare drum, and cymbals are used, all of which are held in reserve and play only three times in the piece, the timpani not playing at all until the final cadence. This spare use of percussion contributes to the piece's solemn and song-like quality, but will probably not keep middle school percussionists engaged. Jay Gilbert suggests adding triangle or creating mallet parts from the oboe line, a workable solution to that problem, but one that will obviously alter the character of the piece somewhat.

Expression/Dynamics

Dynamics in the piece are generally not dramatic or used for special effect, but rather, they grow organically out of the rise and fall of the melodic material and the phrase structure. The piece would be almost as effective played at one dynamic, so much does it rely on its melody and harmony.

A sensitive attention to Erickson's dynamics, however, creates a powerfully expressive effect, especially the sudden drop in dynamics that sets up the B section, the expanding *mf* that opens wide the C section, and the final climactic *crescendo* that brings the piece to its heroic conclusion. These printed dynamics are basic, but of course need to be enriched with expressive dynamic phrase shaping that serves the ebb and flow of the melodic line.

A variety of articulations is not part of the expressive palette of the piece. Most needed is a lovely tone quality and an exquisite *legato*, soft tongue style that enhances the piece's flowing style.

The Heart

The heart of *Balladair* is its three attractive melodies and especially the way Erickson has scored them. *Balladair* is perfectly crafted to be tuneful, memorable, playable, and musically satisfying, while still challenging young players to meet its technical and expressive demands.

Introducing the Piece

1. Give students a sheet with various definitions of "ballad" and "air" culled from dictionaries:

   ballad *n.* a simple song or poem, especially one telling a story

   ballad *n.* a song or poem that tells a story in short stanzas and simple words with repetition and refrain. Most old ballads are of unknown authorship and have been handed down orally, usually with additions and changes.

   ballad *n.* a popular song, esp. a slow, romantic, or sentimental song

air *n.* a melody or tune

air *n.* in music, a melody or tune, especially the main melody of a harmonized composition, usually the soprano or treble part.

After students have read and discussed these definitions for clarity, write the word "Balladair" on the board. Tell students that this is the title of a famous work for band. "Why would a composer create this title for his piece? What would you expect the piece to sound like? What musical elements would you not include in a piece called "Balladair?" Students may expect a piece with words—keep them guessing about this.

2. Play a recording of *Balladair* and have students listen for how the music reflects their ideas about its title. "Why would Frank Erickson call it "Balladair" when there are no words? Could you imagine this piece being sung? What might the words be about? Does the title give us clues about how to play the piece?"

3. Later in the rehearsal process, revisit this discussion. Have students write a brief description of the lyrics they might set to this melody. Or, for a more in depth assignment, have them actually write lyrics that fit the tune exactly and match it in spirit.

Skill Outcome

Students will perform the eight bar melodies in *Balladair* with expressive phrasing and staggered breathing.

Strategies

What's a Phrase?

1. Give students a copy of the complete melody to *Balladair* transposed for their instrument. This will become material for warm-ups, intonation exercises, and rhythmic understanding.

2. Ask students to define "phrase" (a complete musical idea, like a sentence). Have them listen while you play the first 16 measures of *Balladair* and have them mark a tick on their melody sheet whenever they think a phrase ends. Have them compare and discuss their

answers. How did they know when a phrase was over? Some may feel that the first two bars are a complete musical thought—help them to hear that the "longer view" hears the piece in four-bar or eight-bar units.

Help students discover that the piece is built in eight-bar sections, that are themselves built of four-bar phrases that have a kind of "question-answer" relationship. Have them draw long slurs over each four-bar phrase, and another overarching slur over each eight bar section.

The Longer View

1. Play the melody for students on your own instrument, demonstrating long phrasing (breathing around slurs and in unexpected places) and choppy phrasing (breathing every two measures) for students to compare and discuss.

2. Play for students other examples of expressive long phrases, either band, orchestral, or solo excerpts. Some horn examples include Mendelssohn's "Nocturne" from *A Midsummer Night's Dream,* and Tchaikovsky's Symphony No. 5, (Second Movement).

   Ask students what sensation or mood is created by the long phrase? What skills are required of a musician to be able to play this way?

Staggered Breathing

1. Play a version of the phrase and have students mark their melody sheet exactly where breaths are taken. Have them perform the same phrase accordingly.

2. Have selected students perform their version of the melody (from the melody sheet), choosing to breath/phrase where they believe it is appropriate. The rest of the band listens, selects the version they prefer and defends their choice.

3. Choose a small group of three to five strong players or section leaders to stand together in front of the band and perform the melody in unison, attempting to create an eight-bar phrase with no audible breath breaks. If they are successful, have the rest of the band discuss why. If they are not successful, give them an opportunity to plan a strategy for staggered breathing and let them play again, asking

classmates to notice if there is a difference. Explain to students the term "staggered breathing."

4. Working with their stand partner, have the band devise rules for staggered breathing, such as:

   a) Player one breathes first, player two must wait and follow.

   b) Player one breathes at the slurs, player two breaks slurs to cover player one's breaths.

   c) Player one and two "fight over" who breathes where and then mark in their parts the initials of each player at the places where they will breathe.

5. Have students work in larger groups of four-six to rehearse their parts, planning for and marking in appropriate staggered breaths. Have them perform for the entire band and be evaluated for the effectiveness of their breathing choices.

Assessment

Continue strategy five above. Let student groups evaluate each other by listening for telltale unison breaths. Evaluation is pass/fail—when a group can effectively perform the eight-bar phrase with no audible break in the musical line, they have succeeded.

Cognitive Outcome

Students will recognize ABA structure and its frequent use as an artistic form.

Strategies

1. Help students discover the form of *Balladair*. Remind them how to label form: first section is always called "A," whenever it repeats, it's also called A. New sections get labeled "B," then "C," etc. Have them listen to a recording of *Balladair* and jot down their version (with letter names) on a 3x5 card. When finished listening, ask students how many sections they heard and how they were labeled. This should provoke a lively discussion.

2. Remind students to listen for repetitions in the piece and repeat

the above activity, without giving students the correct answer. Guide students to hear the piece as AABCAA

3. As students get more familiar with *Balladair* have them listen and label in different ways, to show that they can really hear the various sections. One assessment tool would be a worksheet with blanks in which they fill in the section and the exact time on the classroom clock when the section begins. Their completed worksheet might look like this:

1) A	begins at	10:12 and	11 seconds
2) A	begins at	10:12 and	41 seconds
3) B	begins at	10:13 and	9 seconds
4) C	begins at	10:13 and	39 seconds
5) A	begins at	10:14 and	10 seconds
6) A	begins at	10:14 and	54 seconds

Have students mark the letter names of the sections in their parts and as rehearsals progress, use these letter names as rehearsal letters rather than the printed measure numbers: "Let's begin at the C section."

4. After students are familiar with the AABCAA form of *Balladair*, ask them how they might simplify the form by combining sections. Field their suggestions and show by graphing on the board how sections can be grouped together to create an overall ABA form.

Explain to them that ABA form is probably the most common form in music and in all kinds of other art and architecture. Have them brainstorm for visual examples right in the classroom. Encourage them to think creatively. Make sure to show them examples on the human body (your own!) such as eye/nose/eye or ear/mouth/ear or arm/head/arm, etc.

Invite students to share their ideas about why ABA is such a popular form. What makes it work so well? Tell them that this will be their artistic task over the next few days: to come up with artistic reasons why ABA is so popular.

As homework, have students find as many examples as they can of ABA form outside the classroom, which will be shared as part of a game the next day. On the following day, divide the group into teams and award points as follows:

ABA example in architecture or household items (quite common)	1 point
ABA example found in nature	2 points
ABA example found in visual art/painting/sculpture	3 points
ABA example in a poem or story	5 points
ABA example in a song or piece of music	10 points

5. Continue the discussion of why ABA form is effective and popular and encourage students to keep speculating about it. At some point, invite students to reflect on these questions and share their thoughts, either aloud or in their journals:

> Think about the best vacation you have ever taken. Why is it that we like to take vacations? Have you ever had a great vacation, but still been glad to come home? Describe that feeling of coming home. What does your familiar, old bed feel like to sleep in, after you've been away from it? Why doesn't it feel that "special" way all the time?

6. After all the above activities, playing through *Balladair* should be a new experience. Have students play all the way through to the downbeat of measure 33 (the return of the A section) and then try to describe the feeling in the music of "coming home." Ask for their suggestions about ways to make the "coming home" even more expressive in their performance. (e.g. the diminuendo which sets it up, the possibility of connecting measures 32 and 33 with no breath, or taking a group phrasing breath and a little rubato before m. 32, etc.). Try a *crescendo* in m. 32 instead of Erickson's diminuendo, and have students compare the effect of both. Which do you like better? Why do you suppose he chose diminuendo?

7. Play or perform other works in ABA form for students to compare. Some examples: *Portrait of a Clown* (Ticheli), *Chanson* (Kinyon), *Pevensey Castle* (Sheldon), *Two Minute Symphony* (Margolis).

Assessment

1. To demonstrate that they can hear *Balladair's* AABCAA structure, have students repeat strategy three above, with classroom clock timings.

2. Have students compose a melody of nine to 12 measures in ABA form, with each phrase about three to four measures in length. Set other parameters of key, meter, and note values, and emphasize to students that they will have to be able to perform the melody on their own instrument. Evaluation can be according to the following rubric:

A	*5 points*	Piece follows all guidelines of key, meter, and length. Is clearly in ABA form. Melody is interesting and effective. Notation is correct. Performance is expressive and accurate.
B	*4 points*	Piece follows all guidelines of key, meter, and length. Is fairly clearly in ABA form. Melody is somewhat interesting. Notation is almost all correct with only a few errors. Performance is mostly accurate and expressive.
C	*3 points*	Piece mostly follows guidelines of key, meter, and length with a few problems. Melody could be more interesting or effective. two-five notation errors. Performance needed more rehearsal.
D	*2 points*	Assignment was completed but showed little evidence of careful planning or thought, OR performance was not accurate or effective.
F	*0 points*	Assignment not completed.

3. Have students write a journal entry about what makes ABA form effective, using two examples to support their opinion, one of them *Balladair* and the other a non-musical example.

TEACHING PLANS
BAND

Affective Outcome

Students will analyze and appreciate their individual role in the scoring and harmonies of *Balladair.*

Strategies

The Melody in Context

1. During initial rehearsals of *Balladair*, have students make comparisons between the unaccompanied melody (as printed on their melody sheet) and the fully scored original. They should have both the melody sheet and their part side by side on their stand.

    Step One: Before playing either, ask students to compare the two versions on sight alone. One may look easier, higher, more interesting, "boring," etc.

    Step Two: After playing the A section in both versions (Melody Sheet and their part), have students compare for the relative difficulty of each.

    Step Three: Play the A section again from both versions, and have students compare their part to a specific other part. Encourage them to be as specific as possible in describing what is happening in the other part (e.g. "it's harmonizing with the melody," or "it's playing a little echo of the melody," etc.)

    Step Four: Play the A section from both versions again, and invite any observations.

    After several repetitions of this activity, students will have accumulated a wide variety of impressions and ideas about the variety of material in the piece beyond their own part.

2. Have a single student (preferably a player who doesn't already play mostly melody in the piece, i.e. horn, alto sax, trombone, tuba, etc.) play the tune from the Melody Sheet as a solo, accompanied by piano. The piano plays only a simple, half note chordal accompaniment based on the harmonic progression of *Balladair.* (This is more easily accomplished with the "Conductor's Score" of the piece, rather than the "Full Score." Write out the chord symbols and play it yourself, or

write out simply voiced chords in half notes for a student pianist to play.)

Ask students to describe the similarities and differences between what they just heard and the full band version. After several students have had the opportunity to play the melody (or part of it) as a solo with piano, try having them play it as a solo with the full band accompaniment (in very reduced numbers) playing their parts. Again, ask students to note similarities and differences. Guide students to hear the beauty of the thick scoring and the brief moments of contrapuntal movement in the inner parts.

3. With you or a competent student playing the half-note chords on piano (as above), have students hum along with the harmonic progression, improvising on sustained pitches. Start by playing each of the three notes of the B-flat triad, to let them find a note that fits their voice range and to get them started on a note that works. Invite them to do one of three things when they hear the chord change:

   a) go up just a step

   b) go down a step

   c) stay on the same note

   Tell them it's OK if they hum a note that doesn't seem right—they will get better the more they do it. Encourage the choir students to take the lead and sing confidently. After several tries going through just the A section, they should become more confident. Have students sing it again, this time on "loo" (which is actually easier than a hum). The important thing is not the quality of their performance but their experience of the rich harmonies of *Balladair.* Repeat this activity again in subsequent rehearsals as a break from playing the piece and to remind students of the harmonies.

4. Invite students to create analogies for a beautiful unaccompanied melody as opposed to the same beautiful melody with a richly scored accompaniment. For example:

   a) A beautiful painting or portrait alone, versus the same painting in an ornate or decorative frame.

b) A story line embellished with less important but equally interesting subplots.

How much more interesting is the main story when accompanied by the other sub-plots?

Suspensions

1. As a warm-up activity, use the major scale and refer to the pitches by solfege syllables or numbers. Use hand signs to guide their playing slowly up or down the scale (use either traditional Curwen solfege hand signs or just a simple gesture that moves "up" or "down.")

   When students can play the scale by following your gesture, divide the band by stand partners into two groups. Have both groups start on five (sol) and have group one follow your left hand, group two your right hand.

2. Introduce the term "suspension" by writing it on the board and having students copy it in their portfolios. Explain that a suspension always has both a tension and a release, and the release always happens by the lower voice moving down, to "get away from the upper note, which is touching it." Have them play the suspension exercise again listening for the tension and release.

3. Show on the board what a single suspension looks like in notation, in a simple example (as above). Have students copy it on a piece of staff paper of their own. Erase the example and have students write another one of their own, starting on different note. (Key or key signature does not matter at this point.)

4. Ask students which part of the suspension should be louder, the tension or the release? Try playing it based on their suggestions. Have them lean forward slightly during the suspension and relax backward slightly on the release.

5. Have half the band play and the other half cup their hand and grab their stand partner's cupped hand, gently pulling on their partner's hand during the tension and relaxing their grip during the release. Switch parts, so the players become the "pullers."

6. Try the same activity, but instead of pulling on their partner's cupped hand, have them press the palm of their hand against their partner's, pushing gently on the suspension, relaxing on the release. Do this several times, until the sound of the suspension/release expresses the feeling of tension and release, and students have a strong sensation of how the tension feels and sounds.

7. Have the band play *Balladair* with student listening teams identifying when the suspensions occur and in which part. Have students apply their experiences with the strategies above to *Balladair*, and periodically ask them to listen for the effective shaping of the suspensions. As a reminder, have those with suspensions in their parts stand up when they play them.

Shaping the Inner Lines

1. Write the following on the board before rehearsal:
   - The smaller the note value, the louder the note.
   - The larger the note value, the softer the note.

      Have students scan their parts for *Balladair* and determine which notes will be softest (whole-notes) and which loudest (eighth-notes) and try playing it with this in mind.

2. Have students color code their parts with a large dot to show important parts and help them bring out moving lines:

Eighth-notes	red	loudest
Quarter-notes	blue	medium loud
Half-notes	green	soft
Whole-notes	yellow	very soft

3. Pass out photocopies of a mostly non-melodic part (e.g. tenor sax, horn, trombone one, etc.) to a select group of students as a listening team. As the band plays *Balladair*, have the listening team evaluate the section's dynamic shadings and mark their copies with comments and suggestions. This can be repeated with any part of the piece or any section.

Assessment

1. Informal assessment of the band's performance should be ongoing throughout the rehearsal process, evaluated both by students and by you.

2. Have students write a definition of suspension including an example in notation.

3. Have students write a short journal entry (two or three sentences) identifying their favorite part in the piece (other than their own) and describing why they like it. Let several students share their opinions about this each day and include some of these statements in the concert program.

Music Selection

The music of Frank Erickson is well known as quality works for young musicians. His compositions feature parts for all instruments that are perfectly idiomatic for the limited abilities of second and third year players. Ranges are easily accessible while the scoring is complex enough that the piece sounds far more difficult than it actually is to perform. Eighth graders will not feel as though they are being "programmed down to."

Middle school band students need well-written and accessible works that foster the development of a beautiful tone and challenge their ability to sustain a phrase over more than two measures. Unfortunately, young musicians are often quick to dismiss works of this genre as "slow and totally boring." This piece is a good one to change their opinion to "slow and amazingly beautiful."

In many middle schools, there is a high percentage of band students who also participate in choir and this piece provides many opportunities to vocalize beautiful melodic writing.

Finally, this is not the typical kind of piece usually selected for the CMP process. It is a very traditional band work (and a staple of the band repertoire) but, as a piece of absolute music, it does not "tell a story," refer to extra-musical ideas, or find its basis in literature, folksong, theatre, or opera. As such, it does not lend itself as easily to creating learning outcomes of cultural, historical, improvisational, or programmatic concepts. The challenge is to find an approach or "hook" that will motivate students to accept and treasure this piece as the great work it is, and the outcomes of this teaching plan are written toward that end.

Resources

Miles, Richard, ed. *Teaching Music through Performance in Band: Volume 3.* Chicago: GIA Publications, Inc., 2000.
Includes Jay Gilbert's thorough analysis and discussion of *Balladair*.

Balent, Andrew. *"Frank Erickson-The Composer's Point of View."* The Instrumentalist, XI, April 1986, 28-34.

Frank Erickson *Band Classics.* The Virginia Wind Symphony, Dennis J. Zeisler, Conductor. Walking Frog Records.
Compact Disc available from Southern Music Company (www.southernmusic.com)

THE HEADLESS HORSEMAN

Timothy Broege (b. 1947)

Manhattan Beach Music

Background Information

Timothy Broege's background as a public school instrumental music teacher is evident in his many compositions for young bands. Their evocative titles and compelling musical ideas engage the imagination of young players and provide both appropriate technical challenges and gratifying musical experiences. Many of his more than 30 works for band are suggestively titled including *Peace Song, Dreams and Fancies, Streets and Inroads, Jody*, and *No Sun, No Shadow* (Elegy for Charles Mingus), as well as a series of numbered sinfonias, all extended works that also bear intriguing subtitles.

Broege taught at the Manasquan Elementary School in Manasquan, New Jersey, from 1971 to 1980, and *The Headless Horseman* was written in 1973 for the students in the Manasquan Summer School Concert Band. Its title refers, of course, to "The Legend of Sleepy Hollow," the immortal short story by Washington Irving (1783-1859).

The tale was first published serially between in 1819 and 1820 and then in a collection of short stories (including "Rip Van Winkle") called *The Sketch Book of Geoffrey Caryon, Gent* (London, 1820). It is a brief, simple story with just a few characters: the prim, proper, and slightly nervous bachelor schoolmaster, Ichabod Crane; the coquettish young lady Katrina Van Tassel who has captured his fancy; her father Baltus Van Tassel, a generous and jolly old man who hosts a grand party in the story; and Brom Bones, the strapping, handsome, and roguish rival to Ichabod for Katrina's hand.

As the classic American "ghost story," it has been told and retold in many ways, and has been the subject of painting, poetry, and drama. It has also inspired numerous films: most notably Disney's animated short classic *Ichabod and Mr. Toad* (1949) narrated by Bing Crosby, (still considered by many the finest and truly frightening adaptation of Irving's story), Pierre Gang's *The Legend of Sleepy Hollow* (1999), and Tim

Burton's *Sleepy Hollow* (1999), which featured Johnny Depp and Christina Ricci in the roles of Ichabod and Katrina, but departed significantly from Irving's original tale.

Broege's *The Headless Horseman* is essentially a miniature tone poem that focuses on one character in the very last portion of the tale, the mysterious horseman on his midnight ride. Although the piece is quite short (only about 90 seconds) it is packed with musical ideas, which contribute to its breathless, suspenseful, high-energy ride.

Elements of Music

Form

The piece is a series of musical events that can be described as an arch form (ABCBA) with an introduction.

1-9	Introduction	Percussion *crescendo*, trombone tritone wails, wind/brass dissonant "shrieks"
10-19	A	"Riding theme" in saxophone /clarinet driven by snare drum (suggests G minor) More lyrical melody in flute, oboe and bells (suggests D minor) Brief interruption by trombones uses tritone motif This section is punctuated by a *tutti* D-minor triad.
20-23	B	Brass/saxophone *forte* rhythmic theme Woodwinds continue to develop lyrical melody from A
24-25	Transition	Dissonant shrieks from Introduction; "riding rhythm" in snare drum
26-32	C	Chorale in quartal harmonies passed between

		winds and brass "Riding rhythm" in snare drum continues
33-35	B	Shortened version of first B section
35-38	Transition	B section is punctuated by *forte* statements of "D" and "A," followed by a grand pause
39-45	A	Shortened version of first A, including all its elements Added woodblock and solo trumpet, baritone, flute, oboe

Rhythm

A piece about a wild ride through the night is necessarily rhythmic. Lack of recognizable rhythm, for example in the amorphous introduction, creates an uneasy, foreboding mood. Once the ride begins (m. 10), the piece remains consistently rhythmic, mostly through a specific rhythmic motif in the snare drum, which appears in 23 of the 36 remaining measures, including even the sustained chorale (mm. 26-32).

Much of the energy of the piece is derived from the nature of its rhythms: they are short figures that are often repeated in an *ostinato* fashion. This makes the piece accessible to young players, but also has the effect of creating momentum and tension. The rhythms are not unusual and all are duple patterns, except for the final trumpet solo, which plays broad triplets—an unusually expressive touch.

Melody

The supernatural subject matter of the piece compelled the composer to avoid lyrical melodic material in favor of special effects of timbre, texture, dynamics, and rhythm. There is one exception—the one lyrical melody used in the A and B sections that relies on thirds and a tuneful closing figure of eighth-notes—which is the only "hummable" tune in the piece. Indeed, the only other use of melodic material is specifically un-

237

lyrical: the opening trombone glissando on a tritone, which evolves into an aggressive, spiky theme in mm. 14-15, reprised by solo baritone in mm. 41-42.

Harmony

The piece is ostensibly in G-natural minor, which is reinforced by the main lyrical melody. The eighth-note "riding theme" in the clarinet/alto sax (m. 10) also suggests G minor. Other harmonic elements in the piece conspire to upset its harmonic stability. Of these, the thorough use of dissonance is most striking. Sharply dissonant shrieks and wails and the quartal harmonies in the chorale not only contribute to its eerie instability—they provide young players with opportunities to play a piece that is expressively "modern" in its sound.

Timbre

Instrumental colors and their frequent and sudden changes are an important feature in this piece. Percussion colors are used evocatively, both for their stereotypic rhythmic contributions and also for tone painting effects (e.g. the opening *crescendo*), the galloping snare drum, and the woodblock hoofbeats. Idiomatic uses of instruments include the unsettling trombone *glissandos* in the introduction, the agile "riding theme" in the woodwinds (*piano, staccato, allegro*), and the menacing low brass interjections (mm. 14-15).

A peculiarly unidiomatic use is made of the bells, which are prominent in the piece, usually doubling the lyrical woodwind melody. Why such a traditionally cheerful color is used so often in an otherwise dark piece is another mystery of the *Headless Horseman*!

Another interesting use of color is the chorale (mm. 26-32) where a brass choir is briefly contrasted with a woodwind choir before they are brought together. Mention should also be made of the special use of soloists, especially the muted trumpet, in the closing bars of the piece— lonely voices that fade away as the rider disappears in the night.

Texture

Textures vary widely and change suddenly and frequently, like the other elements of the piece. Even a quick glance through the score reveals changes in texture that happen in almost every measure. Dark, thick textures (m. 9) are often contrasted by high, thin ones (m. 10). Unison writing or tall octave doublings are frequently used to add an exclamation point to a section (examples include mm. 14-15, 19, 36-37, 40-41).

In fact, the texture is rarely complex in terms of number of voices; only two sections of the piece rely on polyphony—mm. 33-35, where the combining of contrapuntal lines creates a tense, climactic effect (an exclamation point); and mm. 42-45, where the combining of three familiar strands of material creates a coda "finale" feeling, albeit a atentative one (a question mark).

The use of solos has already been mentioned—this sound is a fresh one when it appears, even in a piece that features a panoply of textures.

Expression/Dynamics

Dynamics are as varied and changeable as the other elements of the piece and range from intense *fortissimo* blasts (m. 24) to the mere vibration of the opening *pianissomo* bass drum roll. Silence, too, is a powerfully effective dynamic, used at the Grand Pause (m. 38). Dynamic changes are usually subito, for shock effect, but *crescendos* are used to mark transitions to new sections (mm. 9, 19, 32, 37). If students are taught to see the *crescendos* for their structural function, it is more likely they will remember them and play them expressively. The same is true of the final diminuendo, expressive of the vanishing Horseman.

Another aspect of expression—articulation—plays an important role in the piece's dramatic and coloristic effects. So many different articulations are needed that the piece is practically a compact etude of articulation styles for all instruments. (See skill outcome below.)

The Heart

The heart of the piece is the breathless, wild ride of suspense and surprise created by not one musical element, but rather the effect of rapid changes among many musical elements, especially timbre, texture (homophonic versus polyphonic), harmony (consonance versus dissonance), and dynamics.

Introducing the Piece

This introduction features the percussion section. Before passing out the parts to the band, rehearse the percussionists privately on the opening six measures (including the cymbal crash). Tell the band to close their eyes and listen to the introduction to this "mystery piece" and be able to describe the mood that they feel is being created. Discussion will most likely include the effect of suspense, of mystery, of something impending. Invite students to speculate on what the piece might be about, without telling them its title.

During the next rehearsal, do the same thing but include the trombones. Ask the band again to describe the effect on the music's mood and to guess again what the piece might be about.

Tell them the title of the piece and let them share their knowledge of "The Legend of Sleepy Hollow." Piece together as much of the story as they might know and invite speculation about how a piece based on such a story might sound.

Skill Outcome

Students will perform a variety of articulations including *staccato, legato,* and accented.

Strategies

1. *Warm-up*

   Begin rehearsal by warming-up on a scale that is easy and familiar to students. Ask them how many different ways they can play it without changing tempo or dynamics. Guide the discussion to the subject of articulation and ask them to describe three different kinds of articulation or tonguing styles (*staccato, legato* or soft tonguing, and accented). Try all student suggestions with the scale or part of it, and encourage students to use the terms *"staccato," "legato,"* and "accented." Explain that the next few weeks of rehearsal will be focused on developing their articulation technique.

2. *Focusing on Staccato*

Have students play scale warm-ups in repeated *staccato* eighth notes, alternating with a snare drum, which serves as a model.

Ask students, "how short is *staccato?*" and let them debate until they realize that "short" is a relative term and the answer to the question is: it depends on how short is musically appropriate. Instead of snare drum, have another student play a hand drum, a conga, a cabasa, or some other percussive instrument, (these need not be percussion players), and repeat the scale exercise above. Compare the different lengths of *staccato,* and challenge students to really listen to the length of the percussion sound and imitate it. (This will of course always involve lots of "instrument-specific" comments about tongue placement, embouchure, air flow, etc.—that is, plain old technical tips for wind and brass articulation.)

3. *Focusing on Legato*

Begin rehearsal by singing the following and having students repeat after you:

After students have sung well (this may take several tries), have them describe the articulation style (*legato*). Help them see the connection between *legato* and singing, that *legato* is essentially a singing style. Review how *legato* is performed technically, reminding students of the various specific techniques idiomatic to their instrument.

TEACHING PLANS BAND

Continue using both *staccato* and *legato* articulations in scale warm-ups to begin each rehearsal.

4. *Focusing on the Accent*

Begin rehearsal by asking students, "Is accented articulation a *staccato* thing or a *legato* thing?" After students debate, help them see (by playing) that both styles can be performed with an accented "front edge" on each note.

Again, explain how accents are performed properly on different instruments and let students try out the various kinds of accents and note lengths. Make these articulation styles part of the daily scale warm-up: *staccato* and no accent, *staccato* with accent, *legato* and no accent, *legato* with accent.

While playing warm-up scales, involve individual students in three ways:

a) Letting them choose the articulation style.

b) Letting them come to the front of the room to evaluate articulations they hear according to evenness, uniformity of style, precision, expressiveness, etc. Require them to be prescriptive about which sections need to be shorter, longer, etc.

c) Letting them conduct, requiring them to show the articulation without verbalizing it. This is something the entire band should practice with your coaching.

5. *The Verbal Imagination*

Assign students individually or as part of a small group to come up with new descriptors that go beyond the words "*staccato, legato,* and accented." Challenge them to make all three related in some way. For example:

- Water: tranquil pool (*legato*), a drippy faucet (*staccato*), chunks of ice hitting a hard sidewalk (accented)
- Sports: hitting a tennis ball and watching it soar (accented and *legato*), rowing with long oars (*legato*), ping-pong (*staccato*)
- Food: popcorn (*staccato*), caramel (*legato*), crunching celery (accented)

Have each student or group write their descriptors on a 3x5 card to turn in. Draw one from a bag each day and use them as a new way to play warm-up scales.

6. *Back to Broege*

As rehearsals continue for *The Headless Horseman*, continually invite students to make decisions about articulations in the piece. Where articulations are specified (e.g. *staccato* at m. 10, *legato* at m. 20, accented at m. 24) ask students why. Encourage them to consider what the composer may have had in mind with the articulation he indicated.

Where no specific articulation is indicated (most of the piece) ask students to make decisions about articulation style. For example, is the flute/oboe melody at m. 11 *legato* or slightly detached? Accented or soft tongue? Should measures 14-15 be accented and detached, or loud but smooth? Try student suggestions and let the group discuss the effectiveness of their ideas.

As the group works its way toward effective articulations, invite them to write new descriptors in their parts, which they can decide as a group. If they relate to the story of the Headless Horseman, even better. For example, m. 10: "clip of distant hoofbeats."

Assessment

1. Record the piece at various stages throughout the rehearsal process and have students mark places in their parts where articulations are not uniformly matched in style, not precisely together, not pronounced enough, or not effective in some other way.

2. As a final exam, have students record themselves individually, playing three scales (one each of *legato*, *staccato*, and accented). With a rubric of the group's own devising, have them evaluate themselves, as well as a peer.

Cognitive Outcome

Students will analyze and describe compositional devices that create tension, suspense, and surprise.

Strategies

1. *Composer's Tool Box*

    Remind students about the day the piece was introduced to them by the percussion section and the effect of the opening percussion *crescendo* (suspense, mystery, etc.). "Which musical elements are being used for effect here?" (Dynamics and Timbre). If students have not learned these words, introduce them and explain that over the next few weeks they will be exploring all the musical elements, that create suspense and surprise in the piece. They will be examining all the different musical tools that Timothy Broege used and what they are called.

    Pass out a worksheet with the words "Composer's Tool Box" at the top. This will be kept in their folder or portfolio as a place to record new vocabulary they learn as they explore the compositional devices in the piece.

    Have students write the word "timbre" on the sheet and come up with a definition as a group. (Timbre: the unique color of a musical sound.)

2. *Dissonance*

    At any point while giving directions or announcements during a rehearsal, move near the piano. Surprise students in the middle of your speaking by coming down loudly on a random tone cluster with both hands. "We have a word for that kind of chord—raise your hand if you know it." Students share their ideas ("crunchy" or "ugly" or "harsh," etc.)—if no one offers the word dissonance, teach it to them. Write it on the board and have them write it on their "Composer's Tool Box" sheet, to be defined later.

    "How does a composer create a dissonant chord?" Let students offer their opinions. Invite a volunteer to come to the podium and "create" a dissonant chord by having the band play the notes they suggest. Have a second student do the same. Ask students to explain how the dissonance was created (by notes that lie close to each other—the more notes and the closer they are to each other, generally the more dissonance).

244

Ask students to compare the two chords they played: "Which one was more dissonant?" Let students voice their opinion, without correcting them.

Assign everyone in the band one of these three notes, in their own range, and have them play this chord:

(concert pitches)

This can be done quickly by dividing the group into three and giving them each a pitch (concert) to play. "How dissonant was this chord compared with the others?" Write the chord on the board in notation, as above, so students can see it. "The knowledge that it fits the definition of dissonance—two notes touching—but it doesn't sound as painfully dissonant to our ears. Explain to them that dissonance is a very relative term, and what sounds dissonant to one ear might not be so to another. Explain that it's like salsa—you can think of it as "mild," "spicy," or "extra hot."

Have students write a definition of dissonance in their own words on their "Composer's Tool Box" sheet.

As rehearsals progress, let students evaluate the relative dissonance of certain sonorities in *The Headless Horseman.* For example, have the band listen to the alto sax/clarinet chord at m. 6 and vote on "mild," "spicy," or "extra hot." (Obviously, there need not be consensus.) Try it again with trumpets added in measure eight and again with the final chord of measure nine. Help students hear what makes this chord so dissonant (more pitches, more instruments, loud dynamic, etc.) Have a student from each section name the concert pitch they play and have another student notate it on the board (or have all students notate on their own staff paper) so they can see how dissonant the chord is:

3. *Consonance (Thirds and Intervals)*

At the beginning of another rehearsal, have a different student come to the piano and play a chord of their devising. Tell them to make it as dissonant or "un-dissonant" as they wish. Have the band decide if it's "mild," "spicy," or "extra hot."

Next, have another student come to the piano and play a chord of their own devising that's "not at all dissonant." Have the band evaluate their chord. Most likely it will be a triad. If it is not, ask the student to keep making it less and less dissonant, until he is playing a simple triad. Ask the student to spell the chord he is playing (if he can) or have the band figure out (by ear) what the notes are. Have another student notate the pitches on the board. "Does anyone know the name for the distance between notes?" (Interval). "What are the intervals between these three notes?" (All thirds).

Explain to students that traditionally thirds have come to be associated with "sweet," non-dissonant sounding music. Show them how thirds are notated (always line-to-line or space-to-space). "What is the word for the opposite of dissonance?" (Consonance).

Have students write a definition of consonance on their "Composer's Tool Box" sheet. Also have them define as a group, and write a definition on their sheet of interval, (the distance between two notes) and third (two notes from a scale that skip one note between them or two notes on adjacent lines or adjacent spaces).

As part of their introduction to the word interval, show them how intervals are determined (by counting lines and spaces, or using letter names). Let them practice naming some intervals to assess understanding. For example, you say "fourth" and they spell a fourth within a scale. Use the same scale they are playing as a daily warm-up, to reinforce understanding.

For practice in hearing thirds and playing them in tune, play warm-up scales in thirds. Divide the band into two groups (by stand partners works well). Have the band play half-notes, with group two playing in canon two notes after group one. As students get comfortable and begin to play more in tune, add a third part in canon, so there are triads sounding.

During rehearsal of *The Headless Horseman*, have clarinets play their first note in m. 10 for the band to hear. Explain the difference between harmonic thirds (sounding together, in harmony) versus melodic thirds (sounding one after the other; e.g. flute and oboe in m. 11). As you rehearse *The Headless Horseman*, have students look for thirds throughout their parts, pointing them out whenever possible.

4. *Triads*

As a warm-up/tuning drill over the next few rehearsals, have students build chords in thirds in the band in the following way. Choose a student to name any concert pitch (for example D-natural). Choose another student to add the next note (a third above), and another student to add another pitch, also a third, to create a triad. This can be done by simply having the three students play their notes on their own instruments (and having the band evaluate their choices), or by having the students name the notes they want and having the rest of the band (in three groups) play them.

Always have another student at the board notating what the group is playing. At some point, after students are familiar with the above process, call attention to the notated triad on the board. "There is actually a specific word for this kind of chord, with only three notes, all a third apart. Does anyone know it?" (triad). Have them write it and define it on their "Composer's Tool Box" sheet. (Triad: a chord of three notes in thirds.)

After students are familiar with the above process ask them, "Have we been playing melodic or harmonic triads?" (harmonic). "How would we play a triad melodically?" Have a student answer by demonstrating (an arpeggiated triad). Have the entire band try it. You may choose to introduce the word arpeggio as part of the "Composer's Tool Box" vocabulary sheet.

During rehearsal of *The Headless Horseman*, have a spur-of-the-moment contest to see who can find a melodic triad in their part. Examples are m. 19 (*tutti*) and m. 20 (baritone/bass).

5. *The Devil's Interval*

Remind students that just as certain chords are more dissonant than others, so are intervals themselves considered more or less dissonant. Help them hear this by asking a trumpet player to play a concert B flat. Ask the player next to her to play another note at the same time, which is dissonant. Guide the second student to discover that the most dissonant interval is the one a half-step away. Have students practice finding these dissonant minor seconds by a quick ear-training drill. Divide the band in half. Name a pitch and have group one play it, and group two quickly find the note a half-step away and play it. The raucous sound that ensues should be entertaining (at least for a short time).

Ask students to listen for any other intervals that sound "weird" or dissonant. Play the first 19 measures of *The Headless Horseman*. Most students will probably recognize the opening trombone pitches as somehow "weird." Have them play these notes without the *glissando* to hear that they still have a strangeness.

Explain to students briefly the history of this interval, the tritone. For centuries it was considered too dissonant, even demonic, hence its medieval nickname "diabolus in musica" (the devil in music). Have a trombone notate it on the board and have the entire band play it. Without going into too much music theory detail, help students discover what a tritone looks like (a slightly larger fourth, or a slightly smaller fifth). Remind them of how to count lines and spaces to name intervals. Have them practice finding some tritones on their instrument, spelling some as a group, etc.

Do the same ear-training drill as above, except instead of minor seconds use tritones. It will take students a little longer to figure out the "theory" of finding them; emphasize the listening aspect so students will recognize them when they hear them.

Play the first 19 measures of *The Headless Horseman* and ask students to listen for tritones. When they identify mm. 14-15, have the low brass figure out exactly how many tritones are in this passage and circle them. (This is a great activity for them to work on for several minutes while you are rehearsing another section.)

Have students add tritone and a definition of their own (the devil's interval, a large fourth or small fifth, dissonant, etc.) to their "Composer's Tool Box" sheet.

6. *Dynamics*

Ask students for the proper name for louds and softs in music. (dynamics). Have them write this word and its definition as one of the tools on their "Composer's Tool Box" sheet.

Ask students to think about places in *The Headless Horseman* where dynamics have a special effect. Play through the piece and field their ideas, always compelling them to explain the "why?" of their answer and also the kind of effect that the particular dynamic has on the music. For example, "the piano at m. 10—it sounds mysterious." Check student opinions by playing passages at the "wrong" dynamic to compare for effectiveness. "Does m. 10 work as well when we play it *forte?*" "What is the effect of m. 19 (shock, sudden surprise.)

As each section of the piece is rehearsed and refined, study the dynamic this way, inviting student opinions about the "why?" of each indicated dynamic. Help students discover that many of the most effective moments in the piece involve a sudden dynamic change. Invite them to discuss why this might be so (the shock effect, keep the listener off-guard, emphasize the weirdness and supernatural element of the story, etc.).

7. *Timbre*

Ask students for the proper name for instrumental color (timbre). Remind them of their first experience of *The Headless Horseman*, and the effect of hearing the opening percussion introduction before they knew the piece.

Ask them to think about other places in *The Headless Horseman* where a peculiar timbre or a sudden change in timbre has a special effect. Play through the piece and then field their ideas. Again, always encourage them to uncover the "why?" of their answer, and to describe the effect that the particular timbre has on the music.

Some examples:

- The trombone gliss in mm. 4-6. What does it "mean?" Is Broege depicting something or just trying to "weird us out?"
- The use of low brass in mm. 14-15. Why not woodwinds?
- The solo instruments in mm. 40-45. Why not the whole section?
- Why temple blocks or woodblocks in mm. 42-45?

As each section of the piece is rehearsed and refined, study the timbres this way, inviting student opinions about the "why?" of each indicated timbral choice. Just as with dynamics, many of the most effective moments in the piece involve a sudden change in timbres. Again, invite them to speculate why this might be so.

8. Homophonic Versus Polyphonic

Begin rehearsal with a chorale for band. Write the word "homophonic" on the board and tell students that this short piece is homophonic. Ask them to explain why. Help them to hear that all the (usually four) parts are moving in the same rhythm, playing in chords. Another way to think about it is "melody with accompaniment." Still another way is to imagine it being sung: all the voices would sing the same words at the same time.

Ask students to find a chorale in *The Headless Horseman.* Play through the piece completely and let them discover the chorale, which begins at m. 26. "Why did Timothy Broege put a chorale in the middle of this piece?" (perhaps for some relief from the intensity of the surrounding material, or to symbolize "pleading for salvation.")

This kind of music is homophonic. Add this word and a definition (all parts moving in the same rhythm, playing chords; melody plus accompaniment) to the "Composer's Tool Box" sheet.

The next day, begin by singing a simple round with the band. After they have sung it, have them play it. "Is this song homophonic? Why not?" (All parts have the melody at different times, moving in different rhythms at the same time, different words are being sung simultaneously, etc.). This kind of music is called polyphonic. Add this word to the "Composer's Tool Box" sheet, with its definition (several melodies sounding at once, or the same melody starting at different times).

Ask students to listen for examples of polyphonic music in *The Headless Horseman.* Play through the piece completely and let them debate their ideas. For example, in measures 17-19, is this music polyphonic, or is it merely melody (woodwinds) plus accompaniment (brass and saxes)? This depends on how important you view the brass/sax material. Is the section from mm. 20-23 polyphonic or homophonic? Again, it depends on how relatively important you view the various materials. The indisputable polyphonic passage is the last four measures. Have students listen carefully and "tease out" the various strands of melody.

Polyphonic and homophonic are descriptions of texture. Introduce this word and add it to the "Composer's Tool Box" sheet.

Reinforce the concepts of homophony versus polyphony in follow-up activities:

1. As a take-home assignment, have students design and draw visual pictures of each texture.

2. Send several groups of five students each out of the room and give them this assignment: create a moving or frozen sculpture, using all five people, to depict homophony and polyphony. (This works well with a section that isn't busy while another is being rehearsed.) Give them only five to seven minutes to create their picture. Have them "perform" for the band, and make the band guess which texture they are representing.

9. *Putting It All Together*

After five or six weeks of rehearsing *The Headless Horseman* and discovering the variety of compositional devices in the piece, do a summary activity. "There is a lot to this piece, and we've discovered lots of musical tools a composer can use to create an interesting piece of music."

"Another way to think about the piece is as a big pot of stew, with lots of separate ingredients tossed in. Today we're going to pull out each ingredient and take a look at it to see exactly how many different "music's" there are in the piece."

Brainstorm as a band to generate a long list that accounts for every different kind of musical material. Give each "music" a descriptive name, created by students, and encourage them to consider the "meaning" or effect of each one. If appropriate, share examples from the composer's notes. The students' list might look something like this:

1. Mysterious percussion intro: sets the mysterious mood
2. Trombone glissando: eerie feeling, moaning of trees? Wolves?
3. Dissonant chords: shrieks, the whinnying of the stallion
4. Eighth notes in thirds: the horseman rides, but still far away
5. Woodwind melody: inner fear, creates momentum
6. Low brass interjections: Beware!
7. Tutti unison m. 19: Bigger Beware!
8. First polyphonic section: the ride gets wilder, the Horseman gets closer
9. The chorale: "Maybe I can escape"
10. Unison fifths mm. 36-37: the riders stop.
11. Solo trumpet mm. 43-45: Ichabod disappears.

During the above process, two things may become obvious:

1. There is some repetition of musical material.
2. The musical material changes rapidly. (This may not be apparent to young students, who are used to short, segmented pieces.)

Have students create a giant "call chart" that outlines the exact form of the piece based on the list they generated, but using letter names to discover the overall form of the piece. (Introduction-ABCBA).

Discuss with students why the composer created a piece with so many sudden and extreme changes of texture, dynamics, etc.

"Although there is a lot of variety in the piece, there are some things that help hold the piece together. Is there anything that remains the same through much of the piece?" (the snare drum rhythm). "What might that symbolize?" (the horse's hoofbeats?).

Assessment

1. As a check up, give students a written quiz on all the terms they have learned from this piece (timbre, consonance, dissonance, interval, third, triad, arpeggio, tritone, dynamics, homophonic, polyphonic, texture). A quick quiz would list all the definitions and have students fill in the word being defined. A longer quiz (to write and correct) would list the terms and ask students to write definitions. In either case, have students describe examples of the term from the music itself, to check for understanding.

2. Have students write a short journal entry on the this question: What is your favorite compositional device from the "Composer's Tool Box" that Timothy Broege used in *The Headless Horseman*? Why? (This question could be the final question on the written quiz above.)

3. As part of a playing quiz, have students play scales in melodic thirds or arpeggiated triads, as in strategies three and four above.

Affective Outcome

Students will speculate on the appeal of experiences that evoke fear.

Strategies

1. The Granddaddy of Ghost Stories

After they have begun rehearsing the piece, have students read Irving's "The Legend of Sleepy Hollow." This could be done in class in small chunks, or as short homework assignments. (The complete story is available several places online; see Resources at the end of the chapter.)

Help students with difficult vocabulary words and ask questions to guide their reading, especially questions that ask "why?" At the beginning, there may be some resistance to the florid 19th-century prose and the fact that the "ghost story" part of the story doesn't appear until the end. Ask students to ponder the motivations of the characters, the nature of their relationships with each other, and the choices they make. Halfway through the story, after they have been introduced to the three main characters, have them write a short journal entry that answers these two questions:

a) Which of the three characters (Ichabod, Katrina, or Brom) is most like your own personality? Why?

b) Do you know someone who is like Katrina? Ichabod? Brom? How so?

After reading the final scene, have students journal on the following question and then share their ideas in a group discussion:

c) What do you think actually happened in the final scene? Do you think the Headless Horseman was "real?" Why or why not?

2. *Around the Campfire*

"The Legend of Sleepy Hollow" is a ghost story about ghost stories. That is, the delight in telling spooky stories characterizes the people of Sleepy Hollow, and the cumulative effect of all their stories and superstitions on Ichabod (and on the reader) is what gives the final climactic scene its power and psychological effectiveness.

Give students a week to research and find a ghost story of their own, which they will memorize and be able to tell. (Several Web sites are wonderful resources—see "Resources" below. Typically there are also good collections of ghost stories and urban legends in school libraries.) Divide students into groups of four or five and have them sit in small circles, "around a campfire," and share their stories. For extra motivation, a prize could be offered: each small group chooses their best story, each of which is then shared with the whole group, who votes on its favorite.

This activity could be combined with a trip to a nearby park, beach, or woods, or even done on the school lawn. Including "campfire snacks" would help make it a memorable day in band.

3. *Taking It Personally*

Have students journal again, this time on these questions: Do you enjoy ghost stories? Why or why not? Why do you think people like stories that make them afraid?

Discuss as a group. Invite students to think of examples of things people do that evoke fear (e.g. haunted houses at Halloween, scary rides at theme parks, scary movies, etc.).

Encourage students to ponder the psychology of why people do things that are intended to scare them. Give them opportunities to briefly share their thoughts at various times throughout the rehearsal process.

Assessment

Have students write a final journal entry, reflecting on this question: Why do many people like scary stories, movies, music, rides, etc? Evaluate their writing for its thoughtfulness, coherence, and how well it reflects the previous group discussions.

Music Selection

The Headless Horseman is an ideal piece for the young band, especially students at about the third year of playing. Technical demands are not excessive, but do include a few challenges (repeated *staccato* and piano eighth-notes, first trumpet range, exposed solos, chromatics, etc.). Although only 90 seconds long, the piece is chock-full of possible learning outcomes beyond technique—at the top of the list is the rich interdisciplinary aspect of its source material: a piece of classic American literature.

Other Possible Outcomes

1. Scary music: Is it possible for music to be scary in itself, or is it only scary when we associate it with something else? (Musical examples: *A Night on Bald Mountain* by Mussorgsky, "Dream of a Witches' Sabbath" from the *Symphonie Fantastique* by Berlioz, music from favorite horror films, etc.)
2. Programmatic Music: Music that is "about something" other than itself. Study other examples. How effective is music at relating the plot of a story?

Resources

"The Headless Horseman" in *Teaching Music through Performance in Band.* Richard Miles, editor. 1997. Chicago: GIA Publications. Includes biographical information on Timothy Broege and brief analyses of the piece, as well as additional references and resources.

"The Legend of Sleepy Hollow" by Washington Irving
Online versions of the complete story:

The Bridge Library
www.bri-dge.com/short_takes/short24.html

The Project Gutenberg E-text
www.hyland.org/sleepyhollow/sleep10.txt

Classic Ghost Stories and Urban Legends
www.castleofspirits.com/classic.html

Sleepy Hollow. Directed by Tim Burton. Rated R
www.sleepyhollowmovie.com. Paramount Pictures, 1999.

The Legend of Sleepy Hollow. Directed by Pierre Gant.
Hallmark television movie also available on video,
www.odysseychannel.com/sleepyhollow/home.html, includes a study guide. Hallmark Pictures, 1999.

The Legend of Sleepy Hollow. Directed by Clyde Geonimi.
Disney Productions, 1949.

The MacScouter - Scouting Resources Online
Stories for Scouts and Scouters: Ghost Stories
http://www.macscouter.com/stories/GhostStories.html

The Moonlit Road
Ghost stories and strange folktales of the American South
www.themoonlitroad.com

Classic Ghost Stories and Urban Legends
www.castleofspirits.com/classic.html

The Sleepy Hollow Movie Website
Includes links to "True Tales of the Supernatural"
www.sleepyhollowmovie.com

Upper Middle School/High School Band

CAJUN FOLK SONGS

Frank Ticheli (b. 1958)

Manhattan Beach Music (1991)

Background Information

In 1934 and 1937, anthropologist and American folk song collector John Lomax and his son, Alan, set out to make field recordings of Cajun and Creole music as part of a nationwide folk song survey funded by the Library of Congress. It was part of many New Deal projects intended to encourage interest in the native arts of Americans as a way of boosting national morale and the economy. These recordings were made at a critical time, as traditional rural Cajun music of Louisiana was disappearing and being replaced by the more urbanized sounds of commercially recorded, thickly textured music such as "swamp pop" and zydeco—styles influenced by the new sounds of rock and roll and rhythm and blues. The Lomaxes also transcribed several of the songs they heard and included them in a special chapter dedicated to "French Songs and Ballads from Southwestern Louisiana" in their 1941 folk song collection, *Our Singing Country* (see Resources at end of chapter).

Composer Frank Ticheli was himself born in Louisiana, and as part of his own desire to pay tribute to the people and songs of the old Cajun culture arranged two of the songs from the Lomax recordings in his two-movement suite, *Cajun Folk Songs*. The two songs he selected are contrasting in style and content: "La Belle et la Capitaine" (Movement I) is a slow melody in Dorian mode and "Belle" is a more modern sounding, almost bluesy tune, with a cheerful, pentatonic feeling. It is impossible, however, to fully appreciate the songs without hearing the original Lomax recordings and studying the lyrics to the songs. (See Resources at end of chapter.)

La Belle et La Capitaine

This ballad was sung on the Lomax recording by Julien Hoffpauir in New Iberia, Louisiana. The Hoffpauir family scratched out a poor existence through agricultural labor and Mr. Hoffpauir taught his daughters many of the ballads that had been passed down for generations among Louisiana Cajuns. Many of these songs date from before the days when the French speaking Cajuns (Acadians) were exiled from Nova Scotia in 1755, and this song is probably even older. Its similarity to old French ballads reveals its origins in Normandy, from where the Cajuns emigrated to Canada in the 18th century, bringing with them their music, their language, and their way of life.

Hoffpauir sings the song unaccompanied with a hard, nasal tone and precise, even delivery without special vocal effects—putting focus on the lyrics and the story. The story is an unusual one: a maiden is about to be kidnapped and seduced by a caption when she falls dead. Her father mourns her death bitterly, but three days later she knocks on the door, explaining that she only pretended to be dead to save her honor. In the published transcription of the song in *Our Singing Country*, the title of the song is given as "Blanche comme la neige" (White as the Snow), referring apparently to the maiden's unsullied virtue.

The song is sung in Cajun French, the regional dialect spoken in South Louisiana. An English translation might be:

1. The youngest of all three (soldiers?) took her white hand and said, "Fair maiden, mount up, mount up on my gray horse and I will take you straight to my father's house, where we will stay together."

2. When the maiden heard this, she began to weep. He said, "Eat, eat, fair maiden, with a hearty appetite! Tonight you will sleep next to a fine captain!"

3. When the maiden heard these words, she fell to the ground dead. "Ring out bells! Sound the drums and violins! My little girl is dead. My heart is filled with grief."

4. "And where shall she be buried?"
   "In her father's garden, beneath the three leaves of the lily. We pray to God, dear brother, that she may fly to Paradise."

5. When three days had passed, the maiden knocked on the door. "Open, open the door, dearest and beloved father, for three days ago I chose death to save my honor."

Belle

This song was sung by a Mr. Bornu in Kaplan, Louisiana, who performs in a rapid, clearly-enunciated style with a swinging, regular meter with lots of "blue" notes and a syncopated, "raggy rhythmic" style. Its jazzy melody and lilting rhythm is well-suited to the tragic/comic irony in the lyrics: a man is ready to pawn his cow pony to save his sweetheart's life. The man has gone to Texas (he doesn't tell us why), but is apparently caught between a new love and an old one, who sends word that she is dying. He returns from Texas, only to find her unconscious. He pawns his horse, Henry, but presumably to no avail, and returns to Texas.

The theme of going away to Texas is a common one in old Cajun songs. In Cajun lore, Texas has long symbolized trouble as well as a place of opportunity. In southern Louisiana, just after the Civil War, vigilante groups drove out many "undesirable" Cajun families, forcing them to settle in Texas. Texas also provided work for Cajun cowboys who went there on cattle drives, and for laborers in the early 20th century who worked in the shipbuilding, construction, and petroleum industries.

The melody and lyrics to "Belle" show both European and African influences. The phrases are of regular lengths and always end with the word "Belle." In fact, about half of the text is repeated, a characteristic of African song. Here is a translation of the Cajun French:

1. If I have a sweetheart here, belle (sweetheart),
   It's because of you, belle.
   If I have a sweetheart here, belle,
   It's because of you, belle.

2. I took this very train, belle,
   To go to Texas, belle,
   I took this very train, etc.

3. Only three days, belle,
   After I arrived, belle,

I received a letter from you, belle,

Saying that you were very ill, belle.

4. That you were very ill, belle,

   In danger of dying, belle, etc.

5. I took this train again, belle,

   To come back here, belle, etc.

6. When I reached you, belle,

   You were unconscious, belle, etc.

7. I turned right around, belle,

   And returned there, belle.

8. I pawned my horse, belle,

   To save your life, belle, etc.

9. Oh, if I no longer have Henry, belle,

   It's because I loved you, belle, etc.

10. Parting is hard, belle,

    But forgetting takes long, belle, etc.

When he transcribed the song for *Our Singing Country*, John Lomax chose the meter of 10/8. Ticheli does accordingly in his arrangement, which also uses eighth notes for the tune, but set in a 5/4 meter. However, it is interesting to note that the Lomax transcription place the pitches quite differently within the meter, with Ticheli beginning the melody on a downbeat and the Lomax transcription taking the first three eighths as upbeats.

An evocative picture of Bornu is included in the CD liner notes to *Cajun and Creole Music II* (See Resources at end of chapter.)

In arranging these two unaccompanied vocal songs for concert band, Ticheli has lovingly reinterpreted and re-clothed them. They might be titled "Cajun Song and Dance" for "La Belle et la Capitaine" is set as a lyrical and richly-textured song without words, and "Belle" becomes a spirited dance.

Elements of Music

Form

Both songs are strophic and include many verses. Ticheli has pre-served this aspect of the material and sets both movements as essentially strophic songs for band. It is helpful to talk about their form in terms of verses. Each movement will be discussed separately.

I. *La Belle et la Capitaine*

Each verse of the melody is made of three phrases repeated in this pattern: AABCBC. Hoffpauir occasionally shortens or augments this basic structure, reshaping the musical material to fit his narrative. Ticheli used the same material, setting it in this way:

Verse I

A	1-6	Solo alto sax, unaccompanied
B	7-11	Alto sax is joined by first clarinet in counterpoint
C	12-16	Sax and clarinet finish verse in two-part counterpoint

Verse II

A	17-22	Thicker texture, melody shared by first clarinet, first alto, first trumpet; sustained homophonic accompaniment with occasional movement in inner voices; Pedal D in tuba, bassoon, bass clarinet
A	23-28	Same as above
B	29-33	Orchestration changes slightly, oboe joins melody, Trumpets tacet
C	34-38	Similar to beginning of Verse II; oboe tacet, trumpets join
B	39-43	Flutes/clarinets lightly scored; high *tessitura*
C	45-49	Same as above; alto sax joins; an added measure at the end of the phrase plus a sustained cymbal roll usher in final verse

Verse III

A	50-55	Full, rich orchestration; melody in octaves enriched with moving contrapuntal lines above and below it; Pedal D in low voices
A	56-61	Same as above
B	62-66	More rhythmic activity in accompaniment; *tutti crescendo*, timpani roll, prominent xylophone entrance
C	67-71	Building to climax; *tutti crescendo*

Codetta

72-74	Thinly scored repeat of the last two measures of the melody brings the movement to a quiet close; decorated suspension figure in tenor saxaphone like "Amen."

II. Belle

The melody of "Belle" is a simple four-bar tune in an antecedent/consequent plus antecedent/consequent relationship, the second and fourth measures responding to the first and third measures. Ticheli creates new material for this movement in the form of an original melody, which retains "Belle's" rhythmic feeling, but contrasts with it in melodic direction: where "Belle's" melody leaps up in three of its four measures, Ticheli's melody begins with a downward contour. There are ten statements of "Belle" (A theme) and five statements of Ticheli's melody (B theme).

Intro	1-4	Pedal F and *ostinato* establish key; Percussion establishes 5/4 metrical feel
A	5-9	First statement in memorable timbre: muted trumpet

Interlude

	9-12	Like Introduction
B	12-22	Two statements of B, plus two bars of *ostinato*
A	22-28	Still in F major, plus two bars of *ostinato*
B	28-30	Fragment of B theme
A	31-37	Sudden modulation to A-flat; three bar extension
A	38-52	C major; modified rhythmically to a 6/8 + 3/4 feeling; seven bar phrase extension develops A theme material

Interlude

	53-58	B-flat major; based on material from A
B	58-64	E-flat major
A	65-68	A-flat major (fragments)
B	69-73	D-flat major
A	74-81	Pedal C provides prolonged dominant tension; fragments of A tossed about in various keys

Interlude

	82-88	F major; aggressive interlude combines unison *ostinato* and descending chromatic figure; *ritardando* leads to next section.
A	88-92	F major; slow, reflective statement of tune in brass
A	92-101	Two statements of tune; same orchestration as beginning gives feeling of recapitulation
B	101-104	F major
A	104-114	Similar effects as m. 38; eight-bar phrase extension over pedal C generates tension and pull toward finale
A	120-126	Tutti climax; whooping horn *glissandi*; *fortissimo*
Coda	126-132	Based on A material; whirling polyphony for four bars, Grand Pause, final unison button (with trombone *glissandi*).

Melody

In spite of their common origins, the two melodies used in *Cajun Folk Songs* are quite different in shape and mood. "La Belle et la Capitaine" is in Dorian mode, which contributes to its antique feeling and although it is notated with changing meters does not feel like a mixed meter piece. It is the text that shapes the melody—the changing meters are simply used to accommodate the lyrics.

Although the melodic shape of "La Belle et la Capitaine" seems freely shaped, it is actually a quite unified, organic structure, based on ascending thirds and descending tonic triads. A close comparison of selected measures reveals a tight construction. (Compare for example mm. 1, 7, 12, 15, or mm. 6, 9, and 14.

The melody of "Belle" is more foursquare, in spite of its jaunty meter of five. As mentioned, the four measures alternate in a reflexive relationship, the second and fourth bars "answering" the first and third. This is a pentatonic melody. which, combined with its tonic triad leaps, no doubt contributes to its light-hearted affect. Ticheli's second, original melody is decidedly not pentatonic, its first gesture being a strong downbeat leading tone. In this way, it is a good foil for the "Belle" melody, setting it in relief and providing contrast—the "Belle" melody alone is probably not enough material to support a piece of this length.

Rhythm

"La Belle et la Capitaine," in spite of its mixed meter notation, feels steady and regular, and has a dirge-like quality in keeping with its story.

"Belle" is a 5/4 meter tune, but actually feels like 6/8 plus 2/4. (In fact, the composer recommends conducting it this way.) Ticheli takes a tune that already boasts an asymmetrical meter and distorts it further as the piece progresses, usually by adding a beat at the end of the phrase (e.g. measures 39 and 41, etc.) or by displacing the downbeat (e.g. measures 53-58), which creates a tipsy, off-balance sensation. In the climactic finale to the movement (mm. 120-125), Ticheli gives each of the first three phrases its own unique length, and turns the fourth phrase into a mad, polyphonic scramble.

It is obvious that rhythm is one of the most beguiling features of "La Belle et la Capitaine" and it is the constant metrical shifting which lends the piece its playfulness. Mastering these meter changes and playing with a vital, driving rhythmic integrity is one of the great thrills of playing this piece.

Harmony

"La Belle et La Capitaine" is harmonized in D Dorian, from which it never departs during the course of its three verses. The lack of modulation contributes to its somber mood and Ticheli restricts his harmonization to simple diatonic chords with very little chromaticism. This has the effect of a chorale setting of the tune, which is further enhanced by the relatively restrained movement of the accompanying parts, and the occasional use of cadential suspensions which round out these phrases with an "Amen" feeling.

Harmonic twists, combined with changes of timbre and meter, give "Belle" a saucy character. Because the folk melody is itself so short and tonally static, Ticheli relies on two devices to keep it interesting:

1. Re-harmonizing it over and over with slightly more dissonant settings, especially the use of mildly dissonant ostinati, upon which he lays the tune

2. Changing the key altogether, usually in a sudden, static modulation

Other favorite harmonic devices of the composer include pedal tones (both long tones and rhythmic *ostinati*), and tone clusters, especially setting the melody in dissonant, parallel motion seconds. Ticheli is well aware of the humor in unexpected harmonies, especially when combined with displaced downbeats. One such off-kilter moment begins at m. 38, where the low voices interject an obscene tritone at the end of the phrase.

Timbre

Most of "La Belle et la Capitaine" is scored for full band and the timbre changes are subtle and serve to delineate phrases. For example, the woodwind phrases (mm. 39-50) provide a poignant change of color. The notable exception is the expressive choice of the solo alto saxophone, which sings the opening verse. Most of the rest of the piece features dark, heavy scoring that keeps with the solemn mood of the song. One puzzling exception is the prominent use of xylophone (mm. 62-68) which seems an odd choice, like someone who showed up at the funeral dressed in a party hat. This would make an interesting topic for students to discuss: why did Ticheli introduce the xylophone at this serious moment?

"Belle," on the other hand, depends on a kaleidoscopic whirling of color for its effect. There are hardly two measures of the piece that sound the same in terms of timbre—a delight for the listener and also for the players (the percussion section alone will be kept hopping!). A measure-by-measure look at all the timbre changes is beyond the scope of this teaching plan, but definitely would reveal a clever arranger who makes full use of the concert band, mixing primary and complementary colors like a master painter.

Texture

The whirling colors of "Belle" are closely dependent on changes of texture which happen equally spontaneously, varying from the single line of edgy muted trumpet which introduces the "Belle" tune to the bright and thin textures of the woodwind version of it (mm. 22-28). A favorite texture of Ticheli is the drone pedal tone, sustained under the flurry of melodic activity above it. (e.g. mm. 1-12, 110-114 and other places).

Although the texture's relative thinness or thickness changes with each verse (or more), it is almost uniformly homophonic, in keeping with the strong rhythmic drive of the tune, which would be too cluttered with contrapuntal decoration. It is easy to see a variety of rhythmic activity by glancing down any page of the score, but a closer look shows that it is almost exclusively homorhythmic, intended not to work against the tune contrapuntally, but rather to accentuate its rhythmic contour.

The one truly polyphonic moment in "Belle" occurs in its climactic coda (mm. 126-129), where a pentatonic scramble among the voices begins imitatively on four consecutive beats—a noisy mess that needs a Grand Pause for its dust to settle. The final unison *tutti* is an appropriate exclamation point.

"La Belle et la Capitaine" is almost exclusively thickly-textured homophony with one notable exception: the tender alto sax solo that introduces the melody. This is an obvious choice, considering the piece's origins as an unaccompanied vocal solo. It also has the added effect of focusing the attention on the movement's strongest feature: a powerfully beautiful melody.

Expression/Dynamics

The dynamic shape of "La Belle et la Capitaine" can be thought of as a giant arc that rises out of the single line alto sax solo and ends with a similar, intimate *pianissimo.* Its central peak (mm. 67-71) is approached by various hills and valleys along the way, and each phrase, of course, calls for its own expressive dynamic shape and climax.

"Belle" also begins with a hushed intensity, but calls for a much wider and quickly changing dynamic range, in keeping with its spirited tempo and "quick change" timbres.

Articulation styles can be summarized easily: "La Belle et la Capitaine" depends on a *cantabile* style and smooth tonguing. "Belle," on the other hand, is about quick, agile articulation and especially accents. It is a wide variety of accents, large and small, which etch the angles and edges of this very rhythmic tune.

The Heart

The heart of each movement of *Cajun Folk Songs* is unique. In "La Belle et la Capitaine" it is a nostalgic longing for a "folky," traditional past created by the plaintive, modal melody that evokes the sentiment of its lyrics. The heart is the rhythmic playfulness of its melody, enhanced in the arrangement by continuous, colorful surprises of texture and timbre.

Introducing the Piece

Grab students' attention at the beginning of band by singing for them, without any spoken introduction, the melody of "La Belle et la Capitaine" in a comfortable key on a neutral vowel ("oo" works well). When finished, ask students from where and when they think the melody might come. Sing it for them again and let them continue to speculate on the same questions. "What might the song be about? What kind of mood or feeling does it suggest to you?"

Sing the first verse in French and then invite more theorizing about the origins of the piece. Tell them that it's an old Cajun folk song and that they will be performing it. By now, students have heard the song several times and hopefully are enjoying and are intrigued by its melody. Continue with the Skill Outcome below.

Skill Outcome

Students will sing "La Belle et la Capitaine" and play it in a singing style.

Strategies

1. Teach students to sing "La Belle et la Capitaine" by rote over the course of several rehearsals. Use a neutral syllable like "loo." As they are learning the pitches, use your hand to draw the melodic direction in the air as a guide and have them imitate it as they sing, as a kinesthetic reinforcement. Break the piece into two- or three-measure segments (half a phrase) and have them echo you. Gradually combine these smaller segments into full phrases and finally into an entire verse.

    As students are learning, be unfailingly positive and give them lots of encouragement for their efforts, especially if they are not used to singing. Remind them to use enough energy to make a good sound as they sing, and model this. Model also a natural rise and fall in the phrase shaping, so it is expressive and *legato*, with appropriate intensity, energy, and direction. Be more demanding in your expectation of the students' singing as they get more comfortable: when they are lackluster or not expressive, sing it again for them exaggerating the tension and release of the phrase, without stopping to verbalize instructions. In this way, communicate musical expectations only by singing and conducting. Practice singing the melody this way for several rehearsals until students are confident and enjoy the sound of their singing.

2. After students can sing the entire song from memory, add a drone accompaniment. Have part of the band sustain the first note of the song on "oo" with staggered breathing, while the rest sing the melody. Switch parts. In this new context, students should continue to grow in their appreciation of the melody's beauty.

3. After the melody is quite familiar (this may take any number of rehearsals), begin rehearsal by playing the melody in D Dorian (concert). Repeat the same process as above, but instead with students playing, learning to play the melody by ear. As above, focus on expressive playing, rather than mere note accuracy—do not wait until everyone is playing every note perfectly before expecting beautiful phrasing. After students have learned to make the melody "their own," it is time to pass out the parts to *Cajun Folk Songs* and sight-read the first movement. It should be an effective first reading—not only will the melody hopefully be played expressively, but the accompanying parts should be sensitive to the melody in the texture around them.

4. Follow up rehearsals should include occasional singing of "La Belle et la Capitaine" as well as opportunities to listen to Julien Hoffpauir singing it on the Lomax recording. By this time, students may have more opinions about what the song is about—share with them the French text and translation from the CD liner notes or from *Our Singing Country*, and discuss the lyrics so the story is clear.

5. Teach the band to sing a verse of the song in French. If you are not comfortable with the French yourself, have a French student learn it, practice singing it, and teach the band.

    Have the band sing a verse of the song on the concert before they play *Cajun Folk Songs*.

6. Try singing "Belle" with the band. This can be done in several steps. First, let the band listen to the recording of Bornu singing. They will quickly pick up the "belle" at the end of each line and will be able to sing along after hearing a couple of verses. A couple of confident singers who know French could practice the verses and then lead the group, with the band always jumping in on the "belle" at the end of the line. Another

way would be to have the band sing the entire song in English, using John Lomax's charming translation in *Our Singing Country*.

Assessment

1. On going assessment will include observing students singing, assessing their success and level of comfort, and encouraging those who are reluctant.

2. As a final assessment, have each student record themselves playing the melody of "La Belle et la Capitaine" on their portfolio cassette. Evaluate their performance by this rubric:

    A *5 points* Melody is accurate and in tune, consistently expressive, *legato*, and phrase well. Expressive use of *vibrato* (if applicable).

    B *4 points* Melody is accurate and mostly in tune; Mostly *legato*; some expressive moments. Some *vibrato* noted (if applicable).

    C *3 points* Several note problems in melody or more serious intonation problems. Not very *legato* or expressive; phrasing not clear or intentional. No *vibrato*.

    D *1 point* Assignment completed but many problems with note accuracy, intonation, expressivity, *legato,* use of *vibrato*.

Cognitive Outcome

Students will explore Cajun culture: history, geography, folklore, food, and music.

Strategies

1. Early in the rehearsal process, ask students what the word "Cajun" means and where it came from. Let them share various ideas—they may only know that there is such a thing as Cajun music and food. As homework, assign them to find out everything they can about the word "Cajun," its history, and all the things that it might refer to

TEACHING PLANS BAND

besides food and music. They should be prepared to answer the question: what do we mean when we say "Cajun?" They can use the Internet, the library, or any other resources available to them.

2. The next day, have students share what they learned. As they explain what they discovered, write it as a topic word on the board, to be explored later. Make sure the discussion includes such basic ideas as Acadia, Nova Scotia, the expulsion of 1755, Louisiana, French language, and any other aspects of Cajun culture that students have discovered.

   With student input, group the topics they have mentioned into related groups (language, geography, history, music, culture, etc.) to get a sense of the variety of topics related to Cajun culture.

   Have each student choose a smaller topic to study in depth and share with the class over the six to eight weeks. This could be in the form of a brief (five to eight minutes maximum) presentation or, if students prefer, a wall poster/sketch/graph/collage of their own creation that summarizes and presents the same information in a visual way that is clear and shows thoughtful research. Ask students to select their topic from the list, or come up with a different, related topic of their own. As much as possible let each student have their own topic, so the class experience will be broader and richer. Remind students that their research should involve more than just a couple of sources whenever possible. The Internet will be a valuable source of information, but encourage them to be discerning in what information they use.

   A list of possible topics and questions to be addressed:

   The French

   • Where did the Cajuns originate in France? What aspects of their culture reflect this?

   The Canadians

   • What were the events that drove the Cajuns out of Nova Scotia?

   Louisiana

   • Why did the Cajuns settle in Louisiana? Where did they settle? Describe the geography and culture of "Cajun country."

- How did the early Cajuns support themselves? What occupations are still associated with Louisiana Cajuns?
- Trace the most important developments in the 20th century that influenced traditional Cajun culture (e.g. the recording industry, the discovery of oil in Louisiana, etc.).

Creoles

- Creole Culture
- New Orleans
- Who are the Creoles and how do they relate to a study of Cajuns?

Music

- Zydeco
- Juré
- Fais Do Do
- Swamp Pop
- Conjunto
- What are differences between old Cajun music (before 1930s) and more modern styles?
- What sparked the "Cajun Revival" in the 1960s?
- What are the various influences on Cajun music (African, Native American, French, Spanish, Caribbean, rock and roll, rhythm and blues, country western, pop, etc.)? Pick one and show how it influenced Cajun style.
- What instruments are typically associated with Cajun music? Pick one and trace its history in Cajun culture (accordion, guitar, steel guitar, banjo, fiddle, mandolin, etc.).
- What are common themes in old Cajun folk songs? Pick one theme and share a few examples of songs that reflect it. (e.g. prison songs, story ballads, songs about loneliness, death, etc.).
- What are some popular Cajun music groups? Pick one and research them and their style.
- Pick a piece from a recording and do an in-depth analysis of it: history, meaning, what influences it reveals of other musical styles, etc.

Culture

- Cajun food
- Legends and folklore
- Manners, customs, beliefs (e.g. the charivari)

Assessment

Student presentations could begin after a week or so of research and take the form of a daily "Cajun Minute" (a calendar is drawn up and each person assigned a day to make a short presentation) or even a class "CajunFest" where food, music, and sharing of research fills a whole rehearsal or several.

Assess students on the thoughtfulness and depth of preparation in their presentations. When all presentations are completed, have students write a short essay on these questions:

Has our in depth study of Cajun culture in any way changed the way you hear Ticheli's piece? If so, how?

What is the most important idea you have taken away from our study of Cajun culture? Why?

Encourage students to be as specific as possible in describing their experience and to use details from the presentations as examples in their essay.

Affective Outcome

Students will consider musical traditions and how they are preserved, changed, or lost.

Strategies

1. If they have not already heard it, play the Lomax recordings for students. Explain to them how the recordings were made. Ask them to discuss why they think this father and son team worked so hard to make these recordings of unknown people living in poverty in a place that most Americans didn't know or care much about. Share with them information about the Library of Congress Archive of Folk Song Project. "Why do you think this project came out of the

275

Depression?"

2. Ask students to ponder Ticheli's intentions in arranging these two songs for band. What might have motivated him to choose Cajun songs versus one of the many other kinds of folk music? Read students this paragraph from the composer's notes: *Cajun Folk Songs* is composed as a tribute to the people of the old Cajun folksong culture with hopes that their contributions will not be forgotten.

3. Ask students to name some examples of musical cultures that may have been lost completely. Guide them to see the connection between various facets of modernization and the loss of indigenous musical cultures: the urbanization of 20th-century American life and disappearance of rural cultures; the recording industry and its influence on home music-making and more passive music listening; the assimilation of people groups into mainstream society (Native Americans, first-generation immigrants, etc.) with the subsequent loss of individual cultural identities.

   Invite students to share stories of music they might remember from their childhood that their own children will never experience. Let the discussion go in whatever direction it will, helping students to understand the ways musical traditions disappear or are changed, and hopefully to feel some of the sense of loss themselves.

4. As an outside rehearsal project, have students interview and record someone sharing a musical tradition with which they themselves are not very familiar. This could be a grandparent, elderly relative or neighbor, an immigrant, or a student from another culture. The student's task is to interview the person and record them singing or playing a song from another place or especially another time. Besides making a recording, the student should ask as many questions of their subject as possible: How and when did you learn the song? What's it about? Why do you remember it? What does it/did it mean to you?

   The answers to these questions should be included as part of two-three page essay that students write, reflecting on their experience of preserving an older or foreign musical tradition. The essay should be turned in along with the recording. Ask willing students to share their experiences with the rest of the class and discuss them as a group.

Assessment

As part of their essay, ask students to reflect on the meaning of this project with regard to their own understanding of musical traditions. These projects can be evaluated by their thoughtfulness, and depth of musical understanding.

Music Selection

Cajun Folk Songs has already become something of a classic in band literature and with good reason. It provides opportunities for musical and technical challenges in both cantabile and rhythmic styles. Most importantly, it gives students a window into a musical culture which is most likely not familiar to them

Other Possible Outcomes

1. Pedal tone
2. Improvising in pentatonic
3. Suspension

TEACHING PLANS
BAND

Resources

Books

Lomax, John and Alan. *Our Singing Country*. New York: Macmillan, 1944.

    A collection of folksongs which includes the Lomax's transcriptions of "Belle" (p. 194) and "La Belle et la Capitaine" (p. 182, here titled "Blanche Comme la Neige"), based on their field recordings.

Compact Discs

Allen and John Lomax Classic Louisiana Recordings, *Cajun and Creole Music*. Rounder Records Corp., 1999.
http://www.rounder.com

    Contains "La Belle et la Capitaine" and other recordings by the Hoffpauir Family as well as a number of Cajun waltzes, blues, and two-steps with fiddles and accordions

Allen and John Lomax Classic Louisiana Recordings, *Cajun and Creole Music II*. Rounder Records Corp., 1999.
http://www.rounder.com

    Contains "Belle" and other ballads, laments, and drinking songs, plus examples of zydeco, juré, and the blues.

    Beausoleil is probably the most popular and well known Cajun music band today. Its leader, Michael Doucet, began borrowing from the Lomax recordings in the 1970s, and Beausoleil's version of "Belle" can be heard on Beausoleil: The Spirit of Cajun Music (Swallow 6031)

Other recordings by Beausoleil on Rhino Records:
Buausoleil, *L'Amour ou la Folie,* compact disc R272622

_____, *Cajun Conga,* compact disc 70525.

_____, *La Danse de la Vie,* compact disc 71221.

_____, *L' Écho* compact disc 71808.

_____, *Bayou Deluxe: The Best of Michael Doucet and Beausoleil*

Video

Alan Lomax's American Patchwork: Cajun Country: Don't Drop the Potato, PBS series "American Patchwork: Songs and Stories about America" $24.98 available at www.rounder.com/rounder/artists/lomax_alan/patchwrk.html, (Vestepol Video, 1990).

Websites

There are many websites dedicated to Cajun and Creole culture, music, and food.

http://www.cajunculture.com
The Encyclopedia of Cajun Culture: a gigantic alphabetized index.

http://CajunZydeco.net/
Many links, especially info on current Cajun and Zydeco groups

http://www.randols.com/cfbands.html
Randol's CajunFest
Links to Cajun and Zydeco bands, food, cultural trivia

Elementary/ Middle Level Choir

BASHANA HABA-A

Nurit Hirsh

Arranged by Velvel Pasternak

Edited by Henry Leck

Two-part treble

Posthorn Press (1990)

Background Information

"Bashana Haba-a" is a song composed by the prolific Israeli composer, Nurit Hirsh. It was first performed in 1969 and quite well known throughout North America and Israel, but it is the arrangement by Velvel Pasternak with editing by Henry Leck that has recently grown in popularity among children's choirs and their audiences.

Hirsh's compositions are considered to be "contemporary Israeli folk" style. She has written more than a thousand songs, including some specifically for children, in addition to some film scores. Her original version of "Bashana Haba-a" sounds like a fusion of Klezmer and modern popular music styles, but the Pasternak-Leck edition is much slower in tempo and emphasizes the simpler, melodic aspect of the song.

Songwriter and poet, Ehud Manor, penned the contemplative, hopeful lyrics. Here is one translation:

In the years to come, as I sit on my porch and count
the birds flying around, I will see children playing:
running between houses and in the fields.
You will see, you will see how good it will be in the year to come.

Another translation of the Hebrew text begins, "If I live another year..." Both translations allude to a simple and carefree peace that will come in the next year. The melody and text seem to combine a somber thoughtfulness with an optimistic hopefulness.

281

Elements of Music

Form

   The form is a very simply a verse (mm. 9-24) that leads to a refrain (mm. 25-32) that is repeated. There are four eight-measure phrases in the song, in addition to the eight-measure piano introduction. The first two phrases are in the verse section and have parallel beginnings, but differ after the first two measures, as the melody takes wing and soars upward in preparation for the emotional climax in the refrain. The eight measures of the refrain repeat exactly, with only a slight change for the second ending.

Rhythm

   In the vocal melodic line (part one), a pulsing rhythmic motif is used throughout the verse and is even more emphatic in the refrain. This vocal line is supported rhythmically by the piano accompaniment. The vocal harmony line (part two) provides a rhythmic contrast to the melodic line. The complementary rhythm juxtaposed with the more dominant in the melody creates a rhythmic "echo" effect, a strong pulsing of continuous eighth notes that gives the piece tremendous forward momentum.

Melody

   The verse and refrain, while both in minor keys, are distinguished by contrasting melodic shapes.

   The ascending minor sixth, followed by the descending minor third is the prominent feature of the melody of the verse and its large upward leap is not only emotionally charged but a unique pleasure to sing, especially for young voices. Other interval leaps of fourths and thirds are simple in their melodic context and give the feel of carefree movement.

   The refrain is entirely stepwise in its melodic shape and has a more driving feel. It is the second vocal line, however, that contains some interesting melodic challenges. It begins as a simple countermelody that contrasts the leaps of the melody with an intense, ascending stepwise line. Its pulsing ""Ba-sha-na ha-ba-a" rhythm pushes the phrase steadily forward and works rhythmically against a dotted rhythm in m. 11, creating a moment of rhythmic interest.

It is also the second vocal line that features the only chromatic pitch in the piece, the A-natural in m. 24 that creates a secondary dominant on F, propelling the piece to a iv chord (B-flat minor) and providing another momentary tension. (There are many other written accidentals, but they are all diatonic pitches in F-harmonic minor.) Finally, the second vocal line also contains the only augmented second in the piece, mm. 29-30 (a diatonic *fa, si, la* in F-harmonic minor)—a challenge to sing in tune, but a characteristic interval of this type of Israeli song.

Harmony

Harmonies change in each measure and are outlined in the piano accompaniment. The piece never strays from its F-harmonic minor tonality, and includes only one secondary dominant (in m. 24) that functions more as a coloristic effect rather than providing any real modulation. While the melody includes much repetition, the harmony continues to change, often giving the familiar intervals a new color.

Timbre and Texture

The polyphonic texture of the two voices in the verse, with contrasting rhythmic and melodic ideas, changes to homophonic movement in the refrain, with more range given to the chordal piano accompaniment. The move from dissimilar rhythmic patterns, to a unified, homophonic texture adds a strength and persuasiveness to the refrain. The key of the piece (F minor) means that the first note sung is middle C—the generally low *tessitura* of the opening creates a dark color, which is attractive in young voices. The piano part is simple enough to be played by a student pianist, but could be easily improvised in a more florid, flowing style by an accomplished older player.

Expression

The score is entirely free of any dynamic suggestions in both the vocal and pianos parts. The rise and fall of the melodic line and the changing harmonic structures give the best indications to the singers and the pianist of how to dynamically shape the phrases. With the harmonic, rhythmic, textural and melodic changes that lead to the refrain, measures 24-25, would arguably be the most dynamically extreme and the musical climax of the song.

The Heart

The combination of text and melody join to elevate the simple and ordinary into a beautiful and peaceful future ideal. Within a minor mode and with the use of short, one measure repeated melodic and rhythmic motifs, "Bashana Haba-a" has an unexpectedly powerful and optimistically hopeful melody.

Introducing the Piece

Play the melody of "Bashana Haba-a" for the students without passing out the music. (Use a suitable solo instrument, such as the flute, violin, oboe or a cappella voice on a neutral vowel.) Ask the students to give descriptions of the melody and encourage those words that depart from the obvious choices (sad, slow, etc.). Have students listen to the melody again and ask the them to consider some of the unanswered questions that may have been raised from their first listening. What is the mode? What makes the melody seem pleasant, uplifting, melancholy, dark, hopeful, or relaxed? Does the emotion remain constant, or does it change or intensify in the melody? If so, where?

Tell students that the composer of the melody, Nurit Hirsh, is also a renowned film score composer. Have the students pretend that this melody was written for a movie and let them describe the scene and story that might be underscored by this melody. Discuss the visual scenes and have the students discover what emotions are behind the actions, story, colors, and visual impressions of their scene. Let them discover that the minor melody can speak about much more than simply sadness.

Read a translation of the text, "Bashana Haba-a." Ask the students to identify which part of the poem is the most affirming and positive. Have them theorize about where in the melody this text will be set and then pass out the music.

Skill Outcomes

- Students will sustain a sense of line throughout an eight-measure phrase.
- Students will demonstrate musical independence needed to sing in two parts with different rhythmic patterns.

Strategies

Sustaining the Musical Line

1. While playing the piano accompaniment, have students mentally sing the melody and audibly sustain an unvoiced consonant ("s" works best) throughout the phrase. Have one or two students stand in front and listen and ask them to sit if the consonant gets softer, or seems to lose intensity. After about two attempts, students will intentionally begin to *crescendo* in places where they anticipate the student might sit (after two or four measures). Have them sing using the same vocal energy in the identified "dead spots."

2. Divide the choir into two groups and have one sing while the other sustains "s." Discuss with students how much breath it takes to sustain the phrase and where they will need to use the most breath, or a little extra "tug" of breath energy to move the phrase along.

3. As a warm up, practice singing up and down the solfège scale with different scale degrees chosen as musical climax spots. Have the students experiment with various ways to approach and move away from a phrase climax.

4. Let the students in a smaller choir (or in smaller groups in a large choir) move using their arms and/or body (when space allows) through the two phrases of the verse. Encourage them to continue physically moving and avoid static positions until the phrase ends. Have some groups sing, while other groups move and then switch.

When students have a sense of the energy it takes to keep moving throughout the entire line, have them stand in one place, and draw a long, slow arc with their arm in front and across their body to show the shape of each phrase in the verse. Encourage them to use the full range of

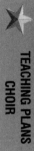

TEACHING PLANS CHOIR

motion in front of them and to never stop the movement. This means they will have to keep the movement slow but constant—a tremendous feat!

Building Melodic and Rhythmic Independence

1. As a warm-up, have the students echo four-beat rhythm patterns that you model with body sounds (hands, feet, whatever). When they have achieved accurate imitation, turn the activity into a canon, where you lead four beats ahead and they repeat whatever vocal or body rhythm you have given while you are performing the next pattern. As they become more proficient, add to the complexity of the activity by putting adding vocal patterns (nonsense sounds) with slightly more advanced rhythms in the canon. Some days, make the canon relatively short (four measures) and have the students notate the rhythms they have performed.

    Use small bits of the text of "Bashana" as part of the canon. Start with a measure of the part one text followed by a measure of the part two text so the students get comfortable hearing the contrasting rhythms layered on top of one another. An added challenge for the very strong musicians is to allow them a chance at being the leader. It is harder than it looks. Most students will find it hard to improvise a rhythm on the spot while watching a classroom of people doing something else!

2. Attach a certain kinesthetic movement to eight notes and another movement to quarter notes. Let students choose these (snaps for eighths, claps on quarters, etc.). Have all of the students sing the second part with these movements. When they are confident, have them sing Part I while still performing the Part II movements, letting them see visually and experience kinesthetically the difference between the parts and how they work together. If students have trouble performing both parts, let them perform only their own part, but with movement, so each part can see how the other one works. If you continue through the entire verse, simply use an elongated motion for the dotted notes in the melody.

Assessment

1. As the score is free of dynamic, tempo or style markings, give the students permission to "edit" a clean copy of the music, with dynamic markings, long phrase markings (slurs or ties), arrows that show direction to "goal" notes, lines under stressed syllables, breath marks, etc. They can describe verbally or in writing the justification for their added markings and explain how their musical decisions help to sustain musical interest throughout the eight measure phrases.

2. Have students compose and notate short melodic or rhythmic patterns of two to four measures in 2/4 meter. With a partner, have them learn both parts and perform their piece for the class, demonstrating their ability to read and perform two or three of these rhythms simultaneously. Good examples could be written on the board for the entire choir to sight-read for warm-ups.

3. Give several rhythms aurally or visually and have students identify which one corresponds to a given section of "Bashana Haba-a," or a piece similar in rhythmic difficulty.

Cognitive Outcome

Students will identify what makes a musical phrase and what determines its length.

Strategies

1. Learn the piece on solfège (beginning *mi-do-la*) and have the students identify repetitions in the music and similarities and differences between the two phrases in the verse. Here is one way to do this: Divide the class into 16 groups of two to five students each (depending on the size of the choir). Give each group a note card numbered 1-16, each with two beats of notated music from the verse. Have them figure out the solfège for their two beats and practice singing it. When they are comfortable performing their one-three notes, have the group line up in order and sing the entire verse on solfège, in "relay style."

   Have the students figure out how many groups need to be put together in order to make a complete musical phrase. Help them discover how long "feels right" by putting together groups one and two; then one, two and three; next one through four, and so on, until they feel like they have assembled a complete phrase. Let them struggle to make a decision without giving them the "correct" answer.

2. Continue the above activity by having the entire choir sing the melody, each student on a different neutral vowel of their choice. (e.g. "loo") Ask them to switch vowels whenever they think they are beginning a new musical thought or phrase (e.g. "lee"). Some may switch every two beats, some every four, and others will go for four or eight measures. Repeat the process a few times until there are two clear groups (encourage them listen and change if they want, but to stand by what they really think). Have each group present the melody using their phrasing ideas and discuss the merits of the eight-measure phrases versus the four-measure phrases. Direct them to look for music indications (such as the chord structure, parallel phrase structure) that point to the eight-measure phrase structure. When students are in agreement about the eight-measure phrase length, they are ready to begin working on shaping the phrase (see "Skill Outcome" above).

Assessment

Repeat the same strategies with the next section of "Bashana Haba-a." The students should be able to analyze the phrase length of the refrain section and transfer this knowledge to other works, similar in scope to "Bashana Haba-a."

Affective Outcome

Students will discover the power of a minor melody to evoke hopeful and positive emotions and analyze the compositional devices that contribute to the affect of this and other works.

Strategies

After the initial introduction, students have decided that the message of this melody and text is essentially hopeful and positive. (This is an affective outcome in itself.) The following strategies will lead students to a greater appreciation for the wide range of feelings and various depths of emotions that music, specifically pieces in minor keys, can portray. In addition, asking the question "why" will encourage them to take a deeper look into intervals, melodic shapes, the interplay between rhythm and melody, placement of texts and countless other compositional ideas. Striving to explain and understand what they find truly beautiful, as well as analyzing melodies that perhaps evoke less of an emotional response, will help students become more aware of, and articulate about, their own affective response.

1. Have students collect minor melodies from popular music, folk songs, past repertoire or wherever they can find them. In a journal, have each student describe their two or three melodies and reflect on the differences. Encourage them to use a wide variety of descriptions, including colors and metaphors. Let them reflect on which, if any, of the melodies makes the strongest emotional statement and ask to explain why. Choose a few contrasting minor melodies to analyze as a class. After collecting first impressions and vivid descriptions, take a closer look at the melody shape, harmonic structures (if applicable), whether there are mostly small or large interval movements, the rhythm, meter, text (if applicable) and other notable features of the melody. Have the students form some hypothesis on how these factors contribute to the emotional content.

2. A story can change dramatically when the ending is changed. Elation can change to tragedy and hope to despair. Let the students alter the emotional impact of "Bashana Haba-a" by composing new ending to the phrases. Given the first four measures (8-12), have them compose a new last four measures (13-16) that they feel significantly changes the musical meaning or mood of that phrase. Have them write or explain what they did that gave the melody a new meaning. It will be helpful to set up some parameters, (e.g. size of interval leaps, rhythms, etc.) depending on how experienced the students are at composing. For example, tell students they can change pitches, but the rhythm must stay the same, or even give them certain pitches, which they must use.

3. Have students find a place in the room where they have a little space around them. (This can also be done on choral risers.) As you speak a word, ask the students to freeze in a body position that describes that emotion. Use words like despair, joy, hope, displeasure, hatred, sadness, relief, excitement, etc. Guide students to see that the more positive emotions generally evoked body postures that were higher and taller than the negative ones.

    Analyze the melody and counter melody in "Bashana Haba-a" and find the many ways that the melody has a "lifted" feel. Compare the number of ascending skips in the verse with the number of descending skips. Find the direction of the largest intervallic skips in the music. What direction does the melody move at the musical climax of the piece? What is the predominant motion in the left hand of the piano part?

4. Using students from within the choir that have instrumental skills (or bringing in students from band or orchestra), have the choir "orchestrate" the piece using instruments that provide the timbres that they feel best suit it. Encourage them to add or subtract instruments to change the timbre. If sequencing software is available and there are students with computer and keyboard skills, let them create their own orchestrated versions of the piece. Have students reflect on how various orchestrations and tempos changed the mood of the piece.

Assessment

In their journals, or as part of a take home written project, ask students to compare and contrast "Bashana Haba-a" and another selection in a minor mode from their repertoire. Have them describe the mood of each piece and use musical terms to give examples of devices in the compositions that contribute to their overall emotional impact. Have them be specific in their descriptions of rhythm, melody, texture, timbre, and form, and encourage them to articulate as clearly as they can the differences and similarities between the two selections.

Resources

Recordings

25th Anniversary Celebration: The Glen Ellyn Children's Chorus 1965-1990.
Sandra Prodan, Music Director; Doreen Rao, Music Director Emerita.
Compact Disc available from:
Glen Ellyn Children's Chorus
799 Roosevelt Rd., Building 6, Suite 100, Glen Ellyn, IL 60137
630/858-2471, fax: 630/858-2476, email: geccsing@earthlink.net
> A wonderful sampling of a wide variety of music for children's choir,
> including *Bashana Haba-a.*

Community Through Song: The Ithaca Children's Choir. Janet Galván,
Conductor. Ithaca, NY.
> Compact Disc with 24 selections for children's choir, including *Bashana Haba-a.*

Web sites

www.hebrewsongs.com
This site gives lists of other songs with words by poet, Ehud Manor,
including seven other collaborations with Nurit Hirsh.

www.nurit-hirsh.com
This gives Hebrew and English video information on Nurit Hirsh. It includes many
photos, a biography and recordings of many of her songs (including one of "Bashana
Haba-a" that is very different from the standard children's choir recordings).

www.rideaumusic.com
This is a site where *Best of Israeli Folk Songs* can be found. It is the largest
collection of Israeli folk music and is arranged by Velvel Pasternak. It is over
165 songs with full Hebrew texts and translations into English.

www.musicbooksplus.com
Velvel Pasternak wrote "Beyond Hava Nagila," which can be ordered from this
site. It is a 170-page book with examples in a 70-minute CD that includes background stories and annotations to many songs and music projects.

NISKA BANJA

Arranged by Nick Page

SSAA or SAAB with Piano three and four hands

Boosey & Hawkes OCTB6517

Background Information

Nick Page describes the origins of *Niska Banja*:

> I first heard "Niska Banja" on a recording by Theodore Bikel and the Pennywhistlers on Electra Records from the late 60s (I think). The translation on the record was "How splendid are the hot springs of Nis! And how fine its ladies! Once and twice, and twice again, many times I kiss you." In 1986 I went to Yugoslavia. In a bar in Belgrade, I heard a Romani group performing. I requested *Niska Banja* and they all burst out laughing because I knew all the words but didn't know all the hidden meanings. I sang it on stage with them, which was great fun. The language is neither Serbian nor Croatian (nor Serbo/Croatian). It is the Romani dialect of that region. The Romani people are the wandering Gypsies who have spread their vibrant culture throughout Europe and the Americas. The roots of the Romani culture are in India and Pakistan. Much of their singing and dancing have roots in Qawwali singing (pronounced Kvah-lee) and Hindu dance. Over hundreds of years these Gypsies spread through Eastern Europe with pockets of them all over. You hear the Gypsy music now with groups like the Gypsy Kings, but you also see their influence with flamenco dancing.
>
> "Niska Banja is a dance." The rhythm, though unusual to Western ears, is very normal in Eastern Europe, where 2+2+2+3 or 3+2+2 meters prevail in much of the music, both fast and slow. Mary Goetze, at Indiana University, did some research on the song. She said that it referred to the local women of Nis, a coastal city in Serbia, as being quite beautiful. The women would go up into the hills to bathe in the hot springs. There they would be joined by men and they would kiss. Sometimes these men were not their husbands. You may want to edit this translation when doing the song with young people. Think of the

song as a spirited song of romance—a dance. In fact, Mary Goetze, who believes in complete authenticity, has her students dance when they sing this. When I arranged the piece, my only attempt for authenticity was in the vocal parts, which are as I sang them on stage in Belgrade. The piano part was inspired by the jazz guitar styles of Pat Metheny.

Practical Concerns

- Though the voicing is listed as either SSAA or SAAB, the piece also works well with mixed voices on all parts—which allows for voice placement in a comfortable tessitura for all singers in any choir.

- General translation information is explained above in the Nick Page notes. A Serbian reader was able to give some specific line translations, but could not translate the "Gypsy" lines. The information below along with the translation given above and the Mary Goetze research provide sufficient insight.

Verse I:
Niska Banja topla voda | Zanis lije | ziva zjoda (or zgoda)
in Nis the spa warm water | for the people of Nis | a very good thing

Refrain:
Emka ravla, emkame ravla | ando nisi name kavla | (Gyspy, not translated)

Verse II:
Nislike su fine dame | Neseta ju nikad same
the ladies of Nis are fine ladies | never go for a walk by themselves

Verse III:
Jek duj de suj duj | cumi davte caje ando muj | (Gyspy, not translated)

- The "PG-13" translation given in the octavo is: Let's go to the baths of Nis where we shall kiss, kiss, kiss.
- Do not underestimate the use of the text here to stimulate student enthusiasm for the piece. It is important to not ignore the translation.

- A clear pronunciation guide is given in the octavo. Please note this correction supplied by Nick Page: At m. 25, the second verse is pronounced, "Choo-me dav-tey Cha-yey."
- The top piano can be played by a student pianist with a strong rhythmic sense.
- Introduce the accompaniment into rehearsal as soon as possible. The piano is helpful with pushing the rhythm along and helps students to feel the underlying eighth note pulse.
- Because this is a dance piece, it needs continual rhythmic excitement. Try adding a clapping part during the long piano interludes and final postlude.
- Let students shout and "yip" and "hey" to create the feeling of a wild party at the Baths of Nis! A final "hey" on the last note will not only bring the house down-it will ensure a clean cut-off.

Elements of Music

Form

The song is the typical verse-refrain form of many folk songs. There is a piano introduction prior to the first verse section at m. 7 and there is a piano interlude before the second and third verse section at m. 23. Each verse section is repeated and immediately followed by the exuberant repeated refrain. The verse sections can be sung by a duet or a small group with the full chorus exploding on the refrain. The piece ends with a short coda in a sudden largo tempo marking. This coda features a notated "cadenza" with an ornamented, improvisatory feeling which stops dead the piece's huge build up of momentum. The piece ends in a flourish: an a tempo final sung chord and the exciting, pulsing rhythm returning in the piano.

TEACHING PLANS CHOIR

Rhythm

The driving 9/8 meter with 2+2+2+3 rhythms is quite easy to pick up, infectious and continuous. This division of meter is a common dance meter in Eastern Europe. The eighth-note pulse never stops in the piano, except for the single a cappella measure (32) for the feeling of free ornamentation just before the ending.

Melody

The melody (top line) has a very narrow range. After the initial leap up to the tonic, the melodic motifs are built of seconds and thirds, all within the limited compass of a fourth. There are many repeated notes and much "back and forth" direction in the tune. Notated ornament figures and suggestions in the score for ascending *glissando* "yelps" give the piece an authentic folk feeling, as if the piece were being improvised.

Harmony

The piece is set in F major with brief relative minor section (D minor) in the accompaniment. The melody is harmonized with a third above in both the verse and refrain sections. Drone harmonies are utilized in the inner voice parts. Drone harmonies are also used in the piano accompaniment in various places (i.e. refrain; second and third verse section, m. 23-30), but set in an *ostinato* rhythm.

Timbre

The singing tone quality should be bright and frontal in production. It is typically a strong, hard voice style. Recordings of Eastern European folk music can provide a model. The piano accompaniment is a bright, driving force in the enthusiastic sound. The program notes in the octavo list the accordion, bouzoukee, mandolin, and tambourine as likely traditional instruments that would have been used to accompany this dance.

Texture

The vocal texture is strictly homophonic; it is thin and clear in the two part sections—primarily using harmonized thirds. Texture becomes thicker in the four-part refrain when the inner voices provide drone harmonies. Duet options create texture contrast at m.23. The timbre of the piano provides other varieties of texture, but most often contributes to the piece's high, bright, thin quality.

Expression

The dynamics match the boisterous rhythms of the piece and only vary from *forte* and *fortissimo* in the ensemble to *mezzo forte* in the solo sections. A sense of driving, robust strength is inherent in the music. There are suggestions for adding glissando "yelps" in the opening section which add to its wild and free feeling.

The Heart

The heart of the piece is the exuberant and infectious dance feeling created by its driving 2+2+2+3 rhythm.

Introducing the Piece

1. Play a recording of "Niska Banja" and invite students to tap along quietly, trying to feel the pulse. Most will probably try to tap quarter-notes. Silently model eighth note tapping until students are following. Ask students to figure out how many taps are in a group (nine) If they are having trouble, count aloud "1-2-1-2-1-2-1-2-3" and have them join you.

2. When the recording is finished, ask students if they have any guesses about where in the world this song might come from. The hard voice style and the unusual meter might be clues. Explain to them the piece's origins, but don't translate the text (leave that a mystery). Underscore the fact that this meter, which feels strange and exciting to us, is actually quite common in Eastern European music and would not be difficult or strange at all there.

Skill Outcome

Students will perform 9/8 meter with the subdivisions of 2+2+2+3.

Strategies:

1. Count and Conduct

    Teach students to conduct a four pattern, counting eighth notes in 4/4. (e.g. "1-2-1-2-1-2-1-2"). After they have practiced it sufficiently, model the 9/8 counting (1-2-1-2-1-2-1-2-3). Have students conduct this meter, with the fourth beat getting a bit more time on the upward "swoop" to accommodate the extra beat. If possible, do this strategy with piano playing the accompaniment to "Niska Banja."

2. Vocalize

    Ask students to find words that reflect the syllabic pattern. Example: "Sun-day Sun-day Sun-day Sa-tur-day." After feeling and speaking several student examples, incorporate the actual text of "Niska Banja." Introducing the accompaniment patterns right away will assist in the subdivision feel.

3. Move

    Have students step the rhythm as suggested in the instructions, lifting their heels off the floor on each beat, or stepping side to side in place with a lift on each beat. Either way, the fourth beat will need a little extra time and a larger gesture. Return to this "dance" often throughout the rehearsal process, even as students are learning their pitches.

Assessment

Each time the choir counts, conducts, vocalizes, moves, or sings "Niska Banja," the director can assess the accuracy of the subdivision and the exuberant feel of the dance meter. Students should also be asked to assess the character and accuracy during the rehearsals by having half the group sing and the other half tap and listen for accuracy. Record the choir and have students tap silently to monitor the rhythmic accuracy for places where the choir rushes (not common) or drags (quite common).

Cognitive Outcome

The student will identify and recognize thirds as a common harmonic device.

Strategies:

1. Discover

    Begin with this warm-up:

    do   mi   re   fa   mi   sol   fa   re   do

    and then switch to this one:

    do   re   mi   fa   sol   fa   mi   re   do

    Ask students to describe the difference. Focus on the aspect of steps versus leaps. Ask if anyone knows the name of the interval in the second warm-up (thirds). On the board, show what thirds look like notated (a line to a line, or a space to a space). Have students practice writing thirds.

2. Write a Warm-up

    Use thirds in many ways for warm-ups. Ask students to explain the difference between melodic (consecutive) thirds and harmonic thirds (sounding together). Devise warm-ups that use harmonic thirds. For example:

    a) One section begins on *do.* When the singers reach *mi,* the next group joins on *do,* and all sing the ascending and descending scale in thirds.

    b) Using solfége or numbers, you sing a pitch anywhere in the scale and the choir finds the note a third above. As students gain familiarity, have the first note sung by a student and the third above it sung by the group.

c) Have students create their own warm-ups using thirds. They should notate them on staff paper, and then teach them to the choir, either by rote or by putting their notated versions on the board. Have a different student teach a "Third Warm-up" each day.

3. Improvise Thirds

Have students think of other songs that can easily be harmonized in thirds. Improvise harmonizations with their suggestions. ("Michael Row the Boat Ashore" works very easily, if they are not coming up with examples. Key of C major: everyone sings the first two notes together. The altos stay on *mi* and continue a third below the sopranos for the remainder of the song. Join the sopranos on the last note.)

4. Stair Step Sport

If you have access to steps, you can place several "melody" students on a step and place the "harmony part" students a "third" away. Have them "perform" measures eight, nine and ten by jumping steps.

5. At some point in the learning, ask students if they can guess which interval, of all the possible intervals in the scale, is most common in our Western music (thirds). Ask them why they think this is so (perhaps the sweetness of the sound to our ears).

Assessment

Have the students write a simple four-bar melody and harmonize the tune with thirds. When the compositions are played, decide which melodies lend themselves the best to third harmonizations. Some examples will sound better with fourths, fifths, or sixths. Experiment. Assess student comprehension via the composition. Students can locate other examples of thirds, both melodic and harmonic in other repertoire. Challenge them to always be on the lookout and to feel free to point out examples in future rehearsals.

Affective Outcome

Students will explore their ideas about the relationship between dance, music, and romance.

Strategies:

1. Shall We Dance?

   Over the quarter or semester, bring dance into the classroom. Ideally, bring in an ethnic dance specialist who can teach group dances to the entire class from different traditions (this could be a special whole day workshop.) On another day ask a faculty member who ballroom dances with her spouse to come in and share their expertise and demonstrate for the class. Short video clips of dances could also be shared to broaden the styles and ethnic diversity. Help students to discover the connection between the movement styles and musical styles. There may be some trained dancers in the choir who would be willing to share their expertise, e.g. Irish dancers, ballet dancers, hip hop dancers, swing dancers, etc.

2. Isn't It Romantic?

   Ask students to journal their thoughts on some of the following:

   • Describe or name romantic dances that come immediately come to mind. What kind of music is used? Encourage students to think beyond the latest popular dance or dirty dancing. Hopefully you will get answers like: tango, waltz, pas de deux (ballet), flamenco, etc.

   • Can you think of any fast dance music that is romantic?

   • Do you think that any group dances (i.e. line dances, square dances, folk dances, Renaissance dances) can be romantic or even alluring? How?

   • If you could wonderfully dance in any style, what would your ideal romantic dance be?

   Ask willing students to share some of their thoughts on the above with the class. It is important that this activity not be merely discussion and thought, but as much kinesthetic activity as possible, so students begin to feel the connection between movement and musical expression.

TEACHING PLANS
CHOIR

Assessment

After this unit of study, ask students to journal on how their experiences with different dances as well as their reflections on the connection of music, dance, and romance affected their understanding and performance of "Niska Banja."

Music Selection

In the past decade, "Niska Banja" has become a "standard" in children's choirs, middle school choirs, and high school choirs. Its voicing versatility and its infectious dance rhythm makes for an exciting addition to nearly any program—but especially for concert programs that feature music from many different lands.

High School Choir

HARK I HEAR THE HARPS ETERNAL

Traditional Hymn Tune

Arranged by Alice Parker.

Lawson-Gould Music Publishers, Inc. (1967)

Practical Concerns

- "Hark I Hear the Harps Eternal" is arranged by Alice Parker for a cappella SATB choir with *divisi*. It is appropriate for average and above average high school choirs with a good number of singers.

- The melody crossings at mm. 28 and 44-45 can be taken out for choirs where the baritones/altos are not comfortable taking over the melody part-way through in such a high *tessitura*. Or, one can divide the sections in half and have some stay on the melody throughout. Either option allows for a more consistent sound and for the comfort of young baritones and altos.

- In choirs where the men have trouble singing *divisi* and the women can sing *divisi* easily, the alto two section can sing the baritone part (the range is fine!) on the refrains throughout and at m. 54, beat three-jump up to the tenor line while the tenor sings the melody. Adjustments in the *divisi* can be made to fit many different choirs!

- "Hark I Hear the Harps Eternal" in the Alice Parker arrangement is recorded by Robert Shaw and the Robert Shaw Festival Singers of The Ohio State University on the CD *Amazing Grace: American Hymns and Spirituals* (Telarc CD-80325).

Background

"Hark I Hear the Harps Eternal" is from the American singing school tradition of the 19th century. The tune and text can be found in the William Hauser *Olive Leaf,* a shape-note hymnal, with a tune titled "Invitation" (new) #247. The same tune, with a different hymn text, can be found in William Walker's *Southern Harmony*, #303 titled "Invitation" (new), and B.F. White's *Sacred Harp* 3rd ed., #335 titled "Return Again."

Arranger Alice Parker has written about American congregational singing and shape-note hymnals: "They praise the Holy Trinity in language, which is often truly poetic. The strong and beautiful tunes, some of them centuries old, have a quality of inevitability about them that is the mark of great music."

Popular throughout the South and the frontier states since early in the 19th century, shape-note hymnbooks encourage congregational reading of even unfamiliar hymns by using notes with heads of different elementary shapes—triangles, squares, circles, diamonds—corresponding to the various degrees of the scales. The key-note *"do"* is always one shape, regardless of key; *"re"* is another shape, *"mi"*another, and so forth. "Singings," or gatherings to sing beloved old hymns from these books in the traditional hearty, full-throated style, continue to this day in many Southern communities. They are often called Sacred Harp singings after the best-known of the shape-note hymnbooks, *The Sacred Harp,* first published in 1844.
–Nick Jones

A student of Robert Shaw, Alice Parker became his conducting assistant for the Robert Shaw Chorale. Many well-known arrangements of traditional American religious music, notably African American Spirituals and traditional hymns from congregational traditions bear dual authorship: Robert Shaw and Alice Parker. Nick Jones notes: "In the years since the Chorale disbanded, she has continued to research and disseminate American hymns and religious songs, making of herself an invaluable resource for scholars, congregations, and choruses alike."

Elements of Music
Form

The hymn is set in a typical strophic Verse/Refrain form: VR VR VRR. There are two interesting aspects of the setting of the form in this arrangement. In verse three (mm. 32-40), the refrain melody appears as a solo descant above the verse—perhaps signifying the singing souls/saints that have passed before. The repetition of the final refrain is also of interest—a final, vigorous expression of conviction.

Rhythm

The rhythm is strong throughout – symbolizing the strength of conviction of a faithful people. The meter is 3/2 and the verses and refrains are dominated by a constant "quarter, quarter, half, half" feel that is ornamented with dotted quarter followed by an eighth and eighth followed by dotted quarter patterns. Cadences of the verse and the final cadence of the refrain conclude with identical phrase endings—rhythmically and melodically. The constant repetition of the double quarter-note upbeat figure throughout the piece creates a vital, vigorous mood that reflects the constancy and assurance of faith.

Melody

The melody is pentatonic, typical of many traditional American hymn tunes, and is placed in F major in this arrangement. The verse melody hovers around do with a range of sol above and la below. The powerful refrain melody includes more skips and rises to high do several times with a primary range between *mi* and high *do*. The final segment of the verse and the refrain melody are identical. The repetition of this identical ending contributes to its musical unity and also to the message of strength and constant faithfulness expressed in the hymn.

Harmony

Alice Parker has chosen to set the entire tune in strict pentatonic harmonic treatment – there are no *fa* or *ti* pitches—therefore there are no IV or V chords with their accompanying harmonic colors. The harmony is dominated by I, vi, I (6-4) and V-type chords that are colored with the 9th, and 11th tones and no third (of course). Perhaps Parker chose to use strict pentatonic harmony to honor the hymn singing tradition or to provide an "older" sounding harmonic color. The steady, unwavering harmonic structure of the arrangement adds to the strength and stability of its expressive power.

Texture

The texture is thinner on the verses than on the refrains, putting emphasis on the text of the verses, which naturally changes from verse to verse. The texture of each refrain is varied by using the melody in a different manner. For the first refrain, soprano and tenor sing in unison; for the second refrain, soprano and tenor sing the melody in canon a beat apart; for the third refrain, the tenor begins the canon and the soprano enters a measure later; and on the final refrain, the soprano and tenor are back in unison (with some variation) for a powerful ending. The accompaniment voices vary rhythmically on each refrain, gradually gaining rhythmic complexity and contributing to a growing thickness of texture. This expansion of texture suggests "nearing those swollen waters" or coming closer to the "mansions of the blest" where the heavenly singing is happening.

Timbre

The timbre should be robust and strong throughout; use of "hard voice" singing would be appropriate to its style and tradition.

Expression

There is variation of dynamics as well as texture from verse to refrain. There is always a stronger dynamic on the refrain as one hears the "hallelujahs" of the "farther shore." Overall, the dynamic of each refrain, and therefore the entire piece continue to grow to a *fortissimo* exuberant final refrain. Additionally, there is also the variation of the *poco marcato* and the *poco leggiero* in the second verse that relates directly to the text—the marcato deals with "my soul, stained, sorrow, passing over those waters"; the *legato* deals with the "light of day, and the city far away." In other words, contrast in the textual references is highlighted by articulation styles: sorrow versus light; death versus heaven.

Heart

The heart is the robust expression of the confidence in heaven, through the strong pentatonic melody and the constant vigorous rhythm, especially the repetitive upbeat figure.

Parker creates contrast in this arrangement by varying the treatment of each verse and refrain as indicated above. Contrast is furthered by use of softer dynamics and thinner texture in the verses and fuller dynamics and thicker texture in the refrains.

Unity is created by the strict use of pentatonic harmonization and the traditional Verse/Refrain form.

Introducing the Piece

- Have students learn the opening four measures on solfège syllables—first the melody and then harmony. Immediately involve students with the strength of the rhythm with gesture, stepping, etc, especially the "quarter, quarter, half, half" pattern.
- Ask the students to identify which syllables of the major scale were not used (*fa, ti*). Have students scan entire piece looking for any *fa* or *ti*. Introduce term/concept: pentatonic (penta-five; tonic-sound/tone).
- Have students listen to a recording of the arrangement. Ask them to describe their first impression of the overall effect and mood of the piece, as well as the unique sound of an entirely pentatonic piece. Have them write in their journal first, then have several share their thoughts with the class.

Knowledge Outcome

Students will identify pentatonic melodic and harmonic treatment and compose pentatonic melodies.

Strategies

1. Have students practice singing the pentatonic scale. (Point to syllable names placed on the board in ascending order. Use the key of F major. Include the *la* and *sol* below *do*. Use *la* and *sol* with an arrow down, to differential from the higher *sol* and *la*.) Still pointing to the syllables, begin to mix up them up.
2. After a few days, when students are confident and can sing the pentatonic syllables easily and in tune, ask them to create a pentatonic melody. Ask students to write 16 pentatonic syllables that sound good

to them on a piece of paper. They should start and end on *do.* Encourage them to test them out by singing them as they write them. After all are done, have the entire class sing their melody together in free rhythm and tempo a few times (blissful cacophony), each time allowing them to make minor adjustments. Students can be encouraged to make changes if they find that some of their notes are hard to find (usually because of too large a skip). Some confident soloists may like to share their melody with the class.

3. On the next day, ask students to transfer their solfège syllable pentatonic melody into notation in the key of F major, 4/4 time, using quarter notes. Again, ask them to sing their melodies all together as a student puts her example on the board. Sing the student example and analyze a bit for shape/direction and ease of singing. Continue this process putting other examples on the board and singing the tunes— all learn from the analysis and enjoy hearing "their" composition.

4. Have students transfer their 4/4 quarter-note tunes into 3/2 time (like "Hark I Hear") using various rhythms. They can choose from quarter notes, half notes, dotted half notes, whole notes, and dotted whole notes. If they are feeling very adventurous, they can use the eighth followed by dotted quarter as used in "Hark I Hear." (Note: most will feel adventurous if you phrase it that way.) Encourage students to use a good share of the longer notes—reminding them that the half note is the basic beat. Encourage students to sing as they compose.

5. At the beginning of class each day, have a student put up his or her melody on the board. It becomes the class sight-reading exercise for the day. Affirmation, recognition, and analysis allow all to enjoy and learn.

Improvisation Strategy:

"Black Key Ostinato." Using several keyboard instruments or just the classroom piano, have students create patterns using only the black keys. One student can set up an *ostinato* in the lower portion of the keyboard while another improvises melodic treatment in the middle register and possibly even a third in the high register. Have all students participate over several weeks.

The rest of the singers can improvise additional long-tone harmony with solfège that fits with the *ostinato*, but even without this participation they will be eager listeners to their classmates' improvisations at the piano.

Knowledge Assessment

The pentatonic melodies can be assessed at each stage by rehearsal observation to see:

- If students have facile use of the solfège syllables and understand which syllables are not used in this form of the pentatonic scale.
- If students can transfer solfège to pitch notation in simple quarter notes.
- If students can manipulate and create rhythm in a less familiar time signature.
- If students grasp the sense of direction and "singability" that make a good melody.

All this can be done through the composition process—individually and as the group performs and discusses student compositions.

Skill Outcome

Students will sing with accuracy in a robust and confident non-*legato* singing style.

Skill Strategies

1. Have all parts learn the melody of the refrain (try to get all to sing it high; but lower octave is OK when not possible). Sing it in several different styles: *molto legato*/syrupy; light/bouncy; strongly accented/heavy. Explain a bit of the history of the "singing school" traditions and that songs such as this were sung by ordinary people of strong conviction—people sure of the mansions/cities/harps, of eternity.

2. Use physical gestures to keep the strength deep in the physical act of singing. Strong, powerful downward gestures can help with the visceral feel of this style of singing. Special emphasis on the separated, heavy singing of the quarter, quarter pick-up of each measure. Let

students create appropriate physical gestures to match the vigor of the rhythms. When you see a particularly effective gesture, let that student demonstrate for all the choir to see and try themselves. Discuss how theses gestures change the sound of the choir.

3. Listen to recordings of singers active in Fasola and shapenote singing societies (www.fasola.org). Northern Harmony and Village Harmony have wonderful recordings and songbooks (www.northern-harmony.pair.com). Try the Seth Houston "Big Sky" from the *Village Harmony Endless Light* songbook and recording, which could also serve as a companion study piece. Have students describe this hard voice singing style and work to imitate it in a healthy manner, with good breath usage, in the final refrain of "Hark I Hear the Harps Eternal."

Skill Assessment

Each time the choir sings, the director can assess the strength, vigor, and slight separation/accent that students use while singing this style. Students can also be asked to assess the robust (or lack of) character used by a particular section of the choir during the rehearsals, creating a class rubric to measure and assess its effectiveness.

Affective Outcome

Students will explore the compositional techniques used in this arrangement to express and enhance the meaning of the text.

Affective Strategies

1. Ask questions about the meaning of "farther shore" and "swollen waters." Some students may already know or make connections to the "River Jordan" or "passing over" images. Direct the discussion until all understand the imagery of the first verse. Spend a little time contrasting the desire/hope of the "harps eternal" and the hardship/ difficulty of the "swollen waters with their deep and solemn roar." Finally, ask students how the "Hallelujah" refrain which follows immediately fits with the thoughts of the first verse.

What (or how) does it express? Sing verse one1 and refrain with that understanding. Encourage students to communicate that understanding in their singing.

2. (This is primarily a "cognitive" strategy, but does relate to the affective objective). At some point early in the learning process, help students discover the form of the piece. Using terms verse and refrain, have them find each verse and refrain and mark them in their score. There will be some discussion about verse three, as some will see the refrain melody in the soprano solo. On the board write the form: VR VR VRR. From this point on, use terms like "first verse," and "second refrain," in the rehearsal process to reinforce the understanding of form.

3. Sing the melody to verse two. Ask students to sing with the contrasting *poco marcato* and the *poco leggiero*, explaining these terms. Ask them: Why do you suppose Alice Parker decided to set this verse with that contrast? (Direct the discussion to the contrasting feelings in the text, if necessary.) Again, ask students how the "Hallelujah" refrain that follows fits with the expression of the second verse. Sing verse two and refrain with that understanding. Work to express that understanding in the singing.

4. Learn the verse three section. Ask several people (at least three) to read the text of the verse aloud. Sing the verse with the humming parts. Then sing the verse with the humming parts and a soprano soloist. Ask the question, "Why do you think Alice Parker set this verse in this manner?" (If more questioning is needed, ask what the humming and the soprano descant could represent.) Have students write their ideas in their journals, and then have some share their ideas with the class. Sing verse three and refrain with that understanding and work to express it.

5. During one rehearsal, ask, "Why do we repeat the final refrain? Couldn't we just end at m. 48: VR VR VR?" (Try it with and without the final refrain.) What feeling does the final refrain give? Why? The students could write their thoughts in their journal prior to sharing their ideas with the class.

Affective Assessment

Assessment is done throughout the classroom discussions and journal writing regarding textual meaning and compositional choices. The final assessment comes in the student's ability to express that understanding in performance.

Music Selection

- Part of the traditional music of American heritage
- Great pentatonic melody and an artistically interesting arrangement using all pentatonic harmony
- Arrangement sets text in an artistic manner with variety and sensitivity to textual meaning
- Well-known American woman composer/arranger
- Powerful opening or closing piece
- Robust singing style suits high school students well
- Vocal ranges (with the part switching mentioned above) suit the typical high school choir.

SICUT CERVUS

Giovanni Pierluigi da Palestrina (1525-1594)

ed. Robert Hufstader

SATB

Mercury Music Corp/Theodore Presser (1946)

Background Information

"Sicut Cervus" is the first section of a longer motet of the same name by Giovanni Pierluigi da Palestrina, published in 1581, while he was living and working in Rome. It is a classic, standard piece in the choral repertory and represents the epitome of the high Renaissance polyphonic motet style. For many choral musicians, this piece is the definitive exemplar of Palestrina's craftsmanship and artistry as a composer.

The text comes from Psalm 42 in the Vulgate translation:

Sicut cervus desiderat	*As the heart desires*
ad fontes aquarum	*for springs of water,*
ita desiderat anima measo	*longs my soul*
ad te, Deus.	*for Thee, O God.* (Psalm 42:1)

The complete motet uses verses one, two, and three of the psalm, but modern published versions of the piece are usually limited to just verse one.

The liturgical function of this motet in Palestrina's time was the blessing of the water and the baptismal font on Holy Saturday. This service was a vigil on the night before Easter Sunday. It was an important service in the 16th-century church—indeed, from ancient times—as it marked the baptism of new catechumens who had finished their instruction and initiation during the preceding 40 days of Lent.

"Sicut Cervus" was sung (either as plainchant or as a motet like this example) during the procession to the baptismal font; its references both to the purifying, life-giving powers of water as well as the spiritual longing of the soul after God underscore its symbolic significance for the occasion.

Elements of Music

Form

In typical Renaissance motet fashion, the piece is through-composed and based on the structure of the text. Each phrase of text is given its own, melodically distinct motive and these unfold in points of imitation. There are three large sections: *Sicut cervus* desiderat ad fontes aquarum (mm. 1-23); Ita desiderat (mm. 23-40); and Anima mea ad te Deus (mm. 40-58).

Rhythm

Phrases often begin with long notes and gain rhythmic momentum as they peak. A wide variety of rhythmic figures are used, but all contribute to a smooth, lyrical, flowing mood, without jarring syncopations or angular patterns that would disrupt the mood of tranquility. Rhythmic shape is often determined by syllabic stress. Melismas on important words, some quite long, use a freer, expressive approach to rhythm.

Meter, in Renaissance fashion, is free. Although the notation makes the piece appear to be in 4/4 time, the editor suggests Renaissance performance practice by putting bar lines between the staves (as points of reference) and includes no meter signature. The metric feeling throughout is mostly duple, but is often gently disrupted by word stresses that create many different micro-meters within the phrase.

Melody

Completely diatonic, the melody is as tranquil and smooth as the rhythm, without dramatic leaps. Melodic shape often follows syllabic stress, with important syllables receiving higher notes or melismas or both. Amazingly, the piece relies almost entirely on stepwise movement, which contributes to its tranquility and liquid effect, yet the result is never tedious.

Harmony

Also diatonic, reinforcing a major mode feeling. Harmonies are almost always triadic, (I, IV, and V chords are most common) with occasional suspensions at cadences being the only dissonances. A lone accidental (only one in 58 bars!) creates a fleeting secondary dominant (m. 27) but is quickly re-directed back to the ongoing, constant A-flat major. Overall harmonic rhythm is generally slow.

Timbre

All four parts are predominantly set in the middle or lower half of their voice range, and *tessituras* do not stray from within an octave or ninth. This conservative use of the voices, and their close voicing, creates a mellow, rich, and somewhat dark color.

Texture

Texture is a significant feature of the piece and a hallmark of Palestrina's style. After a monophonic tenor opening statement, the other parts join in turn, after which the texture remains completely polyphonic throughout. Each new motive is introduced in one part, then taken up by all other voice parts, who follow strictly in unfolding points of imitation.

Significantly, there is no relief from this seamless texture. Never does it thin out to less than three voices and never is a new point of imitation revealed clearly but usually "sneaks in," emerging from within a rich texture that remains constantly in motion. This factor contributes to the piece's flowing, liquid feeling, and also reinforces its almost "unearthly," spiritual quality, as if sung by divine beings who never needed to stop and take a breath, as mere mortals must.

Entrances of the points of imitation are, in general, spaciously placed which also creates an effect of tranquility. An exception is the stretto effect in the last four bars, where quicker entrances of the final *"ad te Deus"* create a climactic, albeit a gentle, feeling of conclusion.

Expression

The editor has added word accents in the text and *tenuto* markings on their related pitches to indicate stressed syllables. The rehearsal accompaniment gives good suggestions for dynamic shaping, but the singers' parts are free of extra editing. The editor's suggested dynamics range from *pp* to *f*, but a more historically accurate performance might remain within a more conservative dynamic range, perhaps *p* to *mf*. This would also reinforce the mood of calm reserve, placidity, and balance.

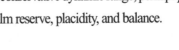

TEACHING PLANS
CHOIR

The Heart

The heart of the piece is the tranquil mood created by the seamless polyphonic texture whose surface is never marred by harmonic, melodic, or rhythmic surprises, and yet continually unfolds in a flowing, almost liquid motion. It is this simultaneous feeling of stasis and motion which makes the piece both a marvel of composition and a continuous delight to the listener.

Introducing the Piece

Give students a copy of the text to "Sicut Cervus" along with a word-by-word translation. Have it read aloud several times in these ways: two students alternate, one reading a phrase in Latin and the other reading the same phrase in English; one student reads the entire text in Latin, another one or two read it aloud in English. Let the sound and meaning of the words sink in. Invite students to share their thoughts about the poem; they may have a reaction to it, a favorite image, a recollection of hearing it before or a special connection to it.

Guide the discussion to focus on the metaphors in the text. What two things are being contrasted in the first phrase? (thirst vs. water). What do they represent in the second phrase? (longing vs. God, or perhaps spiritual hunger vs. nearness to God).

Ask students what kind of music they would write to express this text and why. Encourage them to use specific musical vocabulary in their description.

The next day, recall the previous discussion with students and tell them, "I'm going to play a recording of a piece that was written in the 16th century. I'd like you to listen carefully and decide what overall mood the composer is trying to evoke." After listening, invite them to share their responses, perhaps first by a quick journaling, and then in a group discussion. You may choose to guide the discussion to the question of which of two ideas are being expressed: the soul's longing or the tranquility of peaceful water.

Skill Outcome

Students will make artistic decisions about phrasing based on word stress, phrase shape, and suspensions.

Strategies

Melodic Rise and Fall

1. As students are learning their parts on "loo" for the first phrase (mm.1-11), invite them to make decisions about which notes seem most important, or should have the most stress. Encourage them to try different "peaks" and to shape them smoothly and not abruptly. Ask them how they are making decisions about which notes are most important. Help them to feel the natural ebb and flow created by rising and falling lines.

Word Stress

2. As students are learning text, ask them how composers make decisions about which syllables are set to high notes, long notes, etc. (accented syllables). Ask students to underline accented syllables. They can identify them by the accent marks in the text that have been added to the edition. (This is a good homework assignment.) Invite students to give extra stress to these syllables as they perform, cautioning them to "set up" these stresses carefully by the way they prepare and move out of them, so their effect is not too abrupt or jarring.

Suspensions

3. During warm-ups, students have done ear-training exercises on solfège syllables and know the hand signs for each syllable. Split the choir into two groups, one for each of your hands. Begin with both groups on *sol*. Change right hand to la, creating a dissonance. The choir may "back away" from this, but show through your face, hands, and body energy that they should sing "into" it and vigorously. Move left hand group down to *fa,* resolving to a third. Let students tune. Now move right hand group down to *sol,* creating another dissonance, then resolve left hand to *mi,* etc. Continue this chain of suspensions until the left hand group must resolve to *ti* (right hand group is singing *re*) and then bring both groups to a unison *do.*

317

Group I

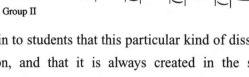

Group II

Explain to students that this particular kind of dissonance is called a suspension, and that it is always created in the same way. One voice creates a dissonance above another, which then lowers itself to resolve.

Use this warm-up for several days, inviting students to "lean into" the dissonances to give them a little extra expressive stress. Notate the warm-up on the board in two-part harmony and show how suspensions are easy to spot if you look for "two notes touching" (a handy definition of dissonance).

Have students find examples of suspensions in their music, both by identifying them in notation and by listening. Suspensions are found in mm. 12, 15-16 (in a chain, like the warm-up), 17, 21-22 (a decorated suspension), 27, 29 (chain), 31, 34, 37 (the suspended note is on top instead of on the bottom), 40, 42, 43, 45, 48, 49, 50, and 54. It may be hard for students to find suspensions in their music when they are not in adjacent voice parts, in different registers or clefs. Some examples are easier to hear or see than others, such as m. 12 (soprano and alto) or m. 27 (tenor and bass). It may be helpful to focus on these examples first, to help students hear and see how Palestrina integrates suspensions into the flow of the counterpoint.

As they are discovered and rehearsed, encourage students to sing these suspensions expressively.

Ebb and Flow

Review with students all the different ways Palestrina creates ebb and flow (tension and release) in the piece (melodic shape, long versus short notes, suspensions). Have students pair up with someone next to them, face them, and grasp a cupped hand. Have them practice a gentle "pulling apart" that should feel like a tensing in their hands and arms. Then have the choir sing a section of the piece this way, pulling and relaxing as they sense the music ebb and flow. Encourage them to use the most pull for the highest point of the phrase, a little pull for the less important stresses, and no pull for the moments when the phrase relaxes.

Another way to create the same feeling is to have students pair up with someone next to them, face them, and put their palms together against their partner's. If this section of the music is memorized they can use both hands (which is ideal); otherwise they can use one hand and hold the music with the other. Have them practice a gentle "lifting and pressing" that should feel like a rise of energy in their arms. Then have the choir sing a section of the piece this way, lifting and relaxing as they sense the music ebb and flow. As their arms drop, they should let them expand outward, creating buoyant circles as their arms rise and fall. Encourage them to use a full extended reach for the highest point of the phrase and less for the lesser stresses. If there is room in the rehearsal space, set up the pairs in a big double circle, so they are more aware visually of the rise and fall of the entire groups' arms.

A third way to create this stretching sensation with the phrases is to give each student an strip of elastic, about two-three feet in length. Have them put one end under their foot and pull up on the other end as they sing, creating more tension as the phrase expands, and relaxing the elastic as the phrase releases. This can also be done with large circles of elastic, which a group of five to ten students hold while standing in a circle. They will pull out to feel tension in the phrase, and relax inward toward the group to release.

Ask students to discuss their experience. Guide the discussion to highlight this idea about phrasing: there is often one most important "peak" of each phrase, but it is usually approached and departed from by other, smaller peaks, very much like the foothills around a single, prominent mountain.

Pick two or three different phrases from the piece and ask students to graph (with a colored marker and paper) the "mountain range" of each of them. Encourage them to capture the shape and relative duration of the high and low points of the phrase, and to make expressive decisions about the relationships among the different "peaks." Remind them of the various factors that contribute to the music's "rise and fall," beyond just high notes and low notes.

Assessment

Students can be informally assessed by transferring their understanding of phrasing to a new piece, especially a slow, lyrical piece where the phrase shape depends on the same factors as "Sicut Cervus" (melodic rise and fall, word stress, suspensions).

Students can also analyze a new section of "Sicut Cervus" on their own (perhaps as homework), drawing a "peaks and valleys" graph in pencil above their part in the music.

Cognitive Outcome

Students will identify examples of melisma and their use as text painting.

Strategies

Melisma warm-up

Teach students this warm-up:

Sing a song of gladness, sing a song of joy.
D R M F S S S F M R D

Modulate through several keys, and emphasize good choral tone, crisp diction, and a bright, energetic style. Next, teach them this warm-up:

Sing_____with joy_____.
D R M F S   S S F M R D

TEACHING PLANS
CHOIR

Discuss with students the difference between the two warm-ups. Introduce the concept of melisma (more than one note per syllable) versus syllabic setting of text. Write the word melisma on the board, with its definition. If students are keeping a vocabulary list, have them write it down.

Melismas and Text Painting

After students have begun learning "Sicut Cervus," ask them to search their music for examples of these melismas:

- The melisma with the most notes. To what word is it set?
- The longest melisma, the one that covers the most beats. To what word is it set?
- The melisma with the widest range of pitches. To what word is it set?
- A melisma that goes up. What word?
- A melisma that goes down. What word?
- A word that is always set as a melisma.
- A word that is never set as a melisma.

This can be done informally as a group activity, as a contest or a race, as homework, or as a small group activity with a worksheet and blanks to be filled in. When finished, solicit student answers and write them on the board.

Ask students to observe which words are set to melismas and to speculate why this is so. (Composers typically underscore important words this way.) Guide students to see relationships between the shape of melismas and possible meanings the composer might intend (e.g. the undulation of "aquarum" suggesting water, the rising shape of *"desiderat"* suggesting longing).

Introduce the term "text painting" and explain its common use as a choral compositional device. Ask students to find other possible examples of text painting in this piece (e.g. the melodic line that ascends on "ad te Deus," the long, sighing note on "anima mea").

Student Composing

Have students compose short warm-ups that use melismas, text painting (to a text of their own) or both. They should be short, easily singable and teachable, and written with correct notation. Use a different one each day as part of the regular warm-up routine. Have the student composer write it on the board and teach it to the choir.

Assessment

1. The Student Composing strategy above may be used as an assessment.
2. Writing definitions of the terms (in their own language) and giving examples (in notation) will demonstrate student understanding.
3. Ask students to find examples of text painting, melismas, or both in another piece they're working on, or a new piece they haven't seen before. They can write a short paragraph describing the composer's use of these techniques, incorporating examples from the music.

Affective Outcome

Students will analyze relationships between compositional devices and mood.

Strategies

Remind students of the earlier discussion of Palestrina's possible intentions in setting the text. The verb in the psalm verse is longing. What are other words that describe this feeling (hoping, praying, discomfort, frustration, anxiety, loneliness, etc.)? Encourage students to include words with both negative and positive connotations.

Discuss with students the water metaphor. What kind of emotional state does this metaphor symbolize? Create a list of words (peaceful, energized, tranquil, confident, relaxed, etc.). Tell students that their job over the next few weeks is to come to a conclusion about Palestrina's possible intentions in "Sicut Cervus:" was he trying to underscore the idea of longing (i.e. discomfort, anxiety), or the idea of water (i.e. peace, tranquility)?

Have the tenors sing their opening line. Ask students to describe the effect of this kind of opening. "How would it be different if all four voices opened together in unison? What about the men in octaves? All four voices entering together in a chord?" Try each of these and compare with the original. "What makes the original so compelling and effective?"

"Do you think Palestrina is depicting thirst and longing or setting up a piece about water and contentment?" Have students jot their ideas in a journal and share them in a brief group discussion.

Over the course of the next few weeks, examine each of the six following features of "Sicut Cervus" in the same way:

1. The gradual unfolding and thickening of texture as each of the four parts enters in the opening eight bars
2. The suspensions
3. The choice of beginning each new point of imitation with a long note
4. The frequent and generous melismas
5. The ascending lines
6. The concluding *stretto* on the words *"ad te"* (bass, alto, tenor in quick succession).

TEACHING PLANS
CHOIR

Have students keep track of their evolving personal theories about Palestrina's possible intention, by jotting in their journal and sharing in class discussions.

After all of the compositional devices have been examined, ask students to vote on either thirst/longing or water/contentment. Hopefully the discussion will be lively and opinions mixed. At the appropriate time, remind students that we really have no way to know for sure about Palestrina's intention and suggest that perhaps the reason it's hard to come to a conclusion about this question is because Palestrina is able to convey both moods at once: the tranquility of gentle waters and the restless longing of a thirsty soul.

As a final journaling activity, invite students to answer the question: What is something you long for? After giving them a chance to write, sing the piece through, with their focus on what they have written. Invite discussion about what may have sounded different or better to them.

Assessment

As a summary activity, have students write a short essay describing their opinion on Palestrina's intentions and why they believe it to be longing/thirst or water/contentment. Tell them to use the musical terms they have learned and that they must defend their opinion with specific examples from the music, as well as their effect on them as a singer.

These essays will be evaluated on the following scale:

3. Excellent connection between musical examples and ideas about Palestrina's intention. Essay was thoughtful, coherent, and persuasive.

2. Essay showed some thoughtful insight about musical examples. Examples were used appropriately and showed understanding, but didn't always make a compelling or reasonable connection.

1. Essay was completed but was missing musical examples or didn't demonstrate a clear understanding of musical examples.

Music Selection

"Sicut Cervus" is a recognized classic in its genre, the Renaissance motet. It represents an a golden era of polyphonic choral music, presents appropriate and satisfying musical challenges, and is supremely rewarding to sing.

Other Possible Outcomes

Renaissance art and architecture

String Orchestra

FOLLOW THE DRINKING GOURD

African American Spiritual

Arr. Katherine W. Punwar

Punwar Publications (2002)

Background Information

The song "Follow the Drinking Gourd" was actually a riddle that urged slaves to escape. They could only travel at night, and the Big Dipper, or the "Drinking Gourd," pointed the way north, through a series of safe houses and hiding places known as the Underground Railroad.

During the era of slavery in the United States, many slaves fled to freedom in the North. In order to reduce the numbers of escaping slaves, their owners kept them illiterate and ignorant of geography. Slave owners even went so far as to try to keep slaves from learning how to tell directions. Their attitude is illustrated by a statement from one of the overseers in the book *Roots*:

> I don't take to slaves off the plantation. This way they don't know which way is east, which way it is to the west. Once they have figured where someplace else is—next thing you know, they'll know which way is the North.

Nonetheless, slaves knew perfectly well that freedom lay to the north, and they knew how to locate north. They used the North Star, or Polaris, its proper name. Polaris lies almost directly north in the sky. Slaves fled using the simple direction "walk towards the North Star." However, unable to plan a route, they risked walking into impassable or dangerous terrain.

Members of the Underground Railroad were fully aware of the predicament of fleeing slaves. The Underground Railroad was a loose confederation of men and women, both white and black, many of them former slaves themselves, who defied the law and risked their own safety to help slaves make their way north to freedom. About 1831 the Railroad began to send travelers into the South to secretly teach slaves

TEACHING PLANS
ORCHESTRA

specific routes they could navigate using Polaris. By the beginning of the Civil War in 1861, about 500 people a year were traveling in the South teaching routes to slaves, and escape routes had been established. Scholars estimate that 60,000 to 100,000 slaves successfully fled to freedom.

Polaris became a symbol of freedom to slaves as well as a guide star. As soon as they were old enough to understand, slave children were taught to locate Polaris by using the stars of the Big Dipper. The two stars at the end of the bowl of the Big Dipper point over to Polaris, the North Star, which is the end of the handle of the Little Dipper.

Instead of a fancy metal dipper, slaves used a hollowed-out gourd to scoop water out of a bucket to get a drink. So they referred to the Big Dipper as the "Drinking Gourd." Slaves passed the travel instructions from plantation to plantation by song. In Africa, tribal cultures often created songs to transmit factual information and history. As slaves in America, they turned song into codes that secretly transmitted information they wished to keep from their white masters.

"Follow the Drinking Gourd" is a coded song that gives the route for an escape from Alabama and Mississippi. Of all the routes out of the Deep South, this is the only one for which the details survive. The route instructions were given to slaves by an old man named Peg Leg Joe. Working as an itinerant carpenter, he spent winters in the South, moving from plantation to plantation, teaching slaves this escape route. Unfortunately, we know nothing more about Peg Leg Joe.

The song and its hidden meanings are as follows:

> *When the sun comes back and the first quail calls,*
> *Follow the Drinking Gourd.*
> *For the old man is a-waiting for to carry you to freedom,*
> *If you follow the Drinking Gourd.*

"When the sun comes back" means winter and spring, when the altitude of the sun at noon is higher each day. Quail are migratory birds wintering in the South. The Drinking Gourd is the Big Dipper. The old man is Peg Leg Joe.

TEACHING PLANS
ORCHESTRA

The verse tells slaves to leave in the winter and walk towards the Drinking Gourd. Eventually they will meet a guide who will escort them for the remainder of the trip.

Most escapees had to cross the Ohio River, which is too wide and too swift to swim. The Railroad struggled with the problem of how to get escapees across, and with experience, came to believe the best crossing time was winter. Then the river was frozen, and escapees could walk across on the ice. Because it took most escapees a year to travel from the South to the Ohio, the Railroad urged slaves to start their trip in winter in order to be at the Ohio the next winter.

> *The riverbank makes a very good road,*
> *The dead trees show you the way,*
> *Left foot, peg foot, traveling on*
> *Follow the Drinking Gourd.*

This verse taught slaves to follow the bank of the Tombighee River north looking for dead trees that were marked with drawings of a left foot and a peg foot. The markings distinguished the Tombighee from other north/south rivers that flow into it.

> *The river ends between two hills,*
> *Follow the Drinking Gourd.*
> *There's another river on the other side,*
> *Follow the Drinking Gourd.*

These words told the slaves that when they reached the headwaters of the Tombighee, they were to continue north over the hills until they met another river. Then they were to travel north along the new river, which is the Tennessee River. A number of the southern escape routes converged on the Tennessee.

TEACHING PLANS ORCHESTRA

Where the great big river meets the little river,
Follow the Drinking Gourd.
For the old man is a-waiting for to carry you to freedom if you
Follow the Drinking Gourd.

This verse told the slaves the Tennessee joined another river. They were to cross that river (the Ohio), and on the north bank, meet a guide from the Underground Railroad.

This arrangement of "Follow the Drinking Gourd" was written for the Wisconsin Youth Symphony's preparatory string orchestra, the Sinfonietta, and Mark Leiser, Conductor. Suggestions for compositional ideas came from the students in the orchestra. They attempted to describe the feelings that a slave, in search of freedom, would experience along the journey. The beginning is more anxious—afraid to set out, yet excited to be leaving slavery. The middle of the journey is more tedious and the traveler is weary, thus the bluesy feel in the music. Finally, as this slave nears the end of long travel, the music is more energetic and driving as it draws closer to its destination—freedom. The only major tonality in the piece is the very last chord—freedom having been achieved! Special coloristic effects at the beginning were also suggestions from these students (i.e. horses in the distance, wind blowing in the trees, birdcall of the quail).

Elements of Music
Form

Like the song on which it is based, the arrangement is strophic—there are three verses or sections, each with a unique character that propels the story. An introduction, filled with programmatic effects such as wind, quail calls, and horse hoof beats, sets an eerie mood.

Intro	mm. 1-16	Coloristic effects, fragments of the melody presented
Verse one	mm. 17-26	Melody in bass, viola, violin, with cello drumbeat *ostinato*
Verse two	mm. 27-46	Slow swing; bluesy feeling

Verse three mm. 47-67 Driving *allegro con fuoco* pushes toward
climax

Coda   mm. 68-77 Broadening creates dramatic ending

Rhythm

Rhythm is a major feature in this arrangement. Lack of clear pulse in the introduction contributes to its unsettling effect. Percussive rhythms in the cello (mm. 17-24) suggest drumbeats. The swing rhythms of verse two create a slow burn, jazzy blues with a walking bass. The violin solo which closes this section is freely rhythmic and improvisatory in feeling. Verse four depends on a driving, straight eighth-note accompaniment for its momentum. A brief coda in 3/4 pulls back the forward motion, as the traveler takes the last large strides toward freedom.

The melody of "Follow the Drinking Gourd" has two characteristic motives, which appear in the arrangement:

1. A syncopated figure (associated with the words "drinking gourd")
2. A chain of straight eighth notes ("for the old man is a-waitin' for to carry you to freedom")

Melody

The melody, in D minor throughout, is a simple call-and-response form, typical of many slave songs. Fragments of the melody are heard in the introduction, but it is not until after the drum beats begin, played by cellos, that we hear the complete melody. It is passed from voice to voice frequently, a favorite device of Punwar's. For example, it is first presented in the bass, followed by violas, and completed by violins. In the second verse, first violins carry the melody, supported by jazzier harmonies in the lower strings and walking bass line. A fragmented *pizzicato* melody between upper and lower strings then leads to a violin solo. This solo may be played as written, and octave higher, or the student may freely improvise or create something new here. In the third verse, the melody occurs in the lower strings, then is transferred to upper strings. The final melody is played by lower strings, while upper strings play fiery *tremolo*.

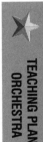

TEACHING PLANS ORCHESTRA

One of the interesting aspects of the arrangement is the transformation of the melody as the piece moves through its various moods, from its tentative beginning to a weary, foot-dragging blues to a robust gallop to the end. By variation of tempo, dynamics, range, and timbre as well as "blue" notes and both swung and straight eighths, the same melodic material assumes a wide variety of personalities.

Harmony

The piece is consistently in D minor, a great key for young string players and also a stabilizing device which suggests tenacity and steadiness in pursuit of a goal. The opening bars are just a whisper of tonality, as the basses sustain a harmonic D. Pedal tones on D and A in the first 21 measures firmly establish the key. As the piece progresses, the harmonic language becomes richer and more confident, from the first thicker harmonies of mm. 22-24 to the jazzier extended harmonies of verse two (as suggested by the C/C-sharp/D dissonance in measure 26).

Verse three uses strictly diatonic harmonies with a notable dissonant blue note (A-flat) in m. 55 and some minor seventh chords (m. 62) providing extra tension. The final tonality, a bright picardy D major, is set up by a powerfully scored four-three suspension in m. 72, an effective set-up for a triumphant ending.

Timbre

One of the recognizable features of Punwar's arrangements is the exceptionally imaginative use of timbre—indeed, nearly every available string color is put to use in this soundscape, plus many non-traditional sounds. As already mentioned, the opening sequence is created by collegno sliding up and down strings (wind), short, cooing, upward *glissandos* (quail), dampened strings played *collegno* (hoof beats), and tapping the body of cellos (rhythmic drums). Harmonics, *pizzicato,* and a wide variety of bowing styles (*staccato, legato,* brush strokes, *tremolo,* etc.) are all featured, making this not only colorful music, but a natural way to teach these techniques within a meaningful musical experience.

Texture

The most commonly used texture is a homophonic, melody-plus-accompaniment. The accompaniment varies from rhythmic *ostinato* to sustained chords or long tones. Even within these textural parameters, and without the use of polyphony, the texture continually feels flexible and varied.

The texture at the beginning is intentionally thin. It evokes an unsettled feeling, one of a solitary person setting out into a great unknown. The thicker texture presented in the middle section creates a more weighed sensation—the heavy load of the traveler, the sense of weariness. A single voice "cries out" in mm. 43-46, with the *tremolo* underscoring anxious despair. Finally, the end of the journey nears, and the richer texture and the driving eighth note rhythm signify renewed energy.

Expression/Dynamics

Dynamics are an integral feature of the piece's story and, along with a variety of articulations (*tremolo,* accents, etc.) help paint the picture of the journey. The subdued dynamics of the opening suggest the precarious nature of the trip. More strength is gained as the travels continue, but wanes somewhat in the solo that follows the more "labored" verse two. Finally, aggressive dynamics and accents highlight the energy and excitement of the final push toward freedom.

The Heart

The heart of this piece is its journey from an uncertain beginning to glorious ending—the spiritual on which it is based is about a journey, and the piece itself becomes a musical journey through the gradual transformation of its music elements (tempo, key, timbre, texture, etc.).

TEACHING PLANS ORCHESTRA

Introducing the Piece

The goal of this introduction is to teach students the spiritual, its lyrics, and its historical context. This introduction should be spread out over several rehearsals.

1. Sing the song "Follow the Drinking Gourd" for students. Ask them if they recognize it. If so, have them share what they know about the song.

2. Pass out copies of the tune and lyrics and teach students to sing the first verse and refrain. (Reproducible copy enclosed in score/packet.)

3. Share with students the background of the song and of the Underground Railroad.

4. Discuss the lyrics and their hidden meaning to those in slavery.

5. Sing again. Have students discover how the verse and chorus are different melodically (and harmonically). Have them suggest some ways an arranger could modify the melody and/or other music elements to help tell the story musically.

6. Have students listen to other arrangements, instrumental or vocal, of this song.

Skill Outcome

Students will use various bowing styles to create mood.

Strategies

1. As each verse of the piece is rehearsed, ask students to identify words
   to describe its mood. For example:

   Verse one: Anxious, dark, spooky, uncertain, etc.

   Verse two: Sad, bluesy, heavy, etc.

   Verse three: Driving, intense, energized, aggressive, etc.

Have students write these words in their parts.

2. In each verse, identify what kind of bowing articulation is needed,
   where in the bow it should be played, and where the contact point on
   the string should be (closer to the bridge or the fingerboard). Create
   warm-ups (on scales or other patterns) that emphasize these aspects.
   Some examples:

   A sustained, floating *mp,* full-bow slur (as in m. 14):

legato

- A weighty, slow swing style (as in verse two):

(heavy)

- A hammered, heavy *staccato* (as in m. 35):

f (heavy staccato)

- Brush stroke in *forte* (as in m. 47):

f (brush)

- *Tremolo* Accented, full bow, *forte* (as in mm. 68-71)

  Assign students to create their own warm-ups which, rehearse these bowing styles and then teach them to the group. Encourage them to be observant of each other's bow placement and articulation, both by watching and listening.

3. As these styles are learned, give each one a code name, which can then be referred to clearly in rehearsal. For traditional bowing styles, like brush stroke or *martel,* teach students these terms, and invent new ones for the other styles/rhythms/articulations. For example, the first one above might be named the "Float" and the second one, the "Swing."

4. Throughout the rehearsal process, continue to invite discussion about how the bowing styles contribute to the character of each section and help tell its story. Consistently refer back to the narrative aspect of the piece as a way of motivating students to be expressive in their bowing.

Assessment

1. Assess students informally throughout the learning process by observing their progress in mastering the various bowing styles.

2. Review with students the complete list of bowing styles learned and their "code names." Do an individual playing test with each student, where they are asked to demonstrate the styles by playing a short version of each of the warm-ups. Use a checklist and assign each performance a rating of 1) Mastered/Consistent, 2) Progressing/Inconsistent, 3) Not Yet.

3. As an alternative to number two above, have students choose a simple melody (e.g. "Twinkle") and create five variations, using different bowing styles, rhythms, dynamics, and articulations. One variation should be in minor. Assign each variation 20 points;

five points each for effective bowing choices, technical mastery, imaginative composition and mood, and intonation.

Cognitive Outcome

Students will recognize compositional devices that enhance music's storytelling ability.

Strategies

Give students a copy of the melody to "Follow the Drinking Gourd." (Enclosed in score/packet.) Play through it as a group. Divide students into heterogeneous groups of four to seven students. Assign each group the task of creating a new verse of "Follow the Drinking Gourd," using their own ideas. Let students experiment and encourage their improvisation without censoring.

If they get stuck, here are a few suggestions (as a way of spurring their imaginations): Try changing something about the melody, by changing some notes, adding extra notes to a phrase, sliding into or out of notes in a jazz style, playing it much faster or much slower, or changing the rhythm. Add a rhythmic *ostinato* figure to accompany the melody. Borrow a short rhythmic motif from the melody or create a contrasting, new one. Add a drone accompaniment on D, or D and A; rhythmicize it. Try playing it in a major key. Have each group perform for the class. Let the class discuss each variation with regard to: the technical and musical means used (this will be a good opportunity to teach any new words such as "drone" or "*ostinato*" that students may not know already) and the mood or character created (encourage students to use rich vocabulary and to verbalize as clearly as possible the affect being created). Return to the Punwar's "Follow the Drinking Gourd." Give each student (or every stand) a copy of the score. Give them a quick primer in score reading and use the scores for discussion, so every student can see what is happening in the other parts. Discuss what makes each verse's compositional devices and techniques "work" and how they advance the story. Have students re-order the various sections of the piece and have the group play it in the re-ordered version. What works and doesn't work? Discuss the difference

TEACHING PLANS ORCHESTRA

between specific sound effects (e.g. horse hooves) and musical styles/ compositional devices (e.g. swing rhythms in the blues, a major chord at the end of a minor key piece, dissonance, tempo changes, etc.). Help students see how one is merely imitating an extra-musical sound and the other is using a less specific musical language to create a mood or suggest an aspect of the story, but not in a literal or pictorial way. Play examples of different kinds of musical storytelling for students, such as Beethoven's symphony no. six (especially Movement IV, Storm) or Vivaldi's *Four Seasons* (where the music to narrative relationship is very close and there is a one-to-one relationship where nearly every musical gesture "means" something extra-musical) versus more general and suggestive kind of musical story-telling, such as Eric Ewazen's *Four Royal Dances* (where each movement suggests the personality of a lord, a lady, a jester, and a knight), or Tchaikvosky's "Romeo and Juliet Overture," in which musical themes suggest characters and events but no attempt is made to tell the entire story.

Assessment

Have students summarize the various compositional devices and strategies they have learned while making a personal connection with the story of "Follow the Drinking Gourd." They will do this by writing a narrative story version of the piece, in the first person, as a slave about to escape to freedom.

On the right-hand side of their paper will be the story they write, and on the left they should keep a running list of the musical devices being used in the piece and how they are created. Encourage students to go beyond the music with their story; in other words, their story may be much longer or include sections that don't correspond exactly in length to the music. All the various sections of the piece should be present in their story, though, and tell them that they will be evaluated on how imaginatively they write a story that features the same "events" as the music.

The final story should be at least five pages long—most students should have no trouble creating a narrative of that length. Depending on time, you may choose to subject the story to at least one revision in the process.

It may be helpful to give all students the starting paragraph of their story, or use it as a suggestion:

Follow the Drinking Gourd

Name_____

Basses hold a pedal tone on D

I don't remember a darker, colder, windier night in my whole life. Maybe because I had never been more afraid in my whole life. Tonight was the night.

Evaluate students' stories on general writing criteria, according to their English classroom writing curriculum. (This project may, in fact, be an interdisciplinary one in which help with the writing could come from the students' English teachers.) Evaluate the "music margins" by how completely and accurately (with correct vocabulary) students describe what is happening in the music, showing what they have learned about the compositional devices used.

Use one or two particularly well-written stories in the concert performance of "Follow the Drinking Gourd."

Affective Outcome

Students will consider the theme of freedom, and how music has been used throughout history to express ideas about freedom.

Strategies

Discuss "freedom" in the context of African American slaves in the 19th century. What, exactly, did a runaway slave mean when he or she used the word "freedom?" Why did slaves risk being killed to escape? Why didn't all slaves try this? Why did other people, both white and black, break the law, even risk their lives, to help slaves escape?

What other kinds of freedom do people long for? What does freedom mean to you? At this point in the discussion, ask students to journal briefly about the meaning of freedom to them.

Ask students to name other books, movies, or songs they know that deal with the subject of freedom, in any way. This may take some reflection time, to think outside the box of 19th-century slavery. Discuss aspects of these works and how they express ideas about freedom.

Over the next four to six weeks, present other songs (especially, but not onlyspirituals) that celebrate or describe a yearning for freedom, such as "O Freedom!" "No More Auction Block for Me," "Deep River," "Go Down Moses," "Now Let Me Fly!" "We Shall Overcome," "If I Had a Hammer," "Free at Last." Help students to notice the frequent use of metaphors for freedom in thesespirituals, e.g. "crossing over Jordan." Guide them to discover various kinds of freedom being described: going north, returning to an African homeland, death. Compare these songs to "Follow the Drinking Gourd" using a Venn diagram. What things do the two songs have in common? How are they different?

Assessment

As part of the first person narrative they write (see Outcome two assessment, above) have students include a reflection on the meaning of freedom, woven into their story. Why is it so important? They should make clear through their storytelling why they are prepared to risk everything for it.

Have students write a short poem about one of the following:

- Experiencing the of loss freedom (either real or imagined)
- Ways in which people are not free today
- Ways in which they themselves have felt enslaved, but not by another person

TEACHING PLANS ORCHESTRA

Music Selection

"Follow the Drinking Gourd" is a beautifully crafted arrangement which not only is highly imaginative and colorful, but also well-suited to the technical abilities of the middle level orchestra. It introduces students to a wide variety of bowing techniques and expressive demands that they will be motivated to achieve. Significantly, it provides firsthand experience with an important musical genre that is often missing in the orchestra classroom: the African American spiritual.

Other Possible Outcomes

Any of the compositional devices mentioned in the strategies for Outcome number two could be studied in depth (e.g. pedal tone, *ostinato,* suspensions, etc.). They could be the jumping off point for a unit of composition or improvisation. Blues style, blue notes, blues harmonies, and minor tonality could also be studied.

Resources

Songbook

Steal Away: Songs of the Underground Railroad. Kim and Reggie Harris. Compact Disc available from Appleseed Records. http://www.appleseedrec.com/underground/
Audio clips available at http://www.amazon.com

Web Sites

http://www.nationalgeographic.com/features/99/railroad/
National Geographic's Underground Railroad Site: thoughtful, interactive introduction to the Underground Railroad and some of its members.

Other pieces by Katherine W. Punwar

These pieces for intermediate level orchestra, all include a conductor's score, a complete CMP teaching plan, background information on the piece, and card stock master copies of each part with permission to copy. Order from kwpunwar@tds.net
Phone 608.220.3178

A Civil War Suite: Three Civil War Songs for String Orchestra (Dixie, One Vacant Chair, Battle Hymn of the Republic)

Sansa Kroma: An Akan Playground Song for String Orchestra and Percussion

Celestial Suite: Four Short Pieces for Young Orchestra

ÅSE'S DEATH

(from Peer Gynt Suite No. 1)

Edvard Grieg (1843-1907)

Background Information

The great Norwegian playwright Henrik Ibsen (1828-1906) originally wrote his epic *Peer Gynt* as a "dramatic poem" to be read only, but by 1874 was exploring the possibility of a staged production in the capital Christiana (now Oslo). On January 23, he wrote to Edvard Grieg about the possibility of composing incidental music for the production. Grieg thought that the material was inherently unmusical, and only agreed reluctantly because he thought the project would demand just a few pieces of music. In fact, his work on *Peer Gynt* occupied him intensely for the year and a half and in the end he delivered 26 musical numbers.

Ibsen had given Grieg some fairly detailed ideas about the where and how he thought music could enhance the play, but also gave him a free hand to use his own creativity. Throughout the process, Grieg was often vexed or overwhelmed by the challenges of writing incidental music for this phantasmagorical drama that seemed to borrow from folk-poetry, Greek tragedy, Shakespeare, the Bible, Romantic fairy stories, and contemporary social commentary, but the music he wrote added immensely to the play's tremendous success when it opened on February 24, 1876, in Christiana.

Although it ran for another 35 performances, and soon became popular throughout Scandinavia, the play caught on only slowly in theatres abroad. Grieg's music, however, quickly became very popular throughout Europe—so much so that in 1888 Grieg assembled four pieces from the incidental music into a suite for concert performance, the *Peer Gynt Suite* No. One, published at the request of C.F. Peters in Leipzig. A second suite was published in 1891. Although productions of *Peer Gynt* are mounted today, it is probably Grieg's music (and specifically these two suites) that most people think of when they hear the name "Peer Gynt."

Synopses of the play (even its entire text) can be found in many dramatic anthologies or on the Web. It is essentially a psychological drama concerned with large questions of personal identity, society's morals and their emptiness, the true nature of being human, and the redemptive power of love. Peer, a handsome, headstrong youth, is driven to world-wide adventures by his ambition for fame. His fantastic escapades include 40 different scenes from the mountains of Norway to the Arabian desert, a Cairo lunatic asylum, and a ship in the stormy North Sea, as well as encounters with the Woman in Green, her father the Troll-King, the giant, invisible Bøyg, a Moroccan chieftan and his daughter, Anitra.

The two women who figure most prominently in Peer's personal evolution are his sweethearts Solveig, who remains faithful to him through-out his selfish wanderlust, and his mother, Åse (pronounced AW-suh). Act III, at the center of the play, involves encounters with Solveig and Åse by Peer, who has briefly returned home. Åse's Death is actually played as the Prelude to Act III, but it is not until the fourth scene of the act where Åse is actually on her deathbed. It is evening and the fireplace glows faintly in Åse's hut, which has been stripped bare. She has been forced to sell everything to pay for Peer's misdeeds. She is encouraged by seeing Peer again after so many years and their talk is of news in the village and reminiscing about happier times. Peer, with his usual high-spirited imagination, turns her bed into a sleigh ride, which ends tenderly as he notices her eyes close in death. It is during this conversation that the entire piece is played again a second time but more quietly, behind the stage, as underscoring, beginning with Peer's words, "Gee-up! Get along, Blackie!" and ending with Peer quoting St. Peter as Åse pulls up to heaven's gate: "An end to all this fuss and bother—Mother Åse can come in free!"

Elements of Music

Form

The form of this miniature is obvious and uncomplicated, which makes it ideal for student study. The first four-bar phrase, based almost entirely on a simple anapest rhythm is repeated ten times, plus a five bar coda, for a total of 45 measures. Each repetition of the opening phrase is varied, either by key, pitch level, harmonization, texture, or dynamics. The phrases are grouped by twos in an antecedent consequent relationship.

One of the marvels of Åse's Death, is its delicate balance between repetition and variation. When described in prose, its ten-fold repetition seems incredibly tedious and dull. The actual effect, however, is powerful: Grieg is able to hold interest through subtle variation, and an inexorable *crescendo* followed by an equally gripping *diminuendo*. Ultimately, it is the repetition of the rhythmic motif that lends the piece its austere power, which might be compared to a pendulum, the giant ticking of a clock, the rhythm of life, or the birth-growth-death circle of life.

Because of its hymn-like style, the piece is easily to analyze traditionally as an example of four-part chorale writing. It is also profitable to do so, as a way of revealing the subtle variations in each repetition, for it is these very subtleties that make a convincing performance of the piece. Because the piece is so short, and the full score is a mere two pages, it could be easily reproduced for students to analyze, at whatever level they are capable. Such an activity which would not only reveal many of Grieg's subtleties, but in so doing would help students overcome a possible aversion to the piece's seemingly dull repetitiveness.

The ten phrases might be outlined as follows:

	Measures	Formal Relationship	Key	Cadence	Dynamic
1)	1-4	A (antecedent)	B minor	V	*p*
2)	5-8	A' (consequent)	B minor	I	*PP*
3)	9-12	A (antecedent)	F-sharp minor	V	*mf*
4)	13-16	A' (consequent)	F-sharp minor	Ip	*cresc.*
5)	17-20	A (antecedent)	B minor	V	*f*
6)	21-24	A' (consequent)	B minor	I	*ff*
7)	25-28	B (antecedent)	D major/ B minor	V	*p/pp*
8)	29-32	B' (consequent)	G major/ B minor	I	*p/pp*
9)	33-36	B (antecedent)	D major/ B minor	V	*piu p*
10)	37-40	B' (consequent)	G major/ B minor	Ip	*iu p*
Coda	41-45	material from A	B minor	I	*morendo*

Rhythm

The rhythmic motif that unifies the piece (example six above) is the primary material in 34 of the piece's 45 measures, and the other measures are variations of it. Even the closing measures use this rhythmic cell to effect a *ritardando*, through augmentation (mm. 42-43). The lack of rhythmic variety is one of the characteristic features of the piece—combined with a slow, unchanging tempo, this rhythmic repetition creates the effect of solemnity.

Melody

The rhythmic motif described above takes two essential melodic shapes:

1) A rising theme, diatonic, which leaps up a fourth and then rises another half-step (A above), which corresponds to the slow *crescendo* of the first half of the piece

2) A falling theme, chromatic, (B above), which corresponds to the piece's *diminuendo* in the second half

Since the piece is in a homophonic, hymn style, the melody is in the uppermost voice. Chromaticism, however, is not only a feature of the violin I melody, but also appears within inner voices, especially in descending chromatic figures in the viola and violin II lines.

Harmony

Because the melodic and rhythmic variation is minimal, Grieg creates interest by harmonic variation. For example, the first two phrases are essentially identical melodic material in the violin I part, set in a parallel relationship. Whereas the first phrase (mm. 1–4) is harmonized simply with i, iv, and V chords, the second one (mm. 5–8) uses a richer palette of chromatics and even a French sixth chord, lending a new pathos to the familiar tune.

Just as the melody seems to rock back and forth in its "short-short-long" patterns (see Form above), the four bar phrases also rock back and forth harmonically between tonic and dominant key areas: every phrase cadences on i or V, and every phrase is set in B minor or F-sharp minor, the latter phrases being mostly strict transpositions of the former. This "harmonic rocking" characteristic is most obvious in the cello and bass lines, especially in the latter half of the piece

Timbre

Grieg's choice of strings alone, played *con sordino*, is significant. There is no other major musical number among the 26 pieces in the *Peer Gynt* score set for strings alone. Even the famous *Anitra's Dance* (associated with a very different sort of woman!), which also uses no winds or brass, makes prominent use of the triangle.

The effect of the full string orchestra, muted, could be described variously as hymn-like, otherworldly, reverent, solemn, and restrained. Certainly there is a purity and simplicity in this timbre, which suits the musical material well, and supports the dramatic action effectively. As underscoring, it serves at least two purposes: by its lack of attention-grabbing colors it does not overwhelm the spoken dialogue, and by its simple austerity it sets in relief Peer's frantic efforts to avoid dealing with his mother's nearing death.

Texture

In spite of its general simplicity, Åse's Death uses a variety of textures, which correspond to its back-and-forth rocking of dynamics and harmonic centers. Some of the textural changes are accomplished through transposition. For example, the third and fourth phrases (which parallel the first and second ones) are simple transpositions up a perfect fifth. This transposition to a higher pitch, combined with an increased dynamic, create a higher, thinner texture the effect of which is a forward leaning tension. The next statement of this same material is the fifth phrase, whose pitches and key are absolutely identical to the first phrase. The change in texture, however, pushes the piece to a heightened intensity, as every line is doubled at the higher octave, and the cellos play a triple divisi. This richer, fuller texture, again combined with an increased dynamic, creates the emotional climax of the piece.

Expression

As mentioned above, dynamics play an important structural role in the arc of the piece. In addition to its overall *crescendo-diminuendo* shape, the piece has many localized moments where dynamics are used to great effect. For example, the fourth phrase (mm. 13-16) begins with a *subito piano* after a *mf* phrase, which not only feels like a sudden introspective retreat from forward momentum, but also helps set up the powerful *forte* of the next phrase. Within this four-bar phrase there are four such "retreats," as each *crescendo* falls back to piano.

Especially poignant is the last note of m. 16, a "sobbing" effect created by dynamics, articulation, and release. Also noteworthy is Grieg's choice of morendo to describe the last note. Through attention to these details, Grieg lifts the piece out of mundane repetitiveness.

The Heart

The heart of the piece is its many repetitions of a simple, hymn-like melody, which create the somber but powerful effect of a funereal procession, which advances and recedes.

Introducing the Piece

(This introduction takes place before music has been passed out to students.) Write this rhythm on the board

 (rhythm only)

Tell students they must think like a composer. Their challenge is to create a piece that is about 45 measures long and that uses this rhythm in at least half of its measures. "What is the danger of using the same rhythm this often?" (Monotony, boredom). "How many different things can you think of that a composer could do to make the piece interesting?"

Students can brainstorm as a class to come up with a long list, or work in small groups and compete for the longest, most complete list. Encourage them to think about the elements of music as they think about the parameters they could change. When they are finished, their list might include such things as "change keys, change pitches, create a melody that uses the rhythm in several ways, use different instruments, etc."

Tell students to compare their list with the piece they are about to hear and see how many of their ideas the composer actually used. Play a recording of Åse's Death. Compare the piece with their list and discuss Grieg's compositional choices. "What mood is created by the piece?" "How is it created?" "How does the repetition of the rhythm contribute to the mood?" "What might the piece be about?"

After discussion of the above questions, tell students the title of the piece. Ask them to speculate on who "Åse" might be. Play the recording again, perhaps with copies of the full score for each student to look at. A final discussion might continue the ideas from above, or focus on a more detailed analysis of Grieg's compositional ideas, as students discover them through listening and following the score.

Skill Outcome

Students will perform with a variety of colors, showing awareness of timbre as an expressive element.

Strategies

1. Start with an Idea

Divide students into groups of three or four; mixed instrumentation is OK. Give each group a 3X5 card with three or four of the following words on it: sigh, hum, howl, sob, moan, sing, scream, chuckle, shriek, croon, guffaw, whisper, wail, giggle, chant, murmur, whimper, mutter. (This list could also be generated as a class brainstorm in response to the question, "How many words can you think of to describe sounds made by the human voice?").

Give each group five to eight minutes to experiment with their instruments to create instrumental versions of these words. Let the class guess which word they are performing. After hearing all the ideas, highlight the technical means used to create the sounds, e.g. pitch levels, dynamics, part of the bow used, contact point on the string, *vibrato* or non-*vibrato*. Remind students of the variety of colors available to them on their instruments and that their job as a musician is to first have an idea of the sound or color they want, and then figure out how to make it happen on their instrument. Use the phrase, "I always have a choice" as a spoken mantra and as a banner or sign in the classroom.

2. Colorful Warm-Ups

Over the course of several weeks, review and/or learn terms for coloristic devices and use the warm-up to apply them to scales or other material. Some examples:

- *sul tasto*
- *ponticello*
- a delicate tone with the bow rolled or tipped
- playing strictly at the tip or strictly at the frog
- playing a G scale *sul* G, to hear the difference in color when high pitches are played on a low string
- changing the amount of weight
- *tremolo*
- *col legno*
- changing the amount or speed of *vibrato*

Write the terms on the board under a heading like "Timbre Choices" as they are mastered and use them throughout the rehearsal.

Let a different student conduct the warm-up each day, choosing the kind of sound they want, and using the proper terms (or other descriptive words when no technical term exists) to request the sound they have in mind. Encourage them to combine various colors in the course of a scale; for example, "Play four eighth-notes on each pitch of the scale, at the tip, ponticello, like a breathy whisper, beginning *pianissomo* and *crescendoing* to the top of the scale, ending in a *forte*."

3. The One-Note Improv

Using A-440 for violins/violas/cellos and A-220 for basses, ask students to review how many different ways they can play this one note. Try each suggestion briefly with the group as a review of possible techniques. Violins and violas may not remember the variety of positions with which they can play this note—encourage them to play it at least three different ways, using different strings.

Do the same thing with the pitch E, but let students choose any octave they like, experimenting briefly with their own instrument for a variety of colors.

Play the recording of "First Impressions" from *Appalachia Waltz* with Yo Yo Ma, Mark O' Connor, and Edgar Meyer. In the first section (0:00 to 1:25), students should use "E" as a pedal tone on their instrument, bow freely, and experiment with timbres and dynamics that "feel right" for the kind of tension or the mood of the piece. In the second section (1:25 to 3:01), they should use A, and return to E again in the last section (3:01 to the end). Have students close their eyes and focus on the mood and timbres provided by the players on the recording, trying to add their own color in a way that feels appropriate. Remind them of the many choices they have.

Repeat this activity with half the group playing and the other half listening, or with groups of three or four playing as a group, with the rest of the class listening. In this experience, groups should rehearse by merely watching and observing each other in a circle as they play, without discussing their choices verbally or choosing a director to make the choices.

Invite students to reflect on this experience, sharing their impressions of the different performances, the moods created by the various choices, colors and ideas that they felt were particularly effective, and their experience of playing together in this unrehearsed way.

4. The Next Step

Give students a copy of the score to Åse's Death and the assignment to number each phrase and label them by form (A, A', B, coda, etc.). (This could be assigned as homework.) A group discussion could determine consensus about the form—it will most likely be ten phrases and a coda (see Form above). Have students transfer these numbers to their parts—they will be used as rehearsal numbers, and make it possible to refer specifically to each particular phrase repetition.

TEACHING PLANS
ORCHESTRA

Throughout the next few weeks of rehearsal, ask for student input about the color of each phrase with regard to contact point ("normal," *sul tasto, ponticello,* etc.), amount of bow hair used, amount of weight, bow placement (tip, middle, or frog), intensity of *vibrato,* fingering and position. Experiment with student ideas and have students justify and debate their choices. When a particular choice seems "right," have students write it in their parts. Encourage students also to assign other more poetic, less technical words to the different phrases, words such as "whisper" or "faint echo" or "intensify." The best words will be the most evocative—encourage students to find the most specific, expressive words possible.

Grieg marked the entire piece *con sordino.* Ask students to reflect on why he did, besides the obvious "he wanted it soft." Help students hear the effect of *con sordino* playing as essentially coloristic, by trying some intense, full-bodied *forte* playing with mutes on. Try playing the piece without mutes and compare.

The intention is to create a sensitive performance of Åse's Death but perhaps more importantly to open students to the wide range of timbral possibilities on their instrument and create a mindset of intentionality, so they see making strong timbral choices as part of their responsibility as an artist.

Assessment

Give students a copy of a short, relatively easy piece in a lyrical style, approximately 16 to 32 bars long, even as easy as "Twinkle, Twinkle." It could be a folk song, a pop song, or a simple Classical melody, or it could be a melody of the student's own choosing. The copy should be clean and unmarked, bare of any dynamic or expressive directions.

Students' assignment is to mark the part with their own ideas for dynamics and colors. Their newly marked part should include at least four dynamic markings, including a *crescendo* or *diminuendo,* and at least five of the following: *sul tasto, ponticello*, at the tip, at the frog, *col legno, molto vibrato,* non-*vibrato*; and an additional evocative phrase or word of their own, such as "whispered" or "biting" or "with edge."

Students should practice their piece and perform it, either privately for the teacher, in class for a peer assessment, on a recording for self-assessment, or several of the above. The following rubric can be used for all three assessments:

5 or A

Part included all required markings and markings were artistic, appropriate, and musically effective; Performance showed attention to markings and a clear understanding of terms and techniques; Performance was creative, imaginative and very effective.

4 or B

Part included all required markings and markings were appropriate, but not always artistic or musically effective; Performance showed attention to markings but they were not always accomplished effectively. Performance showed some creativity or imagination, and was often effective.

3 or C

Part included all but one marking and markings were mostly appropriate, though not particularly artistic or musically effective. Performance was lacking close attention to markings and/or there were technical difficulties in playing them. Performance was occasionally imaginative or effective.

2 or D

Part was marked and performed, but without attention to detail, or artistic/musical effectiveness. Technical problems prevented an artistic performance. Rarely imaginative or effective.

1 or F

Student did not mark part or perform.

Cognitive Outcome

Students will create incidental music for a play.

Strategies

1. Homework in Front of the TV

As homework, students should watch an hour of narrative TV (a movie, sitcom, or other show with a story line) and jot down notes on the following:

- Give examples of different uses of music.
- Give some examples of specific instruments used, when and how they are used, and if they are effective. Why or why not?
- How is the characterization of a specific character accomplished through music?
- Describe some examples of music giving the viewer information that perhaps the characters themselves wouldn't know.
- Any examples of music coming from within the action (e.g. a radio playing, someone playing an instrument, etc.)?

Students can summarize their findings in a written paper, or share them informally in a class discussion. Emphasize through discussion the powerful effect of music on dramatic action and explore with students its various uses, using the questions above as a guide.

2. Coming to Terms

Through class discussion of the films and TV shows that students are watching, create a list of terms to describe the various uses of music in drama and film, and the musical genres and terms unique to each. Some examples: incidental music, soundtrack, underscoring, scene change music, entr'acte, overture, songs, dances, diegetic music (music from within the scene itself, as opposed to underscoring). Emphasize which forms are needed only in stage productions and not film (e.g. scene change music). Particularly effective examples could be viewed as video clips in class.

3. The *Peer Gynt* Story

Explore the script of *Peer Gynt* as a class. This could be done several ways (listed from quickest to most intensive):

a) Teacher provides general overall synopsis.

b) Teacher provides overall synopsis in installments, including playing the eight movements from the *Peer Gynt Suites* as they appear in the play.

c) Students read individually and discuss the entire play, over the course of several weeks.

d) Students, individually or in a group of two-three, read an assigned scene or scenes on their own (as they are divided below) and present a five-minute synopsis for the class, focusing briefly on the action and the meaning of the scene. This could be a daily activity for several weeks, or take several full days. There are about 35 short segments.

Act I:	Scene 1	Åse and Peer (divide in two parts)
	Scene 2	On the Way to the Hegstad Farm
	Scene 3	The Wedding and Ingrid's Abduction
Act II	Scene 1	The Abduction of the Bride/Ingrid's Lament
	Scene 2	Åse and Solveig Search for Peer
	Scenes 3, 4	Peer and the Three Herd Girls
	Scene 5	Peer and the Woman in Green
	Scene 6	In the Hall of the Mountain King
	Scene 7	Peer and the Bøyg
	Scene 8	Peer Returns Home/Scene with Helga
Act III	Scene 1	Peer Alone in the Woods
	Scene 2	Åse and Kari
	Scene 3	Peer, Solveig, the Woman and Her Brat
	Scene 4	Åse's Death
Act IV	Scene 1	A Beach in Morocco (two parts) Morning
	Scenes 2, 3	Peer Alone at Night, Nightmares
	Scenes 4, 5	Peer with the Ape, the Thief
	Scene 6	In the Arab Chief's Tent; Arabian Dance, Anitra's Dance

Scene 7	Anitra's Tent
Scene 8	Anitra Doublecrosses Peer
Scene 9	Peer's Monologue
Scene 10	Solveig's Song
Scenes 11, 12	Peer in Egypt
Scene 13	The Cairo Iinsane Asylum (two parts)

Act V	Scene 1	On the Ship; Peer Gynt's Journey Home
	Scene 2	The Shipwreck
	Scene 3	Funeral Scene
	Scene 4	Auction Scene
	Scene 5	Pentecost Eve; Peer's Monologue
	Scene 6	Threadballs, Leaves, Dewdrops Haunt Peer
	Scene 7	Peer and the Button-Molder First Time
	Scene 8	Reunion with the Troll King
	Scene 9	Button-Molder Second Time
	Scene 10	Scene with the Lean One, Churchgoers, Solveig (two parts)

4. Listening to Peer Gynt

   Movements from the Peer Gynt suites are easily available on recording and listed above in italics. These can be listened to and discussed through the process. Some questions for discussion after listening:

   a) How is the piece used (e.g. as underscoring, scene change music, entr'actes, song, dance, etc.)?

   b) What does the music tell us about the character(s) depicted? The mood of the scene? What does the music tell us about how we should be feeling toward the character(s) or the action?

   c) Describe the musical elements used to create the mood of each piece. What instruments were used? How were they used? Why?

5. The Final Project

   As a semester project, students will create their own incidental music for a play. This might be a play they are reading or have read in English class (such as *Romeo and Juliet*), an excerpt of a full-length play, or even a one-act play. Depending on the intended scope of the project and students' previous experience, they could work individually or in groups.

Also depending on students' previous experience with composition, the project could be as advanced as actually composing pieces of music—ideally, this could be for an actual dramatic production at school or in the community—or merely a narrative prose description of the music they would write and where it would appear in the play. It could also be a combination of both: students write a prose description of their entire "score" for the play, but actually only compose one piece, either for their instrument alone or for a combination of instruments.

For the "score in prose," students would write an in-depth description (two or three paragraphs) of each numbered piece of incidental music as it would appear in the play. For each piece, they should answer questions such as:

a) What instruments or voices would be used? Why?

b) What style of melody, harmony, texture, color, dynamics, etc.?

c) What kinds of familiar compositional devices would the piece use (e.g. *ostinato*, canon, dissonance, polyphony vs. homophony, etc.)?

d) How would the piece function: as underscoring, as a "cue" for the audience to understand the action, as scene change or transitional music, songs, dances, etc.?

e) Will there be any examples of diegetic music or music coming from the stage action?

f) Why would you use music here?

At the end of the term, students can present their "scores" to the class, providing a synopsis of the drama (if it is unfamiliar or different from the other students') and descriptions or actual performances of their score.

Assessment

If students have worked in groups, it would be an ideal opportunity to have them assess each other on criteria of their own choosing, such as completeness, thoughtfulness of approach, creativity, effective musical choices, effective use of instruments, thorough understanding of drama, etc.

Affective Outcome

Students will examine their understanding of and reactions to the subject of death and dying.

Strategies

1. Feelings at a Deathbed

    Ask students, "What might be some feelings you would find in a room where someone was sitting by the bed of someone else whom they loved and who was dying?" Students will likely say "sadness"— help them come up with other ideas such as regret, nostalgia, embarrassment, etc.

    Read *Peer Gynt*, Act III, Scene 4 (Åse's Death) as a group, inviting students to name any emotion they sense is present in the scene. Almost all the feelings are unspoken and would be conveyed by the actors as subtext. Encourage students to probe behind the dialogue for the deeper feelings behind the words. Students should add to their list from above such words as shame, grief, denial, joy, humor, or compassion. (When students suggest "love," compel them to come up with a more creative or expressive word.) By the time the scene reading is finished, the list might contain 15 to 20 words or more.

2. Back to the Music

    Play through Åse's Death or listen to a recording. Ask students, "Which of the feelings on our list do you feel are expressed by the music?" Discussion will hopefully elicit the idea that the music's "expression" is much more general than any of the specific words on the list and music, while perhaps more expressive than words, is harder to pin down in terms of specific meaning.

    If time permits, try this activity: students choose a word or two from the list and "assign" it to the piece or sections of the piece, and then play it with that feeling in mind. Ask them, "Did the way we played the piece change in some way? If so, how?"

3. Making It Personal

    Over several days or weeks, have students journal on these questions and afterwards perhaps share their thoughts in a group discussion:

    a) What has been your experience with death or dying so far in your life? Do you think about death much? Why or why not? When you do think about it, what are some of your thoughts?

    b) Think of someone you love very much. If you knew that you would not see them again after today, what would you tell them? Write a letter to them.

    c) How would you like to be remembered if you were to die today? What would you hope people would say about you or think about you? Write a eulogy for yourself.

    After students have reflected on these writing activities, and when the piece has been sufficiently rehearsed, ask them to play it all the way through, keeping in mind the thoughts and feelings they have expressed about their own understanding of death.

Assessment

Ask students to journal once more, this time on the theme of how the reflecting, journaling, and discussion affected their personal experience of playing Åse's Death, and how they believe it may or may not have affected the group's performance of it (in rehearsal or concert).

Music Selection

Åse's Death is a classic, enduring work for strings by a major 19th-century composer. It is easy enough to be played by an intermediate level orchestra but feels like a "serious," mature piece. Because it is short, the score can be copied for each student. This, along with the fact that it is structurally uncomplicated, makes it a perfect piece for student analysis. Its subject matter, the death of a loved one, is a rare theme in music playable by young orchestras, and opens up profound opportunities for affective experience for them.

Other Possible Outcomes

1. Bow control and phrasing in very slow music (skill)
2. Chromatic scale fingerings/tuning (skill)
3. Transposition (skill or cognitive)
4. Chromatic vs. diatonic harmonies/melodies (cognitive)
5. Tonal center, key, cadences on V and i. (cognitive)
6. Nationalism in music (cognitive)

Resources

Grieg, Edvard. Peer Gynt, op. 23. *Complete Incidental Music*, ed. Finn Benestad. Leipzig: C. F. Peters, 2000.

Peer Gynt *Suites Nos. 1 and 2 in Full Score*, Mineola, New York: Dover Publications, 1997.

Peer Gynt. New Concert Version, Kurt Masur, *Gewandhausorchestra Leipzig*, Philips 422 343-2.

Ibsen, Henrik. Peer Gynt, trans. Rolf Fjelde. Minneapolis: University of Minnesota Press, 1980.

Ibsen, Henrik. Peer Gynt: *A Dramatic Poem*, trans. John Northam. New York: Oxford University Press, 1993.

Meyer, Edgar, "First Impressions," *Appalachia Waltz*, Mark O'Connor, Yo-Yo Ma, Edgar Meyer, Sony SK 68460.

http://eserver.org/drama/peer-gynt.txt
Complete text of play in English

www.home.c2i.net/espenjo/home/ibsen/peergynt/index.htm
Complete text of play in Norwegian and English

OVERTURE TO EGMONT, OP. 84

Ludwig van Beethoven (1770-1827)

Background Information

In 1810, Vienna's Court Theater mounted a revival of *Egmont,* Goethe's great historical tragedy of 1778, and Beethoven was commissioned to write incidental music. On May 10, the play opened, featuring ten separate pieces of Beethoven's music minus the Overture. Beethoven had been slow in finishing it and it was not until the fourth performance, on June 15, that the Overture was added. More than merely an introduction to the drama, the Overture is a narrative drama in itself, telling the *Egmont* story in miniature.

Goethe's drama is based on the heroic true story of a 16th-century Flemish uprising against Spanish overlords. Under Charles V of Spain, the people of the Netherlands had enjoyed a certain amount of self-rule and freedom, but when his son, Philip II, assumed the throne, they found themselves oppressed by a tyrant determined to humiliate them. Under the king's governor, the nefarious Duke of Alba, hundreds Flemish citizens were executed or forced to give up their land and homes to quarter 20,000 Spanish troops. Philip had appointed as Governor of Flanders the Count Lamoral Egmont (1522-1568), a brave general, champion of freedom, and popular hero. Although Egmont generally supported Philip, he challenged the Inquisition and Spain's oppressive policies in the Netherlands. After an uprising, Egmont was captured, imprisoned, and beheaded publicly in Brussels' Grande Palace. As a martyr, he became a fierce rallying symbol for the proud Flemish.

Beethoven's Flemish extraction undoubtedly attracted him to the Egmont story, but more likely it was the values of republican equality and individual freedom in Goethe's drama that excited him most. Known has a hard-driving businessman, Beethoven nonetheless refused to take payment from the theatre for his music, an unprecedented gesture of generosity. Beethoven saw himself as a kind of misunderstood hero who knew the torment of personal struggle, and undoubtedly identified with Egmont.

TEACHING PLANS ORCHESTRA

Elements of Music

Form

An ingenious juxtaposition of *sonata-allegro* form and programmatic elements, both of which contribute to the piece's relentless forward momentum. Cast in three sections, the middle section is itself a three-part structure (Exposition/Development/Recapitulation), framed by a slow introduction (*sostenuto*) and a vigorous concluding coda (*allegro con brio*).

I. Introduction
     (*Sostenuto ma non troppo*)   mm. 1-24

II. Allegro

First Theme	mm. 25-66
Transition	mm. 67-81
Second Theme (Sarabande rhythm)	mm. 82-103
Transition	mm. 104-115
Developmen	mm. 116-162
Recapitulation begins	mm. 157
First Theme	mm. 163-200
Transition	mm. 201-224
Second Theme	mm. 225-246
Transition	mm. 247-286

III. Coda (*Allegro con brio*)   mm. 287-347

Programmatic Elements

The opening Introduction uses the characteristic rhythm of the Sarabande, a dance of Spanish origin and a reference by Beethoven to the Duke of Alba and his henchmen. This rhythm later becomes the Second Theme. In the drama of *sonata-allegro* form, this theme can be seen to do battle with the first theme. In the closing bars of Section II (mm. 275-286), a violent *fortissimo* statement of the Second Theme arrests the entire movement with an enigmatic final shriek in the violins (m. 278, often interpreted as portraying Egmont's death). This is followed by equally mysterious *ppp* harmonies in the woodwinds, perhaps a kind of quiet requiem for Egmont.

The overture's coda is the *siegessinfonie* (*victory symphony*), which concludes the play after a stirring monologue by Egmont. He is about to be led from his prison cell to mount the scaffold, and although he is alone with the prison guards, his words are presumably to the Flemish patriots, and lovers of freedom everywhere, "Protect your possessions! And to save that which is most dear to you, joyfully follow my example!"

Although the programmatic events of the overture do not appear in the same chronology as the play, they serve perfectly to build tension and sustain the musical momentum.

Rhythm

Typical of Beethoven's middle period works, rhythm is a unifying force throughout the piece. In fact, rhythmic drive is such a characteristic of nearly every measure that its sudden cessation is always an event of striking importance (e.g. m. 278 mentioned above). Rhythms are not complicated or unusual—in fact, they are typically short motivic fragments with a simple melodic contour that reinforces their rhythmic character. Rather, it is Beethoven's daring amounts of repetition, which create long stretches of tension.

Interestingly, the main rhythmic motif (short-short-short-long) is the same one Beethoven used in other major works of this so-called "heroic" period, such as the Fifth Symphony and Fourth Piano Concerto.

Melody

Also based on short, fragmentary ideas and repeated melodic motifs, the majority of melodic material is presented in the opening bars. Two main melodic ideas are continually recast in various rhythmic guises throughout the piece. The first, a short scale which traces the interval of a fourth, appears in the opening Sarabande rhythm (mm. 2-4) and reappears in a descending form soon after (violin I, m. 15). This time it is preceded by a lower neighbor tone and it is this three-note neighbor tone figure that dominates thereafter, whether in accompanimental and transitional material (e.g. violin I in m. 25; viola in m. 59), or in the single long-breathed melody in the piece (First Theme in cello, m. 29 with

361

upbeat). This note/lower neighbor note motif (first presented by the oboe in m. 5) becomes an important figure when combined with the main rhythmic motif (violins, mm. 43-44). It is this kind of complex inter-relationships of short motifs that help unify the piece.

Harmony

Key relationships follow traditions associated with the symphonic *sonata-allegro* form movements. The primary key is F minor, established in the slow introduction and by the first theme. The second theme (sarabande rhythm) appears first in A-flat major and later in D-flat major. The coda is in a bright, unclouded F major, which serves to create a kind of harmonic victory over the darker F minor of the previous 286 measures.

Both in key relationships and treatment of dissonance, the "Overture to Egmont" is not particularly experimental or innovative, but a few especially colorful moments are typically Beethoven. For example, the Second Theme is stated in two phrases of unambiguous A-flat major (mm. 82-89). The third phrase, however, ends with a chromatically altered last note (F-flat) This mode mixture to the minor side (D-flat/ C-sharp minor) creates not only a suddenly sinister effect, but facilitates a brief enharmonic modulation to A major for the woodwinds. The use of such third relationships is not without precedent, but the effect is still harmonically disorienting and a perfect transition to the development that follows.

Timbre

The piece uses a standard early 19th-century orchestration with double woodwinds and trumpets, four horns, timpani, and strings. Although it is the strings that typically form the main body of the work, Beethoven uses the winds to greater effect than the mere sustaining of harmonies. The choice of oboe for the plaintive opening solo (m. 5), the rhythmic punctuation of string melodies by winds/brass throughout, the final pounding of the sarabande rhythm (mm. 259-278) by the horns, the soft mourning of the woodwinds (mm. 279-286) and the dark presentation of the first theme by *tutti* cellos—these are insightful choices by a master orchestrator. Even the use of the two trumpets is masterful; although they play throughout, they are not really featured prominently until the exact moment when their presence is inevitable: the martial coda.

One idiomatic use of timbre is Beethoven's typical fragmentation of a long melody into short statements by different instruments or families. For example, the second theme (mm. 82-88) begins in the strings, with its consequent answered by woodwinds who share it in one-measure segments. The development section (m.116) begins exactly this way, tossing melodic bits among the woodwinds, a technique Beethoven had used with great success in the *Eroica Symphony.*

Texture

The overall texture is often quite dense because of three factors: thick-textured string writing with *divisi* and double stops, sustained wind/brass chords, and a general tessitura which often lies low and creates a dark, foreboding effect. With little contrapuntal writing, the texture is often melody versus accompaniment, with the accompaniment either from sustained wind chords or chugging *spiccato* eighth notes. The resulting muddiness and lack of clarity is a problem to be addressed in rehearsal.

Beethoven relies on three essential combinations of textures for the entire piece. Most common is a *tutti* orchestra where the strings provide the body of the sound and winds reinforce melodic material or sustain harmonies. A second texture is the alternation of strings with woodwind choir or brass effects (e.g. mm. 225-240). Only rarely does Beethoven thin the texture to a single line for effect, as in the oboe solo (m. 5), the violins' desperate cry (m. 278) or even the horrific blast of F-natural from the entire orchestra in m. 9.

Closely tied with his choices of timbre (as outlined above), Beethoven's texture changes often signal structural shifts. One inventive example is mm. 153-157. After a stormy development section, the cellos and basses have interrupted with a statement of the first theme, which feels like a recapitulation (mm. 146-152). This is, in turn, interrupted by a thinly scored *pianissimo* dominant seventh chord in the woodwinds, with first violins swirling nervously in the middle of it. This particular texture is unique to the piece and creates an unnerving feeling of stasis in the midst of the tumult.

Expression

Dramatic effects and shocking contrasts are often associated with Beethoven's style and figure prominently in this piece. The wide variety of articulations, percussive effects, and sudden tempo changes contribute to this style, but one of the most important expressive devices in Beethoven's arsenal is dynamics. (See Skill Outcome below.)

The Heart

The heart of the piece is the relentless rhythmic propulsion created by an almost punishing repetition of short, rhythmic cells. This rhythmic energy and the tension it creates are well-suited to an overture for a drama of such epic scope and emotion.

Introducing the Piece

This introduction should be spread out over several days, before the music is distributed.

On the first day, play a recording of the "Overture to Egmont: with this verbal introduction. "I'm going to play one of Beethoven's most famous overtures, composed for a drama called *Egmont*. It's about eight minutes long and in three sections. Listen carefully to the kind of "story" that the music tells and then be prepared to answer two questions.

1) Do you think the play was a tragedy or comedy? Why?
2) Does the music give any clues about what the story might be about? What pictures does it evoke in your imagination?

After playing the recording, let students share their ideas. They may be surprised to learn that the drama is a tragedy, since the overture's ending is so jubilant.

On the next day, begin by sharing a brief synopsis of the Egmont story, as outlined above. With knowledge of the political conflict, the good guy (Egmont), the bad guy (Duke of Alba), and Egmont's death by beheading, ask students again to make analogies between the music they're hearing and the story. Accept any thoughtful answers. Discuss the difficulty of this process and point out the variety of interpretations of the music which "work."

The next day, begin rehearsal with a scale warm-up in the sarabande rhythm. Write the first few measures on the board and demonstrate the bowing style if necessary.

Write the word "sarabande" on the board and explain its origin as a Spanish dance. "Beethoven used the sarabande symbolically in his overture. Which character(s) might it symbolize?" Discuss.

"We're going to listen to the overture once more, but this time follow along with your part. Make a notation in your part whenever you hear the sarabande rhythm and be prepared to tell me how many times you hear it."

Follow-up discussions throughout the next few weeks could focus on other programmatic aspects of the piece, including "Egmont's death," the meaning of the woodwind chords that follow it, the triumphant coda, etc. Compare these pictorial or symbolic aspects of the piece's structure with the *sonata-allegro* structure (which has its own coherent "drama").

Skill Outcome

Students will perform with expressive dynamics, making interpretive decisions about balance, blend, dynamic contour, and the relationship of parts to whole.

Strategies

1. Dynamics Ladder

   During an opening scale warm-up, stop in the middle of the scale and ask, "What dynamic would you say we're playing right now?" Whatever students can agree upon (for example *mezzo forte*), write it on the board. "Okay what's one dynamic louder?" (*forte*). Proceed this way, having students name each of the rungs on the entire ladder of dynamic indications, as you write them above or below the first one, by way of review.

When finished, the side of the board will have the complete ladder:

fff

ff

f

mf

mp

p

pp

ppp

Leave the ladder on the board and use it in successive rehearsal warm-ups. Let a student lead the warm-up by choosing:

• A single dynamic for the entire scale: "Let's play the whole scale at *piano*. What is *piano* for our orchestra?"

• A change of dynamics: "Begin *forte* and *diminuendo* to *piano* on the way up, do the reverse on the way down."

• *Subito* dynamics: "Play the next note of the scale at whatever dynamic I point to."

• Special dynamics (such as *fp* or *sf*):

Help the orchestra develop a sense of group dynamics, e.g. what a *mp* should sound and feel like. Stop often in the rehearsal process (of various pieces) and ask, "What dynamic are we playing right now?."

2. Who's on First?

Focusing only on mm. 29-36, isolate the different material by having each line play as the orchestra decides if it is "first melody" (e.g. most important material), "second melody" (important, but secondary material), "accompaniment," or "special effects."

In this phrase, for example: first melody=cellos; second melody=violin I; accompaniment=violin II, viola; special effects=bass. Hopefully, students will argue the importance of violin I in mm. 31-32 and 35-36 as it takes over primary importance from

TEACHING PLANS
ORCHESTRA

cellos. After students have heard each line and decided their relative importance, remind them to play their own part with the hierarchy in mind, trying to be aware of the relative importance of the different lines and adjusting dynamics accordingly.

In successive rehearsals, choose other similar spots (e.g. mm. 15-24, 116-124, 287-294), isolate separate lines and have students decide their relative importance and play with appropriate dynamics, asking questions such as, "Can you hear the 'First Melody' here?" Throughout the rehearsal process, remind students to keep listening and adjusting dynamics accordingly.

3. Marking Dynamics

As the orchestra moves further along in the rehearsal process, explain to them that a characteristic of Beethoven's style is the use of dramatic dynamics and sudden dynamic changes for effect. To visualize the extent of Beethoven's dynamic markings, have them take their music home and circle all the dynamic markings, using red for *f* markings and blue for *p* markings. A *mf* or *mp* would get one circle, a *f* or *p* would get a darker, double circle for more emphasis, etc. *Crescendos* would be marked with a red dashed line for the duration of the *crescendo, diminuendos* with a blue dashed line, etc. When finished, students should have a graphic depiction of the variety and extremes of dynamics in their part.

4. The Meaning of Dynamics

Rather than merely adhering to a series of abstract, arbitrary markings, encourage students to explore possible interpretive meanings of dynamic markings. Here are some examples:

A M. 1 and m. 9 are identical except one is *f* and the next is *ff*. Why? What is Beethoven's point? Try playing them with reverse dynamics. What's the effect? Do the measures that follow them need to be the same dynamic marking? Compel students to think deeply for the reasons behind the specific dynamic, and discourage answers like "because it's more interesting" or "it adds variety."

TEACHING PLANS
ORCHESTRA

B   Have students create expressive words to attach to specific dynamic markings to give them added expressive meaning. For example, the opening oboe solo's *piano* might be "lonely" or "distant" or "tender." The sixteenth-note figures in the second violin/viola (m. 15) might be "simmering"; the *sfp* in m. 28 might be a "whipcrack." Again, encourage students to see the dynamics as specific and meaningful, a kind of "secret clue" from Beethoven which must be decoded for meaning.

5.   Editing and Interpreting Beethoven

Help students to understand that written dynamics, especially in 18th-and early 19th-century music must be interpreted with discretion. For example, the upbeat to A is marked with the same *fortissimo* in every part, a common practice for composers of Beethoven's time, when the musicians were expected to make the adjustments for balance.

Have individual sections play this note with another section to hear how difficult it is to balance. When two trumpets play their *ff,* they will overpower the entire violin I section playing their own *ff.* Likewise, the strings can easily overpower younger woodwinds unless the woodwinds use tremendous amounts of energy. So a *fortissimo* that's interpreted as "as loud as you can play" might work in this spot for woodwinds and some string sections, but not for horns and trumpets.

The same principle applies to balancing homophonic chords so that all factors are heard. Some examples include the F minor string chord in m. 2, the woodwinds in m. 92, the horns and winds in m. 259 (this chord is often revoiced for four horns). Build these chords from the bottom and let the rest of the orchestra make decisions about balance. Have them use chord factor names ("the third" or "the root," etc.) to describe balance problems.

A different kind of interpretive challenge is the *crescendo* at m. 47. It is very difficult to create a *crescendo* of 12 bars, and most orchestras will offer too much and too soon. Try moving the beginning of the *crescendo* to a later spot, for example eight measures before A (m. 51). Have students create a metaphor to describe this long, carefully-paced *crescendo* (e.g. "do not open till Dec. 25" or "the world's slowest bench press.")

Assessment

1. Collect individual parts and evaluate them on how carefully (or imaginatively) they have been marked in rehearsal. (This can be either at any time during the rehearsal process or after the concert.) Use a simple three-point rubric:

    1 Part includes some markings.

    2 Part shows most markings and is in general carefully and thoughtfully marked.

    3 Part is thoroughly marked and shows evidence of creativity, care, and neatness.

2. Record the orchestra in rehearsal and have students listen and critique their playing in the form of short written comments about specific spots, with special attention to dynamics.

3. Have each student choose three favorite moments in the piece and write a one-page journal entry discussing how dynamics "make or break" each of those moments. They should discuss the context of each dynamic marking and why it is particularly suited to that moment in the music.

4. Assess the orchestra's playing informally for their effective use of dynamics.

Cognitive Outcome

Students will recognize the use of the motif and the sequence as organizing devices.

**TEACHING PLANS
ORCHESTRA**

Strategies

1. Introduction

    "Have you ever been in someone's kitchen or bathroom where there was a particular fruit, say strawberries, everywhere—stenciled on the walls, embroidered on the hand towels, in the curtain fabric design, etc? Maybe it wasn't strawberries but ducks, or hearts, or daffodils—one thing that appears everywhere but in different sizes, shapes and colors." Explain the word motif and invite students to share the kinds of motifs they've seen used this way. "What's the purpose of a motif?" (to unify or "tie different things together").

    "A musical motif also serves the same purpose. It's a short pattern, usually two to six notes, that appears in different forms, just like the motif in interior decorating. Can anyone name the most famous short musical motif in a symphony?" (Beethoven, Symphony No. 5, First Movement). If time permits, listen to the first several minutes of Symphony No. 5.

2. Now we have it, what do we do with it?

    Write a four-note descending motif on the board.

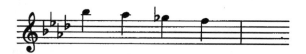

    "This is an example of a motif. Now to use it exactly this way over and over would be boring, so good composers do interesting things with motifs. How many different things can you think of to do with these four notes?" Make a list of student ideas (start on a different note, vary the rhythm of each note, change one of the intervals, use only some of the notes, add more notes, reverse the direction of the notes, etc.).

    Show them how the shape or intervals of the motif might suggest other ideas. For example, these four notes trace the interval of a perfect fourth:

Using staff paper, have students experiment with the motif, notating five different variations of it.

3. The Web of Motifs

Have students search for the above four-note motif in their parts. The first obvious example is violin I (m. 15). Whenever a new example is found, have the student play it for the group to hear and discuss the compositional technique that's being used.

Throughout the rehearsal process, challenge students to uncover other examples of this motif in various guises and help them discover more difficult examples (e.g. the opening sarabande, mm. 2-4: violin I traces an upward scale; the descending lyrical melody mm. 36-42).

4. Breaking It Down

Point out to students that the last two notes of the motif are a minor second or half-step.

Invite them to find other examples of this "micro-motif" in their parts, and have them play each example they find, as before. If no student finds it, point out the violin I melody in mm. 4-5, the first two notes of each successive entrance of oboe, clarinet, and bassoon (mm. 5-6). Another important example is the first three notes of theme I (mm. 28-29) in the cello part. Help students uncover the source of this "idea" (the note-neighbor note-note figure introduced in violin I, m. 15, also used as the transition material in m. 25).

5. The Sequence: Building Tension

Show students, if they haven't noticed already, how in m. 42 (violin I) the two-note minor second motif sets up a chain of patterns just like it. Introduce the word sequence. Have the first violins play mm. 42-47, first alone and then against the bass/cello pedal tone. "What is the effect of these sequences?" (rising tension). Have students search for other examples of sequence in their parts, playing them for everyone to hear.

Assessment

1. Have students create an inventory of motifs and sequences used in the "Overture to Egmont." Using staff paper, notate and group examples as either:

    a) related to the four-note perfect fourth motif or

    b) related to the minor second motif or

    c) an example of a sequence

    Identify each example by measure number. Students without lots of examples in their own part (e.g. timpani, trumpets) could use a copy of the violin I part, or borrow the score and use any part.

2. Have students compose an eight to 16 measure melody that uses a motif in at least three different ways, including a sequence of three segments. Possible letter grades for the assignments might be:

    A No notation errors, melody "works" well and includes at least three interesting uses of the motif including a sequence; melody is good balance of unity and variety; logical structure; satisfying ending

    B Includes one or two notation errors; motif is used in at least three different ways, including a sequence; melody is "correct" but not necessarily satisfying or interesting.

    C Three or more notation errors; motif is not used in three different ways, is missing a sequence, or sequence is incomplete; missing one or more of the following: logical structure, interesting idea, satisfying ending.

D   Assignment turned in but lacking most of the above criteria.

3.   Have students find examples of the use of motifs and sequences in other pieces they are playing in orchestra or in solo repertoire. Have them bring in two examples with a brief explanation of how they are being used by the composer.

Affective Outcome

Students will examine the orchestra as a metaphor for "community."

Strategies

1.   Refer to the "Who's on First?" activity under skill outcome above. After students have had experience with breaking the texture apart into separate lines, discuss the real importance of the various lines compared to their relative prominence in the texture. For example, have the basses play their part mm. 25-37, including counting all the rests, and ask the orchestra to comment on how important the part is, and even if it could be possibly eliminated. What would be the effect? Discuss the relationship between "important" and "unimportant" parts. End the discussion with a short journal writing activity based on the question: "How are relationships between lines in a Beethoven symphony like relationships in the orchestra itself?"

2.   When rehearsing a section like mm. 29-36, ask the accompaniment voices (e.g. violin II/viola) to comment on these questions: "How does it feel playing accompaniment? Do you have any feelings toward those around you with "more interesting" parts (e.g. cello or violin I)? How do you deal with that? How do you stay committed to playing well?" Do a similar discussion with horns/woodwinds at m. 51.

After a brief discussion, invite those with many rests (e.g. timpani, trumpets) to share their perspective on staying committed and interested.

End the discussion with a short journal writing activity based on the question, "Do you ever wish you played in a different section of the orchestra? Which one? Why?"

TEACHING PLANS
ORCHESTRA

3. Ask students to brainstorm and develop a group definition of the word "community." Write ideas on the board. Rehearse the Development section of the piece (mm. 116-157), breaking apart individual lines and inviting students to become more aware of the variety of activities in the different lines of the texture.

Have students journal on the question: "In what ways might this section of the music symbolize "community?" Let students share their ideas aloud.

Assessment

As a final journal activity, have students write on the question, "How has the discussion of "community" changed your understanding of this piece? Your playing of it? Your feelings toward it?"

An alternate assessment might be a piece of visual art (drawing, painting, sculpture, collage, mobile, etc.) created by each student that expressed the idea of community vis-à-vis the "Overture to Egmont" or the orchestra. These would be displayed and presented to the class. The assignment's parameters are intentionally wide and somewhat vague to promote high levels of personal reflection. Evaluate student responses accordingly, and invite them to think both globally and abstractly, as well as personally (that is, how this assignment reveals their own thoughts and feelings about the orchestra as community).

Music Selection

The Overture to Egmont is a wonderful introduction to Beethoven's unique musical style and, of his symphonic works, probably the most accessible to young players. It presents all the challenges of Classical period bowing, articulation, and phrasing styles. In spite of its difficulty, it is always exciting and students seem to never tire of rehearsing it.

Other Possible Outcomes

1. Classical period bowing styles (skill)
2. Incidental music for plays (cognitive)
3. Programmatic effects in music (cognitive)
4. *Sonata-allegro* form (cognitive)

Resources

Goethe, Johann Wolfgang von. *Plays*, New York: Continuum Publishing, 1993.

Block, Glenn. *"Egmont Overture" in Teaching Music through Performance in Orchestra*, ed. David Littrell and Laura Reed Racin, Chicago: GIA Publications, 2001.

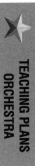

TEACHING PLANS
ORCHESTRA

FINALE (THE DARGASON) FROM
ST. PAUL'S SUITE

Gustav Holst (1874-1934)

Background Information

Even as he gained international recognition as a composer, Gustav Holst never gave up his teaching position at the St. Paul's Girls' School at Brook Green, Hammersmith. The school had opened in January 1904 with a staff of 12 and a student body of 53. Within two years, the enrollment had reached 157 students, and the school was searching for a second music teacher to teach singing, for which Holst was hired in autumn 1905, at that time the only male faculty member.

In 1911, Holst was asked to take over the fledgling school orchestra, which until then had not been a serious ensemble, but under Holst's direction grew and flourished. It was for this string orchestra that Holst began composing the St. Paul's Suite, probably in August 1912, a period during which he was relatively free of other professional composing and conducting obligations. In early March 1913, he left on a trip to Spain and was delighted when he returned to find completed the new Music Wing at St. Paul's. The music department at St. Paul's was now an integral part of the school, and the new wing included 12 sound-proofed practice rooms, a chamber music room, a "singing hall" that could accommodate 300, and another large room which came to be known as "Mr. Holst's Room." This bright and airy chamber, with its two grand pianos, large double windows, long writing desk, and fine acoustics was an inspiration to Holst, but it was the newfangled central heating system, which pleased him most. He could turn the temperature up to 80 degrees, which helped ease the neuritis that plagued him throughout his life.

It was in this room that Holst was to do most of his composing and the first work he completed there was a kind of tribute to the school which had provided him this well-appointed, state-of-the-art facility. The Music Wing was dedicated on July 1, 1913 and the girls' orchestra was duly proud to perform their own St. Paul's Suite. By this time, the orchestra had grown to include a few wind instruments, for which Holst wrote ad lib parts. (These were not included when the piece was published in 1922.) Holst, affectionately called "Gussie" by the girls, enlisted anyone who could play to join the orchestra, including faculty members and even his wife, who played bass. Members of the school who were not in the orchestra were invited to join in the Finale by singing the tune of "The Dargason" to the traditional words "It was a maid of my country, As she came by a hawthorn tree."

The four-movement suite was actually not entirely new. The last movement, entitled "Finale (The Dargason)" was a reworking of the last movement of another, earlier suite, the Second Suite in F for military band where it was titled "Fantasia on the 'Dargason'." In addition to re-scoring the work for strings, Holst transposed it from F major to C major, and expanded it with five additional variations.

Holst was fascinated with music of the Baroque, particularly Purcell, and his fondness for the suite form is but one example of that. In fact, most of the works for which he is best known are suites, including the two Suites for military band and "The Planets," as well as a dozen others. Among the many pieces Holst wrote for school groups, however, the St. Paul's Suite probably most beloved and has earned an unusually distinguished reputation. It even appeared on a program of the Boston Symphony Orchestra, which the composer guest conducted in January 1932. Holst later described the concert in a letter to his wife, where, in his usual dry and understated way, he mentions "breaking a collar stud" while conducting the St. Paul's Suite.

In reviewing the concert, the typically trenchant Phillip Hale of the Boston Globe noticed an aspect of the St. Paul's Suite familiar to every modern school orchestra director: its difficulty. "…It was written for the orchestra of the St. Paul School for Girls. For practice or performance? If for performance, these girls must be singularly accomplished in the use of stringed instruments." Of the same performance, the Boston Massachusetts Transcript said, "He must have taught his pupils well, if they played what is set down for them."

Indeed, the St. Paul's Suite reveals much about Holst's confidence in his pupils and his commitment to them as their teacher. Although untrained,

Holst was evidently a natural teacher whose particular gifts were evidenced by the many tributes paid him over the years by former students, who spanned all ages and abilities. His unstinting enthusiasm, mix of witty humor and passionate intensity, and unusual empathy for students as individuals were unflagging even though he often had reservations about the constant fatigue he suffered as a result trying to be both teacher and composer. On this tension between his two careers, he reflected:

> *The vast majority of great artists of the world have been teachers—usually very good ones. Of course they grumbled when too much time had to be spent in teaching or when their pupils were more stupid than usual. Who wouldn't? But this is very different from despising teaching.*

Elements of Music

Form

The piece is a set of 30 variations on the eight-bar Dargason tune, plus an 11-bar coda. The tune functions as an *ostinato*: it is always presented strictly in its eight-bar form and is never transposed or fundamentally altered. The variations can be summarized as follows:

	"Dargason" Melody	Dynamic	Features
1.	violin I	*pp*	*Soli* presentation of tune without accompaniment
2.	violin II	*pp*	Ornamented G pedal "drone" in violin I
3.	violin I	*pp*	Texture thickens with open string drones and *pizzicato*
4.	viola	*cresc.*	Lilting *pizzicato* accompaniment in thirds
5.	violin II	*mf*	Same as above, but texture thickens
6.	violin I	*f*	Full-textured accompaniment over C pedal
7.	"	*dim.*	Minor harmonies anticipate "Green Sleeves"
8.	viola	*p/mp*	"Green Sleeves" presented as countermelody in cello
9.	violin II	*p/mp*	Violin I joins cello in "Green Sleeves"
10.	viola	*p/mp*	"Green Sleeves" continues in violin I
11.	violin II	*p*	Cello continues "Green Sleeves"
12.	viola	*p*	Cello completes "Green Sleeves"
13.	violin I & II	*f*	Melody in octaves; sturdy, *pesante* accompaniment
14.	"	*ff*	Violent, skipping rhythm in multiple stops
15.	Low strings	*ff*	Marcato melody in violas, cellos, basses
16.	"	*ff*	As above, but violins "run" in duples over tune
17.	All but violin I	*ff*	Most intense statement, violin I *tremolo*

18.	violin I, viola	*sub p*	Intensity remains, Pedal G and rising chromatic scale
19.	violin I; viola I	*cresc.*	Pedal G is released, chromatics intensify
20.	violin II; viola II	*ff*	Chromatic harmony, faster harmonic rhythm
21.	violin I	*ff*	Rising chromatic scale but new, slower rhythm
22.	"	*ff*	Hints of two against three; strong A minor feeling
23.	violin II, viola	*ff*	Melody in 3rds; Violin I "fiddling" open strings
24.	"	*fff*	Soaring, climactic presentation of "Green Sleeves"
25.	viola, cello	*fff*	Violins sing "Green Sleeves" in high octaves
26.	violin II, viola	*fff*	Violin I/ cello continue "Green Sleeves"
27.	violin II	*dim.*	"Green Sleeves" fades and concludes
28.	viola	*p*	Hushed, very slow harmonic rhythm
29.	cello	*pp*	Whispered accompaniment, almost no motion
30.	"	*pp*	Accompaniment floats higher, softer
Coda: Bass, and Violin solos		*pp*	Whimsical duet, four-bar violin scale solo, *tutti* "button"

Holst keeps the players engaged by distributing the tune around the orchestra, but because it is never varied in length, rhythm, or key, he relies on variation in all the other musical elements, which he pushes to the extreme. In fact, it would be hard to think of more possibilities for accompanying the Dargason tune than Holst has already created!

Rhythm

The basic rhythmic cell set up by the Dargason melody is a 6/8 skipping rhythm which is present in nearly every measure of the piece. Holst loved to experiment with rhythmic "tricks" and here juxtaposes several kinds of two against three: the Green Sleeves melody is set in a broad 3/4 time over the 6/8 and a quicker eighth-note duplet figure scampers above and below the tune in variations 16, 17, 22, and the coda.

Rhythmic acuity is one of the principle challenges of the piece. According to the New Grove's Dictionary, "lack of rhythm was one of the few things that made Holst really angry, for rhythm mattered more to him than anything else in life."

Melody

The Daragason melody is contained within a ninth, moves back and forth between *mi-do* to *fa-re* patterns, and is completely diatonic. It is unclear how Holst was acquainted with this melody, except perhaps as a familiar folk tune with various sets of traditional lyrics. The tune is circular: an eight bar melody which never cadences, always turning back on itself. It is first found in printed version in John Playford's *The English Dancing Master* of 1651, (where it is also called "Sedany" or "Sedanny") but probably dates from the 16th century. Playford gives instructions for the dance, a typical English country dance with equal numbers of ladies and gentlemen in a single line. The simple melody would be embellished and varied by the musicians, repeated as many times as necessary until all the dancers had finished the steps. The word "dargason" is possibly derived from the Anglo-Saxon word for "dwarf" or "fairy." "Sedany" means "a woman dressed in silks."

The Dargason melody is catchy but it would have been a formidable challenge to create a piece of length and interest from such scant musical material. It was Holst's knack for quodlibet, the art of combining melodies, which lifts the piece from the mundane. He had already combined two folksongs in counterpoint in other works such as *A Somerset Rhapsody* and *Christmas Day.*

Here the second tune is the familiar "Green Sleeves" (Holst's spelling), which is even today the most well-known of all Elizabethan melodies. It was a brilliant choice. Where the "Dargason" is rustic, dance-like, and frivolous, "Green Sleeves" is lyrical, soaring, and substantial, at least the way Holst presents it. When it appears it comes as a complete surprise and has a way of sounding at once both new and strangely familiar. The staggered entrances of the two melodies also make them feel fresh and less predictable in their phrase structure.

Although quodlibet was a favorite device of Holst and an effective artistic choice, it is not hard to also imagine a pedagogical aim. The New Grove's says: Holst was an unorthodox teacher. He believed in learning by doing and his elementary harmony pupils were encouraged to make up rounds and to spend the rest of the lesson singing them.

Harmony

The Dargason melody suggests only the simplest of tonic and dominant harmonies, but Holst manages to eke out of it every possible harmonic twist. Since this melody and its presentation is unvarying, it is primarily the speed of harmonic rhythm which controls the drive toward tension or release. There are essentially three levels of harmonic rhythm:

1) Slow pedal harmonies, most often built on the tonic (e.g. variations 3, 6, 14) or the dominant (e.g. variation 18) which typically lasts the full eight-bar phrase. Often built on open-string, double stop accompaniments, these variations have the most rustic flavor, suggesting the drone of bagpipes or fiddlers.

2) Medium speed harmonic movement, with chord changes about every one or two bars. These harmonies tend to be richer, diatonic, and flavored with more minor or modal chords, and they are mostly associated with the "Green Sleeves" variations where they support a rhapsodic, singing style (e.g. variations 7-12 and 24 to the end). "Green Sleeves" is here set in D minor.

3) Brisk harmonic movement, with chord changes on every beat, mostly through "walking bass" patterns, either diatonic (e.g. variation 13) or chromatic (e.g. variations 18-20).

The playful interaction of these very different levels of harmonic rhythm, coupled with the variety of textures, timbres, dynamics, and rhythmic activity keep refreshing the Dargason melody and prevent it from sinking into cliché.

Timbre

Because the variations are so short and the Dargason melody so repetitive, quick changes of timbre signal each new variation. In fact, timbral variation is, along with harmonic rhythm, one of the most obvious elements Holst uses to create interest and appeal.

It is instructive to examine Holst's original version of the piece (from the Second Suite in F), written with all the colors of the wind band (including percussion) in mind. Reducing this rich instrumentation to the monochrome string orchestra would seem to impoverish it but the new piece actually works quite happily. Both its melodies are Elizabethan (an important musical period for the English generally and one beloved by

Holst) and the most popular instrumental ensemble for Elizabethans was the string consort.

Holst pulled out all the stops and used an incredible variety of string techniques including *pizzicato/arco* contrasts, open-string drones, a variety of articulations, *tremolo,* quadruple stops, extreme contrasts of range, and even solo violin (versus a stubborn bass *pizzicato*) at the end.

Other simple but equally small touches show Holst's craftsmanship. A few examples: the layering on effect of the opening, where the fiddler is joined by the band, the delay of the first bass entrance, and the simple but effective relocating of the Dargason melody as it travels quickly from part to part, an effect which also provides relief and interest for the players!

Texture

Closely tied to the wide variety of timbres outlined above, wide changes of textures are also important markers for the start of each new variation. The thinnest textures are reserved for the opening and closing bars of the piece, while the thickest ones typically enhance the loudest, most climactic variations.

Throughout most of the variations, where the Dargason melody is presented alone, the accompanying texture is mostly homophonic or at most lightly contrapuntal. The real polyphony appears, of course, when "Green Sleeves" joins the Dargason tune, although it may seem to some listeners that there is still only one melody and its accompaniment—so compelling is "Green Sleeves" that it seems to briefly overshadow its persistent partner tune.

Expression/Dynamics

A wide variety of dynamics serves two important functions besides the obvious one of interest and variety. In close tandem with harmonic or rhythmic devices, they guide the piece's movement through broad swaths of greater or lesser tension (e.g. the first eight variations, a gradual opening up of the piece's energy). Other times they are whimsically arbitrary or sudden, and contribute to the piece's general mood of playfulness (e.g. the subito changes of dynamic that begin variations 13 and 18).

Another expressive aspect worth noting is articulation styles, which vary from the sprightly, detached styles of the Dargason melody to the accented, vigorous, even violent rhythmic figures, which accompany it. These are set in relief by the extreme *legato* cantabile of the "Green Sleeves" sections.

The Heart

The heart of the piece is the juxtaposition of the repetitive, rhythmic and dancing Dargason melody with the singing Green Sleeves melody. This combination is compositionally clever, to be sure, but also creates a joyous whole greater than its parts. The moment the two melodies converge is an unmistakably unique sensation—a kind of circular, floating feeling.

Introducing the Piece

1. Before passing out the music, teach the Dargason melody in C major by rote, first by singing it to students and then having them sing it back until it is familiar. (This could be done on solfége syllables, with hand signs). When students can sing it easily, have them try playing it, practicing under tempo until they are confident.

2. Ask students to play the Dargason melody as a canon. They will need to decide when the second voice should enter. After experimenting until it sounds "right," ask them to discuss why and how the two melodies worked together, and what it is that makes it sound "right." This should introduce the concepts of consonance and dissonance, which can be defined as terms.

3. Have students improvise a simple long-tone accompaniment for the Dargason melody using I and V chords. Start by having basses hold a C, and invite the rest of the students to find notes to create a chord over it. Call this chord a I chord, and explain that it is so called because it's built on the first scale degree. Do the same with a G, and encourage students to change to the note nearest the one they are already playing. Call it the V chord. Rock back and forth between these two chords until students can play them confidently and in tune.

As a final step, have half the orchestra play the "Dargason" melody, and the others improvise long-tone I and V chords underneath it. It will take several attempts before students will be comfortable knowing when to change chords. Ask them to speculate about which chords work at certain points in the melody, relating it to the earlier discussion of consonance and dissonance. (Melody notes work best over chords that contain some of the same notes, and melodies themselves often even suggest certain chords by their outline, e.g. the first three notes of the Dargason melody.)

4. Explain to students the origin of the Dargason melody and tell them about Holst using it for a piece of 30 variations. Invite them to speculate on ways he might have made the piece interesting, in spite of 30 identical repetitions. Pass out the music and read through the piece, or listen to a good recording and discuss student reactions to the question.

Skill Outcome

Students will read and perform rhythmic patterns of two against three.

Strategies

1. Physical First

Begin with eurythmic activity. In a large space, have students begin stepping around the room in a rhythmic "one-two" pattern. (This would be best with music, either improvised by the teacher or a recording.) They should speak "one-two" out loud as they step. Very soon after beginning, have them speak "one-two-three" (and silently clap the same) over their "one-two" stepping, with the music still sounding in a duple meter. Let them continue for a few minutes until they are comfortable.

As they grow in confidence, repeat the process, but this time stepping in threes and speaking/clapping twos. Then have students practice switching from one to the other on your command "Switch!" When they can do it (without too many casualties!), add variety by dividing them into A's and B's, with each half doing one pattern or the other, and switching patterns on your command. (This activity can be done with students standing in place at their orchestra chair, but for the full-body feeling is much better in a large room where they can move through space.)

2. The Next Step

    With students at their seats, have them set up a gentle tapping on their leg with one hand in a duple meter, and speaking "one-two" as above. Add the other hand tapping threes against it. Challenge them by varying the activity: while they continue to tap both twos and threes, have them switch speaking "one-two" and "one-two-three"; as they improve in doing both, challenge them to be able to switch hands. Most students will not be able to switch, at least for the first few days. Make this a homework assignment, something they can practice silently in many places (e.g. on the bus, waiting in the lunch line, during study hall, etc.).

3. Putting It All Together

    Teach students to sing "Green Sleeves." Playing the melody for them, ask if anyone knows lyrics for the tune. Some may know it as the Christmas carol, "What Child is This?" Show them the 16th-century lyrics and have them discuss when they think they were written. Sing "Green Sleeves" with these lyrics and invite discussion.

My Ladye Greensleeves
Alas! My love you do me wrong,
To cast me off discourteously
For I have lov-ed you so long,
Delighting in your company.

Greensleeves was my delight,
Greensleeves was my heart of gold,
Greensleeves was all my joy,
And all for my Lady Greensleeves

Using the large space for movement, review the hands versus feet eurythmics activity (number one above). Add a new twist (actually an easier variation) with students stepping "in one" and alternately clapping silently in two or three, switching on your command.

Ask students which movement describes the Green Sleeves melody (threes). Compare with the Dargason melody (twos). Have them move in one and try singing each melody, clapping silently in twos ("Dargason") or threes ("Green Sleeves").

When students are confident, divide into two groups and try both simultaneously. (Remember: "Green Sleeves" will begin one large beat after the "Dargason"). When the counterpoint breaks down, go back to doing each melody individually. Give each group a chance to succeed at both melodies.

4. Notating

While tapping duple against triple (as in number two above), students will figure out fairly quickly that the composite rhythm of their two hands (with a duple left hand) is:

After they have mastered the rhythm by tapping, ask them to notate the composite rhythm that they hear. They will need to choose the overall meter and the note values to assign within that meter. Check their work and compare answers. (Most students will likely use 3/4 meter.)

Next ask them to notate each hand separately, as two lines of counterpoint. Students may have trouble notating the duple rhythm. Help them discover two alternatives and help them understand the mathematics and the notational conventions that make each possible:

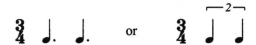

Throughout the next rehearsals, quiz students with quick notational problems for them to solve, such as: "Two triplets in a measure of 2/4" or "Large single triplet in a measure of 2/4." Reverse the questions.

Move back and forth between notating duples and triples of all speeds and meters, helping students to understand the principles of using smaller or larger note values, as the notational convention may be. Always have at least one student writing their answer on the board while the rest work at their seats, and always include performing/speaking the rhythms as part of the process. Particular students will enjoy this type of musical math and should be challenged with more difficult notational puzzles.

At some point in the process, the question will need to be posed: "Is the Dargason melody in twos or threes? Is 6/8 a duple or triple meter?" (Actually it is a composite of both, but in this case, because of its tempo, it is felt in two.) This is important for understanding the relationship between the physical feeling and notation, and vice versa.

5. Scales and Warm-Ups

As part of the daily warm-ups, have students play duples and triples:

a) Alternating duplets and triplets regularly on every other scale degree.

b) Switching randomly from duple to triple on a pre-arranged hand signal from you.

c) Dividing the orchestra in two groups playing together, but alternately duple or triple, so both are heard simultaneously. (This may be more effective if articulations are different—for example, the triplets can be played *spiccato* against a more *legato* duplet, or *pizzicato* versus *arco,* etc.)

Use student conductors as often as possible.

6. Finding Other Examples

Ask students if they have ever listening to windshield wipers that created a cross-rhythm. Invite them to look for other examples, both auditory and visual, of cross-rhythms, especially two against three. Examples might come from architecture, nature, visual arts, furniture, or found objects at school or home. Have them describe or bring in their examples for the class.

7. Knowing the Score

Give each student a photocopied score of the piece. If they are unaccustomed to reading a score, help them see how it is organized. As homework, have them mark the Dargason tune with a highlighter, illustrating how it passes among the parts. Using the Dargason tune as a guide, have them number each variation—these numbers will be used to make discussion of the piece more efficient.

Have students design a score map to show where and how two against three is used in the piece. This should not be musical notation or words, but rather icons or other visual designs. Encourage students to be as artistic and creative as they want, as long as they fairly represent what is in the score. They should also show the difference between the different kinds of two against three.

Encourage students to include as much other information in their score map as they can, such as textures, dynamics, and the location of the Dargason melody.

As the rehearsal process evolves, return to any of the above activities (including having students conduct in one while speaking or singing either or both melodies) to reinforce the two against three feeling. When rhythmic precision breaks down while playing the Holst, have students analyze the problem and use one of the above strategies as a corrective.

Assessment

1. Have students peer assess a partner on the ability to perform two against three by tapping. (see number two above). Their assessment tool could be a checklist:

   _____ Can perform duplets and triplets in alternation (1 point)

   _____ Can perform duplets and triplets simultaneously for 8 repetitions (2 points)

_____ Can perform duplets and triplets simultaneously, switching hand assignments randomly without dropping a beat (3 points)

2. Have students perform in small groups, one on a part, to check for solid internal rhythm and accuracy. This could be teacher-evaluated or peer-evaluated, and the rubric, which could be designed by students, should include evaluation of all types of two against three playing found in the piece. In designing the rubric, students should focus on what problems typically occur when two against three is played incorrectly (rushing the fast part, dragging the slow part, not lining up downbeats, not keeping a steady overall pulse, not subdividing long notes, etc.).

Cognitive Outcome

Students will create a quodlibet.

Strategies

1. Familiar Territory

    Begin rehearsal by teaching students to sing a simple canon such as "Scotland's Burning" or another favorite. Guide a discussion about the difference between homophony and polyphony to help students determine that this music is polyphonic. (You may also introduce the word counterpoint.)

    Divide students into two groups and have them play or sing the Dargason melody and "Green Sleeves" together. Help them determine that this is also polyphony but a slightly different sort. What makes it different? (The independent lines are actually separate melodies, rather than separate lines based on the same musical material.) Explain the concept of quodlibet, the combining of two known melodies that work well together.

2. Funny Combinations

   Ask students why a composer might combine two different but familiar melodies. (The first and most obvious answer is simply, "because they can," i.e. because they discover that the melodies fit together and that's enough reason. Prod students to push this answer further: why would a composer do it, besides the fact that they can? One answer: it's clever and we are intrigued by "clever." Other possible reasons: because each melody is revealed in a unique way when combined with another one, because a melody is set in relief when combined with a different one, because new meaning might be created by combining the meanings of two separate melodies, etc.)

   Tell students that you will play for them a piece that is full of quodlibet, and their task is to listen carefully for possible meanings behind the composition. (This introduction will be more effective if delivered seriously.) Play the *Unbegun Symphony* of PDQ Bach (Peter Schickele). Students may enjoy hearing it a second time; if so, challenge them to name as many tunes as they can. The discussion point should clarify Schickele's intention: humor. Let students discuss briefly how exactly humor is created here (by wildly disparate combinations of completely unrelated melodies, by quick and continual surprise, by constantly thwarting the listener's expectations, by delighting with the unexpected, etc.).

3. A Quick Quodlibet

   Split the class into pairs and give them 15 to 30 minutes, with their instruments, to discover two familiar melodies that work as counterpoint. Suggest to students that they start with a simple folk tune and keep testing tunes against it until they get an idea for one that might work.

   Have the pairs perform for the whole group and ask students to comment on which compositions seemed to work best. Any combinations that seemed particularly meaningful or effective? Strictly from a musical standpoint, what made the most effective combinations? (Obviously, being in the same key, or at least related keys is a preliminary concern.) Need the pieces be in the same meter?

Same style? Same mood?

What if both pieces suggest texts—need the texts be related? If they are not, what new meanings are suggested by their juxtaposition?

Help students hear other aspects of effective combinations, such as rhythmic independence (e.g. one part moves while the other is still), or melodic independence (not too many notes or melodic figures that are the same).

4. Final Project

As a homework project, have students come up with another quodlibet and notate it exactly. As an alternative, some students may want to compose their own countermelody, or even compose both melodies. (Students may actually discover this is easier than creating a quodlibet from known melodies.) Encourage capable students to add a third melody to their counterpoint. Compositions should be at least eight-measures long.

Photocopy these compositions for the entire orchestra, and read through one or two each day for students to critique and discuss. Refer students to their knowledge of I and V chords and, if appropriate, add simple improvised accompaniments in long tones (as in Introducing the Piece above).

Assessment

Have students evaluate their own composition and the composition of one other student. Again, they could develop a rubric that addressed the aspects of an effective contrapuntal work, such as:

Very Effective	Effective	Not Effective
3	2	1

Both melodies are in same key, or related keys.

Melodies are pleasing in their rhythmic independence.

Melodies are pleasing in their pitch independence.

The piece shows thought and imagination.

The piece is notated correctly.

Affective Outcome

Students will evaluate compositional techniques and their effect.

Strategies

1. Have students jot down general aspects of the piece that they feel make it interesting and effective. Compile a list as a class and discuss.

2. Lead a discussion about the tension between repetition and contrast in music generally. What is the purpose of repetition? (To give form, to orient the listener, to help the piece hold together.) What is the effect of too much repetition? (It's boring.) Too much contrast or variety (it's chaotic and also boring, we lose our place in the piece easily). What were some of the potential pitfalls that Holst faced in setting the Dargason melody the way he did? Do you think he succeeds? Why or why not?

   Have students jot down three places in the piece where contrast makes the piece more interesting.

3. Have students listen to the piece with their eyes closed, either by playing a professional recording, or (better) by dividing the orchestra in two and having half play while the other half listens, and vice versa. (This is only effective, of course, if students are sufficiently accomplished to render the piece well.)

   When finished, ask them to briefly journal their thoughts about the moment in the piece where "Green Sleeves" enters, either the first time or the second time or both. How would they describe that musical moment, in terms of their own reaction? What kind of sensation(s) does it evoke? What metaphors or other descriptive language could be used to describe it?

   Invite students to share these thoughts with the group.

Assessment

1. Have students create a more formal presentation of number three above, in some artistic medium such as a poem, a narrative story, or a piece of visual art, etc. The idea is to translate their personal feeling about the piece (and specifically that magic moment in the piece

TEACHING PLANS
ORCHESTRA

which Holst sets up so beautifully) into another mode of expression. These can be displayed at the concert.

2. Have students write a short essay on this question: Describe five of the key compositional devices that Holst uses to create interest in the Finale to the *St. Paul's Suite.* Which one, for you, is most effective? Why?

Music Selection

Written for school musicians, this piece, like the composer's *Brook Green Suite* and Ralph Vaughn Williams' arrangement of *Rhosymedre,* is clear in construction, accessible, and technically playable by younger students. It is representative of the English folk song style and could also integrate well with a folk dance study .

Because of the interesting use of "Green Sleeves," this piece might be useful for programming on a seasonal concert in conjunction with Ralph Vaughn Williams' or Alfred Reed's treatment of "Greensleeves." The simple variation treatment and interesting use of rhythm could also allow the piece to fit into a more extended student composition project, focusing on compositional devices.

Other Possible Outcomes

1. English folk song (cognitive)
2. English country dancing (skill and cognitive)
3. Early 20th-century folk song revival: Holst, Vaughan Williams, Grainger, etc. (cognitive)
4. Music of Elizabethan England (cognitive)

Resources

Holmes, Paul. *Holst: His Life and Times*, London: Omnibus, 1997. Lots of photographs, including St. Paul's School and Holst's room, sketches of the orchestra, etc.

Holst, Imogen. *The Music of Gustav Holst*, 3rd Revised Edition, Oxford: Oxford University Press, 1986.

Playford, John. *John Playford's The English dancing master*: or, Plaine and easie rules for the dancing of country dances, with the tune to each dance : reprinted from the 1933 edition, in which the text was completely reset and the music transcribed into modern notation from the original 1651 edition / with prefaces by Hugh Mellor and Leslie Bridgewater from the 1933 edition. New York : Dance Horizons, 1976.

Web sites about Playford's book and background on the "Dargason:"

www.shipbrook.com/jeff/playford/24.html)

www.pbm.com/~lindahl/lod/vol2/dargason.html

About the Author

As conductor, teacher, clinician, and scholar, Patricia O'Toole has established a reputation for promoting comprehensive music education and a commitment to diversifying music education practices, students and music. She is a frequent conductor and adjudicator for festivals and honor choirs.

O'Toole is presently the Artistic Director for the Columbus Women's Chorus. As a scholar, O'Toole has published in *The Quarterly Journal of Music Education, The Bulletin for the Council of Research in Music Education, The Choral Journal,* and *The Philosophy of Music Education Review,* in addition to several other state teacher journals.

She has presented papers at several national conferences including the College Music Society National Conference, Music Educators National Conference, The Sociology of Music Education Conference, Feminist Theory in Music Conference, Allerton Retreat for Choral Music Education, and the American Educational Research Association National Conference. O'Toole also has a passion for world choral music and she has studied music at the University of Legon in Ghana, West Africa; The Royal Conservatory in Papeete, Tahiti; and at the Irish World Music Center in Limerick, Ireland.

The contributors to this book are a group of outstanding Wisconsin band, choir, and orchestra directors and represent middle school through college level teaching. Each of these teachers has committed to continual growth as a comprehensive music educator, to inspiring young musicians, and to sharing their journeys and discoveries with other teachers in the hopes of offering young musicians every where the most comprehensive music education possible.